KT-572-391

Letts
EDUCATIONAL

ADVANCED
LEVEL

Revise A2
English Literature

Author
Steven Croft

Contents

Chapter 4 Comparing texts

Chapter 5 Texts in context

Chapter 6 The unseen

Chapter 7 Synoptic assessment

Specification lists

AQA A English Literature

MODULE	SPECIFICATION TOPIC	CHAPTER REFERENCE	STUDIED IN CLASS	REVISED	PRACTICE QUESTIONS
Unit 4 (M4) Texts in time	**Section A – Drama pre-1770** Othello: Shakespeare (2006); Henry IV part 2: Shakespeare (2004); The Merchant of Venice: Shakespeare (2005); Noah and his Sons, The Second Shepherd's Play, and Herod the Great from The Complete Plays of the Wakefield Master (2004); The Duchess of Malfi: John Webster (2006); Volpone: Ben Johnson (2005)	1			
	Section B – Poetry pre-1900 Women Romantic Poets;1785–1822, An Anthology (2005); The Prelude: William Wordsworth (2005); Songs of Innocence and Experience: William Blake (2005); Selected Poems: John Keats (2005)	2, 5			
Unit 5 (M5) Literary connections	This module may be taken either as coursework **or** a written unit. The set text options are given below.				
	1 Literary Themes History in Literature (2005) Sacred Hunger: Barrie Unsworth and Hawksmoor: Pete Ackroyd; A Woman's Struggle (2006) Oranges are not the Only Fruit: Jeanette Winterson; The Color Purple: Alice Walker	4			
	2 Time and Place Visions of the Future (2004) Brave New World: Aldous Huxley and Nineteen Eighty-Four: George Orwell Experience of India (2004) A Passage to India: E.M. Forster and Heat and Dust: Ruth Prawer Jhabvala	4			
	3 Ways of Telling Reflections (2006) Precious Bone: Mary Webb and Cold Comfort Farm: Stella Gibbons Humorous Writing (2005) Captain Corelli's Mandolin: Louis de Bernières and Catch 22: Joseph Heller	4			
Unit 6 (M6) Reading for meaning	Theme for reading for 2002 is War in Literature with specific reference to literature written about and during the First World War	6, 7			

Examination analysis

Unit 4	2 questions (closed text)	2 hr	15%
Unit 5	**Either** a) one question on two texts (open text) **or** b) coursework – one essay comparing two text	approx. 2500 words	15%
Unit 6	One question involving several tasks based on unseen material	3 hr	20%

Here is a list of the different specifications for English Literature at A2 Level. If you find the particular specification that you are studying you will see the detail of what you will be studying. Very often, of course, the particular choice of text from those set will be up to your teacher or lecturer but here you will find the full list of those offered. Note that there are **two** specifications, A and B for AQA.

AQA B English Literature

MODULE	SPECIFICATION TOPIC	CHAPTER REFERENCE	STUDIED IN CLASS	REVISED	PRACTICE QUESTIONS
Unit 4 (M4) Comparing texts (coursework)	Coursework – no set texts One prose text and one other text of a different period	4, 5			
Unit 5 (M5) Drama before 1770 Poetry before 1900	**Section A – Poetry before 1900** The General Prologue to the Canterbury Tales: Chaucer; Sonnets: Shakespeare; George Herbert: various poems; Emily Dickinson: specified poems	2, 5			
	Section B – Drama before 1770 Edward II: Marlowe; Measure for Measure: Shakespeare; The White Devil: Webster; Women Beware Women: Thomas Middleton; The Rover: Aphra Behn; The Way of the World: Congreve	1, 5			
Unit 6 (M6) Exploring texts (synoptic module)	Question set on pre-release material distributed to candidates approximately three days before the exam	5, 6, 7			

Examination analysis

Unit 4	Coursework **Either** one essay of 2000–3000 words **or** two essays of 1000–1500 works each		15%
Unit 5	Two questions (closed text)	2 hr	15%
Unit 6	One or more questions	3 hr	20%

Edexcel English Literature

MODULE	SPECIFICATION TOPIC	CHAPTER REFERENCE	STUDIED IN CLASS	REVISED	PRACTICE QUESTIONS
Unit 4a (M4) Modern Prose	This is a coursework option on one named post-1900 prose text				
Unit 4b (M4) Modern Prose	**One text from:** Captain Corelli's Mandolin: Louis de Bernières; Alias Grace: Margaret Atwood; The Man Eater of Malgudi: R.K. Narayan; The Bell: Iris Murdoch; Howard's End: E.M. Forster	3, 5			
Unit 5 (M5) Poetry and Drama	**One question on poetry and one on drama (At least one on a pre-1770 text)**				
	Pre-1770 Poetry The Merchant's Tale: Chaucer; Selected Poems: Milton; Edexcel Poetry Anthology; Eight Metaphysical Poets; Selected Poems: Gray	2, 5			
	Post-1770 Poetry Selected Poems: Tennyson; Selected Poems: Yeats; Selected Poems: Carol Ann Duffy; The Whitsun Welding: Philip Larkin; The Heinemann Book of Caribbean Poetry; New Selected Poems: Heaney	2, 5			
	Pre-1770 Drama Othello: Shakespeare; Dr Faustus: Marlowe; The Duchess of Malfi: Webster; The Way of the World: Congreve; The Recruiting Officer: Farquhar	1, 5			
	Post-1770 Drama The Rivals: Sheridan; The Odyssey: Walcott; Amadeus: Peter Shaffer; Lady Windermere's Fan: Wilde; Our Country's Good – Wertenbaker;	1, 5			
Unit 6 (M6) Criticism and Comparison	Section A – Unprepared Prose or Poetry	5, 6			
	Section B – Comparative Work One area of study to be selected from: **1 The Comic Perspective** – Pride and Prejudice: Austen and either Emma: Austen or Larry's Party: Shields	4, 5, 7			
	2 The Tragic Perspective – Wuthering Heights: Brontë and either The Return of the Native: Hardy, or Petals of Blood: Thiong'o	4, 5, 7			
	3 Divided Societies – North and South: Elizabeth Gaskell and either Hard Times: Charles Dickens or The Slave Girl: Emecheta	4, 5, 7			
	4 Broken Communication – The Tempest: Shakespeare and either Who's Afraid of Virginia Woolf?: Albee or Translations: Friel	4, 5, 7			
	5 Nature and Imagination – The Prelude Books 1 and 2: Wordsworth, and either Selected Poems of John Keats or Selected Poems: Edward Thomas	4, 5, 7			
	6 The Social Observer – The Songs of Innocence and Experience: Blake and either Best of Betjeman (poetry only) or Making Cocoa for Kingsley Amis	4, 5, 7			

Examination analysis

Unit 4a **Unit 4b**	Coursework **or** One question (open text)	1 hr	15%
Unit 5	Two questions (open text)	2 hr	15%
Unit 6	Two questions (closed text)	2 hr	20%

OCR English Literature

MODULE	SPECIFICATION TOPIC	CHAPTER REFERENCE	STUDIED IN CLASS	REVISED	PRACTICE QUESTIONS
Unit 4 (M4) Poetry and Drama Pre-1900	**Section A** The Pardoner's Tale: Chaucer; Selected Poems: Marvell; Paradise Lost Books 1 and 2: Milton; The Rape of the Lock: Pope; Selected Poems: Coleridge; Selected Poems: Dickinson	2, 5			
	Section B King Lear: Shakespeare; The Tempest: Shakespeare; Volpone: Jonson; The Relapse: Vanbrugh; The Rivals: Sheridan; The Importance of Being Ernest: Wilde	1, 5			
Unit 5 (M5) Prose (post-1914) coursework or written paper	Coursework – no set texts **or** one or more post-1914 texts not previously studied for other units Vera Brittain: Testament of Youth; Angela Carter: The Bloody Chamber; Louis de Bernières: Captain Corelli's Mandolin; D. H. Lawrence: The Rainbow; Rian Malin: My Traitor's Heart; Toni Morrison: Beloved; Paul Theroux: The Great Railway Bazaar; Evelyn Waugh: A Handful of Dust	3, 5			
Unit 6 (M6) Comparative and contextual study (synoptic unit)	Candidates choose one of the following contextual areas and at least one of the texts set for that area **Satire** Swift: Gulliver's Travels; Atwood: The Handmaid's Tale	4, 5, 6, 7			
	The Gothic Tradition Lewis: The Monk; Hill: The Woman in Black	4, 5, 6, 7			
	The Victorian Novel Eliot: Middlemarch; Hardy: Tess of the D'Urbervilles	4, 5, 6, 7			
	The Great War in British Literature Faulks: Birdsong; Blunden: Undertones of War	4, 5, 6, 7			
	Twentieth Century American Literature Williams: A Streetcar Named Desire; Walker: The Color Purple	4, 5, 6, 7			
	Post Colonial Literature Ondaatje: The English Patient Roy: The God of Small Things	4, 5, 6, 7			

Examination analysis

Unit 4	Two questions (closed text)	2 hr	15%
Unit 5	Coursework one or two essays max. 3000 words **or** written paper two questions (open text)	2 hr	15%
Unit 6	Two questions (closed text)	2 hr (plus 15 min reading time)	20%

WJEC English Literature

MODULE	SPECIFICATION TOPIC	CHAPTER REFERENCE	STUDIED IN CLASS	REVISED	PRACTICE QUESTIONS
Unit 4 (M4) Poetry (pre-1900)	Chaucer: The Miller's Prologue and Tale; Graham (Ed): Metaphysical Poets; Keats: Selected Poems; Milton: Paradise Lost Books 1 and 2; Rossetti: Selected Poems	2			
Unit 5 (M5) Comparison between texts	Kerouac: On the Road; Minhinnick: Watching the Fire Eater; Glyn Jones: The Island of Apples; D.H. Lawrence: Sons and Lovers; Plath: The Bell Jar; Antonia White: Beyond the Glass; Forster: A Room With a View; Ishiguro: The Remains of the Day; Atwood: The Handmaid's Tale; Orwell: Nineteen Eighty-Four; Banks: The Wasp Factory; Bond: Saved Or centres may select own pair of texts (subject to Board approval)	4			
Unit 6 (M6) Drama pre-1770 (synoptic unit)	Congreve: The Way of the World; Marlowe: Dr Faustus; Marston: The Malcontent; Webster: The Duchess of Malfi Plus unseen linked material	5, 6, 7			

Examination analysis

Unit 4	One question (open text)	1 hr 15 min	15%
Unit 5	One question on one pair of texts (open texts) **or** coursework assessment one essay on two texts	1 hr 30 min (approx 2000 words)	15%
Unit 6	Two questions (closed text)	2 hr 30 min	20%

NICCEA English Literature

MODULE	SPECIFICATION TOPIC	CHAPTER REFERENCE	STUDIED IN CLASS	REVISED	PRACTICE QUESTIONS
Module 4 (M4) *Response to unseen poetry written before 1770*	**Section A** *Response to unseen poetry*	*2, 6*			
	Section B *The study of poetry written before 1770; Chaucer: The Nun's Priest's Tale; Driver (Ed): Penguin English Verse Volume One; Wyatt to Shakespeare; Gardner (Ed): The Metaphysical Poets; Herrick: Selected poems; Milton: Selected poems; Pope: Selected poems*	*2*			
Module 5 (M5) *Twentieth-century Prose*	*Anderson: Winesburgh, Ohio; Bowen: The Last September; Conrad: The Secret Agent; Forster: A Passage to India; Gibbons: Cold Comfort Farm; Heller: Catch 22; Hemmingway: A Farewell to Arms; Lawrence: Women in Love; Murdoch: The Sea, The Sea; O'Brien: Land of Spices; O'Connor: Classic Irish Short Stories; Trevor: The Collected Short Stories; Walker: The Color Purple; Wharton: The Age of Innocence* **or** *coursework option: one assignment on at least one prose text written after 1900*	*3, 5*			
Module 6 (M6) *Drama Synoptic Module*	**Option A** *Miller: Death of a Salesman; Sophocles: Oedipus Tyrannus*	*4, 5, 7*			
	Option B *Farquhar: The Beaux' Stratagem; Wilde: An Ideal Husband*	*4, 5, 7*			
	Option C *Albee: Who's Afraid of Virginia Woolf; Webster: The Duchess of Malfi*	*4, 5, 7*			

Examination analysis

Unit 4	Two questions (closed book)	*2 hr 30 min*	*15%*
Unit 5	One question (open book) **or** coursework one assignment	*1 hr 10 min* *approx 1500 words*	*15%*
Unit 6	One question (open book)	*2 hr 30 min*	*20%*

AS/A2 Level English Literature courses

AS and A2

All English Literature courses being studied from September 2000 are in two parts with three separate units or modules in each part. Most students will start by studying the AS (Advanced Subsidiary) course. Those who wish to will then go on to study the second part of the A Level course called the A2. It is also possible for you to study the full A Level course, both AS and A2 at the same time.

How will you be tested?

Assessment units

For AS English Literature you will be tested by three assessment units. For the A2 English Literature you will take a further three units which will then be added to your AS units give you the full A Level. The AS English Literature forms the first 50% of the assessment weighting for the full A Level and the A2 provides the final 50%.

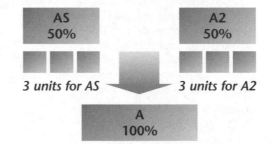

Each unit can normally be taken in either January or June or you can study the whole of each course before taking any of the unit assessments. You can even take the unit assessments for AS and A2 together at the end of your studies if you wish. You can see, then, that there is a good deal of flexibility concerning when you take your exams.

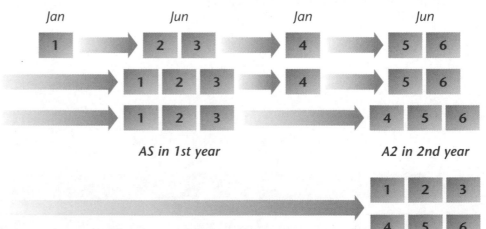

If you are not satisfied with a unit result you can re-sit each unit. It is important to note, though, that each unit may be re-sat once only. The better result will count towards the final award. However, you are allowed to re-sit the whole qualification more than once.

A2 and Synoptic assessment

If you have studied English Literature at AS Level and have decided to go on to study A2 you will study three further units. You will be assessed in a similar way to the way in which you were assessed on the AS course. The final unit that you will study, however, will involve what is known as 'synoptic' assessment. This simply means that the unit will draw together and assess all the assessment objectives that you have studied throughout the course.

Coursework

Depending on the particular specification and the particular options you are studying your course may include coursework assessment. The form and length of the coursework assignments vary but you can consult a copy of the specification you are following for further details.

The aims of the A2 course

There are, however, differences between the AS and the A2 courses and the aims of the A2 course emphasises these differences. At A2 Level, all specifications aim to:

- broaden and deepen the knowledge, skills and understanding developed in the AS, enabling candidates a wider sense of the scope of literary study
- encourage candidates to use detailed knowledge and understanding of individual texts to explore comparisons and connections between them
- encourage candidates to appreciate the significance of cultural and historical influences upon readers and writers.

The differences, therefore, between AS and A Level study and assessment are reflected in both the breadth and depth of the study required.

What will I study?

All specifications for A Level English Literature have the same 'core' of compulsory elements that must be studied. Here are the key areas you will study.
- Prose   • Poetry   • Drama   • One text published before 1900
- One text published before 1770   • Comparison of whole texts
- The cultural, historical and contextual influences on literary texts.

All the texts you study should have been written originally in English and at least one of the exams you will take will be a closed book exam. The final unit you will study will test all the assessment objectives you have studied throughout the course.

It is also worth noting that the quality of your written communication will be assessed in all assessment units. You will be assessed on your ability to:

- select and use a form and style of writing appropriate to purpose and complex subject matter
- organise relevant information clearly and coherently, using specialist vocabulary where appropriate
- ensure text is legible, and spelling, grammar and punctuation accurate so that meaning is clear.

Key skills

Throughout your study you will be developing your key skills and your English Literature course can provide you with the opportunities to develop and generate evidence of attainment in such aspects of key skills as Communication, IT, Improving own learning and performance and Working with others. These areas can contribute towards your achievement of the key skills qualification, which is the equivalent of an AS Level.

Different types of questions in A2 examinations

In A2 English Literature examinations different types of questions are used to assess your abilities and skills. Here are some of the question types you can expect to encounter.

Open book questions

The kind of question that you are asked when you have access to the text in the exam very often begins by referring you to a part of the text that you are asked to re-read. You are then asked a question that is likely to require close analysis of this part of the text, perhaps then relating the specified section to the text as a whole. Open book format allows examiners to set questions that are routed in specific areas of the text and which require detailed text-based answers.

Closed book questions

These tend to be broader in scope than open book questions and do not require the close textual analysis of the open book type question because, obviously, you have not got access to the text in the exam. Such questions often tend to focus on thematic, structural or other issues that involve a consideration of the text as a whole.

Comparison questions

As you will have noticed from the assessment objectives one of the features of the A2 course which was not required at AS Level is the requirement to compare texts with one another. Some of the questions you will encounter, therefore, will ask you to focus on the ways in which texts relate to each other.

Cultural, historical and contextual influence questions

Another feature of the A2 assessment objectives which differ from those for AS is that you will need to consider in greater depth the context within which texts were written and which exerted cultural or historical influences on the text. In questions which address this assessment objective note that the questions will examine context as well as text.

Thematic questions

Some exam boards include a study of texts that are linked through a common theme. This will probably cover the comparison element as well and involve questions that focus on the common themes or links between the specified texts.

Synoptic questions

All specifications involve synoptic questions as we have already mentioned. You will encounter synoptic questions in the final unit of your course. Quite simply, these questions are designed to test all the assessment objectives for the course and because of the broad nature of these questions they may well consist of several parts.

Coursework

As part of your A2 course you will have the option to include coursework for part of your assessment. The exact nature of the coursework will depend on the particular specification that you are studying but it will be assessed against the objectives already given.

Exam technique

Links from AS

The A2 English Literature course builds on the AS course; some of the assessment objectives are common between AS and A2 while others move the study on into new areas. Your study at A2 Level will require both greater breadth and depth founded firmly on your studies at AS Level.

What the examiners are looking for

Bear in mind that 'examiners' are not a special group of people who appear every year to mark examination scripts. The vast majority are teachers just like your own. In fact, some of your teachers may well be examiners. This means that they are well aware of the problems, worries and concerns that you can encounter. Bear in mind is that examiners do not devise questions to try to trick students. Everybody concerned with examining wants you to do as well as you are able and therefore the questions that you will face in the exam will have been designed to be as clear and unambiguous as possible. Here are some points to bear in mind.

- Questions are rarely prescriptive – they are open so as to invite you to discuss the issues involved.
- If the question contains some kind of proposition you are never expected to simply accept it – acceptance or rejection needs to be supported by evidence.
- Read the question carefully and make sure that what you write answers what the question asks.
- Do not paraphrase texts – you get no marks for re-telling the story.
- Never use model or prepared answers. Certainly model answers can be useful to give you ideas or as part of your revision but never try to reproduce them as your own answer. Worse still, never try to 'bend' a question to suit an answer you have in mind.
- Good answers are firmly based on informed analysis and close reference to your text.
- Remember the technical aspects of your written work – technical inaccuracies can detract from your work and at worse obscure what you are wanting to say. You should note that: the quality of written communication is assessed in all assess-ment units where candidates are required to produce extended written material.

What skills will I need?

You will be tested through a series of assessment objectives. These assessment objectives clearly show the skills and abilities that you should have acquired through studying the course. The assessments will assess a candidates ability to:

AO1 Communicate clearly the knowledge, understanding and insight appropriate to literary study, using appropriate terminology and accurate and coherent written expression

AO2ii Respond with knowledge and understanding to literary texts of different types and periods, exploring and commenting on relationships and comparisons between literary texts

AO3 Show detailed understanding of the ways in which writers' choices of form, structure and language shape meanings

AO4 Articulate independent opinions and judgements, informed by different interpretations of literary texts by other readers

AO5ii Evaluate the significance of cultural, historical and other contextual influences on literary texts and study.

Your final A Level grade will depend on the extent to which you meet these assessment objectives.

Four steps to successful revision

Step 1: Understand

- Study the topic to be learned slowly. Make sure you understand the logic or important concepts.
- Mark up the text if necessary – underline, highlight and make notes
- Re-read each paragraph slowly.

GO TO STEP 2

Step 2: Summarise

- Now make your own revision note summary:
  What is the main idea, theme or concept to be learned?
  What are the main points? How does the logic develop?
  Ask questions: Why? How? What next?
- Use bullet points, mind maps, patterned notes.
- Link ideas with mnemonics, mind maps, crazy stories.
- Note the title and date of the revision notes
  (e.g. English Literature: Shakespeare, 3rd March).
- Organise your notes carefully and keep them in a file.

This is now in **short term memory**. You will forget 80% of it if you do not go to Step 3.
GO TO STEP 3, but first take a 10 minute break.

Step 3: Memorise

- Take 25 minute learning 'bites' with 5 minute breaks.
- After each 5 minute break test yourself:
  Cover the original revision note summary
  Write down the main points
  Speak out loud (record on tape)
  Tell someone else
  Repeat many times.

The material is well on its way to **long term memory**
You will forget 40% if you do not do step 4. **GO TO STEP 4**

Step 4: Track/Review

- Create a Revision Diary (one A4 page per day).
- Make a revision plan for the topic, e.g. 1 day later, 1 week later, 1 month later.
- Record your revision in your Revision Diary, e.g.
  English Literature: Shakespeare, 3rd March 25 minutes
  English Literature: Shakespeare, 5th March 15 minutes
  English Literature: Shakespeare, 3rd April 15 minutes
  ... and then at monthly intervals.

Chapter 1

Drama

The following topics are covered in this chapter:

- Drama and A2
- The nature of drama
- The structure of the play
- Opening scenes
- Endings

- Creating characters
- Issues and themes
- Soliloquies and asides
- Text and context
- Approaches to your text

1.1 Drama and A2

AQA A	U4
AQA B	U5
Edexcel	U5
OCR	U4
WJEC	U6
NICCEA	U6

One of the features of the A2 course is that in addition to studying another pre-1900 text, you must also study a text that was written before 1770. Several of the Boards include this option in the drama sections. On some specifications the pre-1770 drama texts include a Shakespeare option so you may find that even if you have studied a Shakespeare text for AS Level, you might study a second one as part of your A2 course. On the other hand you might find that you are studying a pre-1770 dramatist other than Shakespeare. As Shakespearean drama has been thoroughly covered in *Revise AS English Literature*, in this section the main focus will be on pre-1770 dramatists other than Shakespeare.

Some Boards, however, include options that involve studying drama written after this date and so examples of post-1770 and modern drama will also be included in this section. As you will find, though, many of the aspects of drama that will be discussed are common to all drama, no matter when it was written.

Other than Shakespeare texts here are some pre-1770 texts you might study at A2 Level:

John Webster:	*The White Devil*
	The Duchess of Malfi
Ben Jonson:	*Volpone*
Christopher Marlowe:	*Edward II*
	Dr Faustus
William Congreve:	*The Way of the World*
George Farquhar:	*The Recruiting Officer*

Other drama texts written after 1770 but before 1900 that you might encounter include:

Richard Brinsley Sheridan:	*The Rivals*
Oscar Wilde:	*Lady Windermere's Fan*
	The Importance of Being Ernest

Drama texts written in the twentieth century that you might study include:

Peter Shaffer:	*Amadeus*
Tennessee Williams:	*A Streetcar Named Desire*
Edward Albee:	*Who's Afraid of Virginia Woolf?*
Arthur Miller:	*Death of a Salesman*
Brian Friel:	*Translations*

You will find examples from a number of these texts discussed in this chapter.

1.2 The nature of drama

After studying this section you should:

LEARNING SUMMARY

- *have an awareness of how a drama text differs from other kinds of text*
- *have some ideas of how to study a drama text*
- *appreciate the difference between reading the text and seeing it performed*

AQA A	U4
AQA B	U5
Edexcel	U5
OCR	U4
WJEC	U6
NICCEA	U6

If you look up the word 'drama' in a dictionary you will find a definition that says something like:

a play for acting on the stage or for broadcasting.

Such definitions point to one of the main differences between a drama text and the other texts that you will study. The drama text is primarily written to be 'seen' rather than read. In many ways a play can only be fully appreciated when seen in performance. A play, then, is meant to have an audience who share the experience of watching the play and responding to it. When studying the text in the classroom, which very often involves reading the play, it is easy to lose sight of this fact.

When studying your play, therefore, it is vital that you always bear in mind the performance element of the text. You should recognise that it is very different to studying a novel, for example, and that you will need to employ different techniques in approaching it. If at all possible you should try to see a performance of the play in the theatre. If you cannot see a live performance, try to borrow a video tape of the play and watch that. Your public library might be able to help with this. Sometimes, though, it is not possible either to see a live performance or a video production of it. If you cannot 'see' the play you must try to visualise the action in your mind as you are reading it.

Here are some things you can do to help you approach your drama text.

- Work with others when reading the play.
- Take note of the stage directions which will help you to visualise what is happening.
- Try to see a live performance of the play.
- Try to see video performances of it.
- Recognise that each performance presents just one interpretation – a play can be interpreted in lots of different ways.
- Act out with others parts of the play you are studying.
- Listen to audio tapes of the play you are studying.

> **KEY POINT**
>
> Plays are meant to be seen as a shared experience and not read in isolation.

Progress check

Investigate the possibility of seeing a live performance of the play you are studying and check on the availability of video and audio recordings of it.

1.3 The structure of the play

AQA A ▶ U4
AQA B ▶ U5
Edexcel ▶ U5
OCR ▶ U4
WJEC ▶ U6
NICCEA ▶ U6

All plays have some kind of storyline or **plot**. The plot is of central importance to most plays although there are some plays, particularly some modern drama, where the plot is stripped away to a bare minimum and the fact that nothing happens is the very point of the play. In most plays, though, the plot is a highly developed aspect of the play.

However, there is more to the plot of a play than simply a storyline. The plot of a play, and the way that it develops, are closely bound up with the way that the play is put together or the way in which it is structured. The dramatist will have given much thought to the structure and in general terms the plot will perform several functions. For example, an effective plot will:

- keep the audience interested from the opening scene to the final one
- keep the 'action' of the play moving from one scene to another
- introduce and develop the characters in the play
- build up tension to create climaxes or crisis points.

Although every play is different, very often the structure of a play follows a pattern that consists of a number of elements as shown in the following diagram:

> 1 **Exposition:** this is the opening section of the play which introduces the main characters and/or provides background information.

▼

> 2 **Dramatic incitement:** something happens or has happened which provides the starting point for the main action of the play.

▼

> 3 **Complication:** this usually consists of the main action of the play – the characters respond to the dramatic incitement and the developments that stem from it.

▼

> 4 **Crisis point:** this is usually the climax of the play.

▼

> 5 **Resolution:** the final section of the play where things are worked out and the play concludes.

Let's think about how this structure applies to a play that you might already be familiar with, Shakespeare's *Romeo and Juliet*.

1 **Exposition:** The Chorus gives a background to the storyline of the play and the opening scene shows the depth of the quarrel between the Montagues and the Capulets.
2 **Dramatic incitement:** Romeo meets Juliet at the Capulet Ball and they are instantly attracted to each other.
3 **Complication:** various complications arise – the feud between the families; Juliet's arranged marriage to Paris; the secret marriage to Romeo; the death of Tybalt.

4 **Crisis point**: arises through Capulet's insistence his daughter marries Paris and results in the Friar's plan and Juliet's death.

5 **Resolution**: the final scene in the Capulet vault, the death of Romeo and Juliet and the reconciling of the feuding families.

The plot of *Romeo and Juliet* is fairly simple and straightforward but sometimes plays contain secondary storylines that run alongside the main plot and are often linked to it. These secondary storylines are called 'sub-plots' and can contribute to the interest of the play.

> Most plays follow a similar pattern in terms of structure.
>
> **KEY POINT**

Progress check

Now think carefully about the play that you are studying and draw a flow diagram to show how the plot is structured and how it follows the pattern given above.

1.4 Opening scenes

AQA A	U4
AQA B	U5
Edexcel	U5
OCR	U4
WJEC	U6
NICCEA	U6

It is very important that the opening scene of a play engages the audience's attention right from the start. Dramatists can do this in a variety of ways depending on the effects they wish to create. When looking at the opening scene of a play there are two key questions that you should think about.

- What effects does the writer want this scene to have on the audience?
- What purpose does the scene serve to the play as a whole?

Think carefully about these two questions and jot down your ideas on possible answers.

Here are some possible answers.

- The dramatist might want to create a certain mood, or present a particular background to the plot.
- The opening scene is meant to create a certain impact on the audience, perhaps to shock them, or keep them gripped – the tension created in the opening scene of *Hamlet*, followed by the appearance of the ghost is an example of this.
- The opening scene provides the audience with a good deal of background information about what is going on, the characters, etc.
- Characters are introduced and situations and relationships established.
- The opening scene can arouse the audience's curiosity and make them want to know more, therefore sustaining this interest in the play.

> Plays open in many different ways but every opening scene reflects the dramatist's purpose and achieves the particular effects desired.
>
> **KEY POINT**

Now look carefully at the following extract which is the opening from Shakespeare's *Othello*.

Read it through carefully making a note of the following:

- your impression of the two characters
- the information conveyed to the audience here and the technique Shakespeare uses to put it across
- the kind of atmosphere created.

Othello, **Act1, Scene 1**

Enter Roderigo and Iago

1 RODERIGO Tush, never tell me! I take it much unkindly
That thou, Iago, who hast had my purse
As if the strings were thine, shouldst know of this.

IAGO 'Sblood, but you will not hear me!
If ever I did dream of such a matter, Abhor me.

2 RODERIGO Thou told'st me thou didst hold him in thy hate.

IAGO Despise me, if I do not. Three great ones of the city,
In personal suit to make me his Lieutenant,
3 Off-capped to him: and by the faith of man,
I know my price, I am worth no worse a place.
But he, as loving his own pride and purposes,
Evades them with a bombast circumstance
Horribly stuffed with epithets of war,
And in conclusion
Non-suits my mediators. For 'Certes,' says he,
'I have already chose my officer.'
And what was he?
Forsooth, a great arithmetician,
One Michael Cassio, a Florentine –
A fellow almost damned in a fair wife –
That never set a squadron in the field,
Nor the division of a battle knows
More than a spinster – unless the bookish theoric,
Wherein the toged consuls can propose
As masterly as he. Mere prattle without practice
Is all his soldiership. But he, sir, had th'election:
And I, of whom his eyes had seen the proof
At Rhodes, at Cyprus, and on other grounds
Christian and heathen, must be leed and calmed
By debitor and creditor; this counter-caster,
He in good time must his Lieutenant be,
And I – God bless the mark! – his Moorship's Ancient.

RODERIGO By heaven, I rather would have been his
hangman.

4 IAGO Why, there's no remedy. 'Tis the curse of service:
Preferment goes by letter and affection,
And not by old gradation, where each second
Stood heir to th' first. Now sir, be judge yourself
Whether I in any just term am affined
To love the Moor.

RODERIGO I would not follow him then.

IAGO O, Sir, content you:
I follow him to serve my turn upon him.
We cannot all be masters, nor all masters
Cannot be truly followed. You shall mark
Many a duteous and knee-crooking knave
That, doting on his own obsequious bondage,
Wears out his time, much like his master's ass,
For naught but provender, and when he's old –
cashiered!
Whip me such honest knaves. Others there are
Who, trimmed in forms and visages of duty,
Keep yet their hearts attending on themselves,
And, throwing but shows of service on their lords,
Do well thrive by them; and when they have lined
their coats,
Do themselves homage: these fellows have some soul,
And such a one do I profess myself.
For, sir,
It is as sure as you are Roderigo,
Were I the Moor, I would not be Iago:
In following him, I follow but myself.
Heaven is my judge, not I for love and duty,
But seeming so for my peculiar end:
For when my outward action doth demonstrate
The native act and figure of my heart
In compliment extern, 'tis not long after,
But I will wear my heart upon my sleeve
For daws to peck at – I am not what I am.

RODERIGO What a full fortune does the thick-lips owe
If he can carry't thus!

IAGO Call up her father,
Rouse him, make after him, poison his delight,
Proclaim him in the streets; incense her kinsmen,
And, though he in a fertile climate dwell,
Plague him with flies: though that his joy be joy,
Yet throw such chances of vexation on't,
As it may lose some colour.

RODERIGO Here is her father's house; I'll call aloud.

IAGO Do, with like timorous accent and dire yell,
As when, by night and negligence, the fire
Is spied in populous cities.

RODERIGO What, ho, Brabantio! Signor Brabantio, ho!

IAGO Awake! What, ho, Brabantio! Thieves, thieves!
Look to your house, your daughter, and your bags!
Thieves, thieves

Commentary

1 The play opens in the middle of an interchange between Roderigo and Iago so the audience only gradually form an understanding of who the characters are and what is happening – this serves to arouse their curiosity and interest.

2 Although it is apparent that Roderigo is angry with Iago who has difficulty in getting him to listen to his explanation (the audience does not learn the reason for this anger until later in this scene).

3 What is immediately established is that Roderigo has a grievance against Iago who he has trusted with his personal finances – the play therefore opens on a note of betrayal of trust between friends.

4 We also learn that Iago has a grievance himself – against Othello, for being passed over for the post of lieutenant. This post has been given to Michael Cassio. Iago's words suggest his feelings of betrayal.

Progress check

1 Why do you think Shakespeare opens the play in the middle of an interchange between these two characters?

2 What grievance does Roderigo seem to have against Iago?

3 What grievance does Iago have against Othello?

4 What is his grievance against Cassio?

5 What is your impression of Iago?

6 How does Shakespeare convey all this information to the audience/reader?

6 Through the dialogue.
5 Possibly 'two-faced' – prepared to serve Othello and to seek revenge on him.
4 Cassio is inexperienced.
3 Othello has promoted Cassio instead of himself.
2 Roderigo seems to have paid him for something he has not done.
1 To arouse audience's attention.

Now look at this extract which is from the opening of *Translations* by Brian Friel

Read it through carefully, again making a note of:

• your impression of the characters
• the information conveyed to the audience/reader and the techniques used to put it across
• the kind of atmosphere created.

Translations Act One

The hedge-school is held in a disused barn or hay-shed or byre. Along the back wall are the remains of five or six stalls – wooden posts and chains – where cows were once milked and bedded. A double door left, large enough to allow a cart to enter. A window right. A wooden stairway without a banister leads to the upstairs living-quarters (off) of the schoolmaster and his son. Around the room are broken and forgotten implements: a cart-wheel, some lobster-pots, farming tools, a battle of hay, a churn, etc. There are also the stools and bench-seats which the pupils use and a table and chair for the master. At the door a pail of water and a soiled towel. The room is comfortless and dusty and functional – there is no trace of a woman's hand.

When the play opens, MANUS is teaching SARAH to speak. He kneels beside her. She is sitting on a low stool, her head down, very tense, clutching a slate on her knees. He is coaxing her gently and firmly and – as with everything he does – with a kind of zeal.

MANUS is in his late twenties/early thirties; the master's older son. He is pale-faced, lightly built, intense, and works as an unpaid assistant – a monitor – to his father. His clothes are shabby; and when he moves we see that he is lame. SARAH's speech defect is so bad that all her life she has been considered locally to be dumb and she has accepted this: when she wishes to communicate, she grunts and makes unintelligible nasal sounds. She has a waiflike appearance and could be any age from seventeen to thirty-five.

JIMMY JACK CASSIE:–known as the Infant Prodigy–sits by himself, contentedly reading Homer in Greek and smiling to himself. He is a bachelor in his sixties, lives alone, and comes to these evening classes partly for the company and partly for the intellectual stimulation. He is fluent in Latin and Greek but is in no way pedantic – to him it is perfectly normal to speak these tongues. He never washes. His clothes – heavy top coat, hat, mittens, which he wears now – are filthy and he lives in them summer and winter, day and night. He now reads in a quiet voice and smiles in profound satisfaction. For JIMMY the world of the gods and the ancient myths is as real and as immediate as everyday life in the townland of Baile Beag.

MANUS holds SARAH's hand in his and he articulates slowly and distinctly into her face.

MANUS We're doing very well. And we're going to try it once more – just once more. Now – relax and breathe in … deep … and out … in … and out …

(SARAH shakes her head vigorously and stubbornly.)

MANUS Come on, Sarah. This is our secret.

(Again vigorous and stubborn shaking of SARAH'S head.)

MANUS Nobody's listening. Nobody hears you.

JIMMY *Ton d'emeibet epeita thea glaukopis Athene …*

MANUS Get your tongue and your lips working. 'My name—'Come on. One more try. 'My name is—'. Good girl.

SARAH My …

MANUS Great. 'My name—'

SARAH My … my …

MANUS Raise your head. Shout it out. Nobody's listening.

JIMMY *… alla hekelos estai en Atreidao domois…*

MANUS Jimmy, please! Once more—just once more— 'My name—'
Good girl. Come on now. Head up. Mouth open.

SARAH My ...	MANUS YES?
MANUS Good.	*(SARAH pauses. Then in a rush.)*
SARAH My ...	SARAH My name is Sarah.
MANUS Great.	MANUS Marvellous! Bloody marvellous!
4 SARAH My name ...	*(MANUS hugs SARAH. She smiles in shy, embarrassed pleasure)*
MANUS Yes?	Did you hear that, Jimmy? – 'My name is Sarah' – Clear as a bell.
SARAH My name is ...	

Commentary

1 Notice the level of detail Friel gives in his description of the school.

2 Apart from the physical description here we are given insights into the character of Manus – e.g. he has a kind of 'zeal' for everything he does.

3 There are a number of points here that could not be converted into action on the stage. The stage directions, therefore giving more information than could be given to the audience. Who are they aimed at, do you think?

4 See how Friel builds up the tension here and how we get a sense of the relationship between Manus and Sarah – his dedication to making her speak.

Progress check

1 What general impression do you get of the characters in this extract?

2 How do you get this impression?

3 Why do you think Friel included such detailed stage directions?

4 Could all these directions be conveyed on the stage?

1 They are ordinary villagers interested in teaching and learning.
2 Mainly through the stage directions.
3 To give potential actors, and those reading the play, details of how he visualised the play.
4 Not all of them immediately. Some would need to be developed through the action of the play.

Summary

In the *Othello* extract, although it is not immediately obvious from reading it, the first thing that would strike the audience is that the whole scene takes place at night (there are several references to this later). That would have the effect of increasing the sense of intrigue and mystery.

Here, Shakespeare allows the characters to reveal information about what is happening to the audience. This is done naturally so that not everything is revealed at once and therefore the audience's curiosity is aroused. The central character, the Moor (Othello) is mentioned and we are given an insight into how Iago really views him. Another key character, Cassio, is also mentioned here, and again we are given an insight into what Iago thinks of him.

In this opening scene, one of the play's main themes, betrayal, is also raised thus setting the tone for the action that is to follow.

The difference in the opening to *Translations* is immediately apparent. The striking thing is the extensive set of stage directions that Friel gives. He is very precise about the kind of setting that the play opens in and then he goes on to detailed pen portraits of the characters that we see at the beginning. Much of the information that Friel gives us here would be seen by an audience watching a performance of the play on the stage. However, there are some points that could not be conveyed in this way. For example, it would not be possible to convey visually that Manus works as an unpaid assistant to his father, the master of the hedge-school. Nor that Sarah has been considered dumb by the villagers. The audience would pick up most of this information as the play goes on but they would not be aware of it at the opening of the play.

Once the dialogue starts, like Shakespeare, Friel allows the audience to gather information through the dialogue. It is clear that Manus is trying to teach Sarah to speak and that a great breakthrough is made when she finally says 'My name is Sarah'.

> Plays begin in different ways and you should look carefully at the opening scene to determine its purpose and effect.

KEY POINT

Progress check

Now look carefully at the opening section of the drama text that you are studying and answer the following questions.

1 What is the effect of this opening scene on the audience?
2 What do you think the dramatist wanted to achieve by beginning the play in this way?
3 What techniques have been used?
4 What is the purpose of any stage directions?

Specific answers cannot be given for this because it depends on the individual play you are studying. Make sure you have considered all the aspects of the scene.

1.5 Endings

After studying this section you should be able to:

- *develop your ideas on the ways that plays can end*
- *identify techniques that dramatists can use to end their plays*
- *apply these ideas to the text you are studying*

LEARNING SUMMARY

AQA A	U4
AQA B	U5
Edexcel	U5
OCR	U4
WJEC	U6
NICCEA	U6

Just as the opening of the play is an important element in the drama, the way in which a play ends can be important too.

Look at the following two extracts. The first is the ending of *Dr Faustus* by Christopher Marlowe and the second from *The Rivals* by Richard Sheridan.

Dr Faustus, Scene xix

FAUSTUS Ah, Faustus,

Now hast thou but one bare hour to live,
And then thou must be damn'd perpetually.
Stand still, you ever-moving spheres of heaven,
That time may cease, and midnight never come;
Fair nature's eye, rise, rise again, and make
Perpetual day; or let this hour be but
A year, a month, a week, a natural day,
That Faustus may repent and save his soul.
O lente lente currite noctis equi!
The stars move still, time runs, the clock will strike,
The devil will come, and Faustus must be damn'd.
O, I'll leap up to my God! Who pulls me down?
See, see where Christ's blood streams in the firmament!
One drop would save my soul, half a drop. Ah, my
  Christ!

Rend not my heart for naming of my Christ;
Yet will I call on him. O, spare me, Lucifer!
Where is it now? 'Tis gone: and see where God
Stretcheth out his arm and bends his ireful brows,
Mountains and hills, come, come, and fall on me,
And hide me from the heavy wrath of God!
No, no:
Then will I headlong run into the earth.
Earth, gape! O, no, it will not harbour me.
You stars that reign'd at my nativity,
Whose influence hath allotted death and hell,
Now draw up Faustus like a foggy mist
Into the entrails of yon labouring cloud,
That, when you vomit forth into the air,
My limbs may issue from your smoky mouths,
So that my soul may but ascend to heaven.

The watch strikes.

Ah, half the hour is pass'd: 'twill all be pass'd anon.
O God,
If thou wilt not have mercy on my soul,
Yet for Christ's sake, whose blood hath ransom'd me,
Impose some end to my incessant pain;
Let Faustus live in hell a thousand years,
A hundred thousand, and at last be sav'd.
O, no end is limited to damned souls.
Why wert thou not a creature wanting soul?
Or why is this immortal that thou hast?
Ah, Pythagoras' *metempsychosis*, were that true,
This soul should fly from me and I be chang'd
Unto some brutish beast: all beasts are happy,
For when they die
Their souls are soon dissolv'd in elements;
But mine must live still to be plagu'd in hell.
Curs'd be the parents that engender'd me!
No, Faustus, curse thyself, curse Lucifer
That hath depriv'd thee of the joys of heaven.
O, it strikes, it strikes! Now, body, turn to air,
Or Lucifer will bear thee quick to hell!

Thunder and lightning,

O soul, be chang'd into little water drops,
And fall into the ocean, ne'er be found.

3 *Enter Devils.*

My God, my God! Look not so fierce on me!
Adders and serpents, let me breathe awhile!
Ugly hell, gape not! Come not, Lucifer;
I'll burn my books! Ah, Mephostophilis!

Exeunt with him. [Exeunt LUCIFER and BEELZEBUB.]

Scene xx

Enter the Scholars,

1 SCHOLAR Come, gentlemen, let us go visit Faustus,
For such a dreadful night was never seen
Since first the world's creation did begin;
Such fearful shrieks and cries were never heard.
Pray heaven the doctor have escap'd the danger.

2 SCHOLAR O, help us, heaven! see, here are Faustus' limbs,
All torn asunder by the hand of death.

4

3 SCHOLAR The devils whom Faustus serv'd have torn him thus;
For, 'twixt the hours of twelve and one, methought
I heard him shriek and call aloud for help,
At which self time the house seem'd all on fire
With dreadful horror of these damned fiends.

2 SCHOLAR Well, gentlemen, though Faustus' end be such
As every Christian heart laments to think on,
Yet, for he was a scholar, once admir'd
For wondrous knowledge in our German schools,
We'll give his mangled limbs due burial;
And all the students, cloth'd in mourning black,
Shall wait upon his heavy funeral.

Exeunt

[Epilogue]

Enter Chorus.

CHORUS Cut is the branch that might have grown full straight,
And burned is Apollo's laurel bough
That sometime grew within this learned man.
Faustus is gone: regard his hellish fall,
Whose fiendful fortune may exhort the wise
Only to wonder at unlawful things,
Whose deepness doth entice such forward wits
To practise more than heavenly power permits.

[Exit]

Commentary

1 Faustus, who has sold his soul to the Devil, has now reached the last hour of his life before the devils come to claim his soul.

2 The climax approaches as the devils pull, and tear at him. He feels a devil tearing at his heart because he has spoken the name of Christ.

3 He becomes almost insane with desperation as he wants to turn to air or water to hide from the devils before his life is finally torn away.

4 The scholars make comment on Faustus's death, and after the tension and excitement of the climax, the calm dignity of the Chorus sums up Faustus's end. They comment on the tragedy of his death as a lost opportunity for virtue and learning. Their comments end by inviting the audience to learn from Faustus's example and not attempt to transgress divine law.

The Rivals, **Act v, Scene iii**

SIR LUCIUS With your leave, Ma'am, I must put in a word here – I believe I could interpret the young lady's silence. Now mark—

1

LYDIA What is it you mean, Sir?

SIR LUCIUS Come, come, Delia, we must be serious now – this is no time for trifling.

LYDIA 'Tis true, Sir; and your reproof bids me offer this gentleman my hand, and solicit the return of his affections.

ABSOLUTE Oh! my little angel, say you so? – Sir Lucius, I perceive there must be some mistake here with regard to the affront which you affirm I have given you – I can only say, that it could not have been intentional. And as you must be convinced, that I should not fear to support a real injury you shall now see that I am not ashamed to atone for an inadvertency – I ask your pardon. But for this lady, while honoured with her approbation, I will support my claim against any man whatever.

SIR ANTHONY Well said, Jack, and I'll stand by you, my boy.

ACRES Mind, I give up all my claim – I make no pretensions to anything in the world – and if I can't get a wife, without fighting for her, by my valour! I'll live a bachelor.

SIR LUCIUS Captain, give me your hand – an affront handsomely acknowledged becomes an obligation – and as for the lady – if she chooses to deny her own handwriting here – *Taking out letters*

MRS MALAPROP Oh, he will dissolve my mystery! Sir Lucius, perhaps there's some mistake – perhaps, I can illuminate –

SIR LUCIUS Pray, old gentlewoman, don't interfere, where you have no business. Miss Languish, are you my Delia or not?

LYDIA Indeed, Sir Lucius, I am not.

LYDIA and ABSOLUTE walk aside

MRS MALAPROP Sir Lucius O'Trigger – ungrateful as you are – I own the soft impeachment – pardon my blushes, I am Delia.

SIR LUCIUS You Delia – pho! pho! be easy.

MRS MALAPROP Why, thou barbarous Vandyke – those letters are mine. When you are more sensible of my benignity – perhaps I may be brought to encourage your addresses.

SIR LUCIUS Mrs Malaprop, I am extremely sensible of your condescension; and whether you or Lucy have put this trick upon me, I am equally beholden to you. And to show you I'm not ungrateful, Captain Absolute! since you have taken that lady from me, I'll give you my Delia into the bargain.

ABSOLUTE I am much obliged to you, Sir Lucius; but here's our friend, Fighting Bob, unprovided for.

SIR LUCIUS Hah! little Valour – here, will you make your fortune?

ACRES Odds wrinkles! No. But give me your hand, Sir Lucius, forget and forgive; but if ever I give you a chance of pickling me again, say Bob Acres is a dunce, that's all.

SIR ANTHONY Come, Mrs Malaprop, don't be cast down – you are in your bloom yet.

MRS MALAPROP O Sir Anthony! – men are all barbarians—

All retire but JULIA and FAULKLAND

JULIA He seems dejected and unhappy – not sullen – there was some foundation, however, for the tale he told me – O woman! how true should be your judgment, when your resolution is so weak.

FAULKLAND Julia! – how can I sue for what I so little deserve? I dare not presume – yet hope is the child of penitence.

JULIA Oh! Faulkland, you have not been more faulty in your unkind treatment of me, than I am now in wanting inclination to resent it. As my heart honestly bids me place my weakness to the account of love, I should be ungenerous not to admit the same plea for yours.

FAULKLAND Now I shall be blest indeed!

SIR ANTHONY comes forward

SIR ANTHONY What's going on here ? So you have been quarrelling too, I warrant. Come, Julia, I never interfered before; but let me have a hand in the matter at last. All the faults I have ever seen in my friend Faulkland, seemed to proceed from what he calls the *delicacy* and *warmth* of his affection for you – there, marry him directly, Julia, you'll find he'll mend surprisingly!

The rest come forward

SIR LUCIUS Come now, I hope there is no dissatisfied person, but what is content; for as I have been disappointed myself, it will be very hard if I have not the satisfaction of seeing other people succeed better——

ACRES You are right, Sir Lucius. So, Jack, I wish you joy – Mr Faulkland the same. Ladies, come now, to show you I'm neither vexed nor angry, odds tabors and pipes! I'll order the fiddles in half an hour, to the New Rooms – and I insist on your all meeting me there.

SIR ANTHONY Gad! Sir, I like your spirit; and at night we single lads will drink a health to the young couples, and a husband to Mrs Malaprop.

FAULKLAND Our partners are stolen from us. Jack – I hope to be congratulated by each other – yours for having checked in time the errors of an ill-directed imagination, which might have betrayed an innocent heart; and mine, for having, by her gentleness and candour, reformed the unhappy temper of one, who by it made wretched whom he loved most, and tortured the heart he ought to have adored.

ABSOLUTE Well, Faulkland, we have both tasted the bitters, as well as the sweets, of love – with this difference only, that you always prepared the bitter cup for yourself, while I——

LYDIA Was always obliged to me for it, hey! Mr Modesty? – But come, no more of that – our happiness is now as unallayed as general.

JULIA Then let us study to preserve it so: and while hope pictures to us a flattering scene of future bliss, let us deny its pencil those colours which are too bright to be lasting. When hearts deserving happiness would unite their fortunes, virtue would crown them with an unfading garland of modest, hurtless flowers; but ill-judging passion will force the gaudier rose into the wreath, whose thorn offends them, when its leaves are dropped!

2

Commentary

1 'The Rivals' has a quite different ending. The whole drama has been based around the love affairs of two young couples. Throughout the play there has been much mistaken identity and pretending which have led to various confusions. The ending of the play is a time for sorting out the confusions and unravelling the complicated threads of the plot that have developed.

2 The play ends with everything happily resolved for everyone (perhaps with the exception of Mrs Malaprop) and the play ends on a high note hopefully leaving the audience in a similar happy mood.

Progress check

1 How does Marlowe build up the tension in Faustus's final speech?
2 At what point do you think the climax is reached?
3 What function do the scholars serve?
4 What is the function of the Chorus?
5 What techniques has Sheridan used to bring his play to a close?
6 What mood is created?
7 What is the purpose of the closing lines of the play?

Summary

Plays end in different ways depending on the effect the dramatist wants to achieve. In thinking about endings, it is worth asking yourself this question: **How effective do you find this scene as an ending to the play?**

> Different endings serve different purposes.
> The ending is an important element in the play. Look carefully at the techniques that dramatists use to end their plays.

KEY POINTS

Progress check

Now look carefully at the play that you are studying and answer the following questions.

1 What is the effect created by this final scene?
2 What impact do you think that the dramatist wanted to achieve by ending the play in this way?
3 What techniques have been used?
4 What is the purpose of any stage direction?

Specific answers cannot be given for this because it depends on the individual play you are studying. Make sure you have considered all the aspects of the scene.

1.6 Creating characters

After studying this section you should be able to:

- recognise the ways in which dramatists present characters to the audience
- identify the techniques used whereby characters are revealed
- apply these ideas to the play you are studying

LEARNING SUMMARY

AQA A	U4
AQA B	U5
Edexcel	U5
OCR	U4
WJEC	U6
NICCEA	U6

A dramatist can use many different methods of characterisation in order to establish the features and aspects of the characters in the play. Here are some of the techniques they can use.

- Explicit stage directions can be used so the dramatist can define explicitly how the characters in the play should be interpreted.
- The appearance of the characters, the clothes they wear and how they appear physically can tell us about them.
- How the characters speak can reveal important aspects of their characters.
- What other characters say about them can be important.
- What the characters say and do can show a good deal about them.

Now look at the following extract which is taken from *The Duchess of Malfi* by John Webster. The Duchess – whose 'crime' was to remarry after the death of her first husband – has been imprisoned by her wicked brothers and she believes that her second husband is dead. Cariola is her faithful lady-in-waiting and Bosola is a treacherous servant to her brothers.

The Duchess of Malfi, Act iv, Scene ii

DUCHESS Farewell Cariola:
In my last will I have not much to give;
A many hungry guests have fed upon me,
Thine will be a poor reversion.

CARIOLA I will die with her.

1 DUCHESS I pray thee, look thou giv'st my little boy
Some syrup for his cold, and let the girl
Say her prayers, ere she sleep.

[Executioners force CARIOLA off.]

Now what you please—
What death?

BOSOLA Strangling: here are your executioners.

1 DUCHESS I forgive them; The apoplexy, catarrh, or
cough o'th' lungs
Would do as much as they do.

BOSOLA Doth not death fright you?

1 DUCHESS Who would be afraid on't?
Knowing to meet such excellent company
In th' other world.

BOSOLA Yet, methinks,
The manner of your death should much afflict you,
This cord should terrify you?

DUCHESS Not a whit:
What would it pleasure me to have my throat cut
With diamonds? or to be smothered
With cassia? or to be shot to death with pearls?
I know death hath ten thousand several doors
For men to take their exits; and 'tis found
They go on such strange geometrical hinges,

You may open them both ways – any way, for heaven-sake,
So I were out of your whispering – tell my brothers
That I perceive death, now I am well awake,
Best gift is they can give, or I can take.
I would fain put off my last woman's fault,
I'd not be tedious to you.

EXECUTIONER We are ready.

DUCHESS Dispose my breath how please you, but my body
Bestow upon my women, will you?

EXECUTIONER Yes.

DUCHESS Pull, and pull strongly, for your able strength
Must pull down heaven upon me —
Yet stay; heaven-gates are not so highly arch'd
As princes' palaces, they that enter there
Must go upon their knees. *[Kneels]* Come violent death,
Serve for mandragora to make me sleep!
Go tell my brothers, when I am laid out,
They then may feed in quiet.

They strangle her.

BOSOLA Where's the waiting woman?
Fetch her: some other strangle the children.

[Executioners fetch CARIOLA, and one goes to strangle the children.]

Look you, there sleeps your mistress.

CARIOLA O, you are damn'd
Perpetually for this – my turn is next,
Is't not so order'd?

BOSOLA Yes, and I am glad
You are so well prepar'd for't.

2 **CARIOLA** You are deceiv'd sir,
I am not prepar'd for't, I will not die;
I will first come to my answer, and know
How I have offended.

BOSOLA Come, despatch her —
You kept her counsel, now you shall keep ours.

CARIOLA I will not die, I must not, I am contracted
To a young gentleman.

EXECUTIONER Here's your wedding ring.

CARIOLA Let me but speak with the duke: I'll discover
Treason to his person.

BOSOLA Delays —throttle her.

EXECUTIONER She bites, and scratches —

CARIOLA If you kill me now
I am damn'd: I have not been at confession
This two years —

BOSOLA When?

CARIOLA I am quick with child.

BOSOLA Why then,
Your credit's sav'd —

[The Executioners strangle Cariola.]

bear her into th' next room;
Let this lie still.

[Exeunt Executioners with the body of Cariola.]

Commentary

1 Note Duchess's attitude to death.
2 Note Cariola's attitude to death.

Progress check

1 What do you learn about the Duchess's character by her words and behaviour towards the other characters in this extract?

2 What is further shown about her by her references to her children and her brothers?

3 What is her attitude towards death and how does this contrast with both Bosola's and Cariola's?

4 How does Webster create a sense of dignity in the Duchess's character?

5 What is your impression of the character of Bosola and how does Webster create this impression?

1 She is brave and defiant.
2 She is forgiving.
3 Bosola is surprised she is not afraid. Cariola fights against her killers and is afraid.
4 Through the elevated and dignified language she uses.
5 He shows no mercy or feeling for his victims.

Now look at the following extract from *A Streetcar Named Desire*. Blanche has gone to stay with her sister, Stella. Stella's husband and his friends Steve and Mitch arrive home. Read it through carefully.

A Streetcar Named Desire, **Scene 1**

STEVE Playing poker tomorrow night?

STANLEY Yeah – at Mitch's.

MITCH Not at my place. My mother's still sick. *(He starts off)*

STANLEY *(calling after him)* All right, we'll play at my place ... but you bring the beer.

EUNICE *(hollering down from above)* Break it up down there! I made the spaghetti dish and ate it myself.

STEVE *(going upstairs)* I told you and phoned you we was playing. *(To the men.)* Jax beer!

EUNICE You never phoned me once.

STEVE I told you at breakfast – and phoned you at lunch ...

EUNICE Well, never mind about that. You just get yourself home here once in a while.

STEVE You want it in the papers?

More laughter and shouts of parting come from the men. STANLEY throws the screen door of the kitchen open and comes in. He is of medium height, about five feet eight or nine, and strongly, compactly built. Animal joy in his being is implicit in all his movements and attitudes. Since earliest manhood the centre of his life has been pleasure with women, the giving and

taking of it, not with weak indulgence, dependency, but with the power and pride of a richly feathered male bird among hens. Branching out from this complete and satisfying centre are all the auxiliary channels of his life, such as his heartiness with men, his appreciation of rough humour, his love of good drink and food and games, his car, his radio, everything that is his, that bears his emblem of the gaudy seed-bearer. He sizes women up at a glance, with sexual classifications, crude images flashing into his mind and determining the way he smiles at them.

BLANCHE *(drawing involuntarily back from his stare)* You must be Stanley. I'm Blanche.

STANLEY Stella's sister?

BLANCHE Yes.

STANLEY H'lo, Where's the little woman?

BLANCHE In the bathroom.

STANLEY Oh. Didn't know you were coming in town.

BLANCHE I – uh –

STANLEY Where you from, Blanche?

BLANCHE Why, I – live in Laurel.

He has crossed to the closet and removed the whisky bottle.

STANLEY In Laurel, huh? Oh, yeah. Yeah, in Laurel, that's right. Not in my territory. Liquor goes fast in hot weather. *(He holds the bottle to the light to observe its depletion)*

BLANCHE No, I – rarely touch it.

STANLEY Some people rarely touch it but it touches them often.

BLANCHE *(faintly)* Ha-ha.

STANLEY My clothes are stickin' to me. Do you mind if I make myself comfortable? *(He starts to remove his shirt)*

Commentary

1 Note the description of Stanley – a 'macho' character.
2 Note his attitude towards his wife.

Progress check

1 What impression do you form of the character of Stanley?
2 How have you formed that impression?
3 How much have the stage directions contributed towards your impression?

1 He is a 'macho' male chauvinist type of character.
2 The stage directions and the way he speaks about his wife and to Blanche.
3 They create a vivid and detailed impression.

Summary

In the extract from *The Duchess of Malfi* there are very few stage directions except those that simply describe what actions are meant to be taking place. The impression you form of the Duchess (and the other characters) is very much founded on the things that she says and does on stage. In other words, Webster is creating and presenting his characters through the language of the play. Although this is partly true of the extract from *A Street Car Named Desire* – we do learn things about Stanley from the way he acts and the things that he says, Williams has supplemented this with a detailed description through the stage directions. These directions give much more than surface detail, they give an insight into the inner man. Phrases like 'animal joy in his being' and 'the power and pride of a richly feathered male bird among hens' reveal much about the kind of man Stanley is. Remember, then, to gather information about character from as many sources as you can.

Writing about characters

One key point to remember when writing about characters is that you are not writing about 'real' people and so you should avoid describing them as if they were real. They do not have lives of their own and so the 'what if they had done that instead of the other' type of approach is pointless. They act as they do and are what they are because that is the way that the dramatist created them. The question to ask is why did the dramatist create and present them in that way.

> Characters can be created and presented in many ways. Gather all the details you can from the text but remember that they are the creations of the dramatist.
>
> **KEY POINT**

Progress check

Now look at the play you are studying and make notes on the methods used by the dramatist to create and present the characters.

1.7 Issues and themes

After studying this section you should be able to:

LEARNING SUMMARY

- *identify ways in which dramatists present themes in their plays*
- *recognise the themes in the play that you are studying*

AQA A	U4
AQA B	U5
Edexcel	U5
OCR	U4
WJEC	U6
NICCEA	U6

One of the main purposes of a play is to **entertain** the audience. However, very often a play has another purpose too – that of making us think. By reading and watching plays we can learn a great deal about human relationships and the kind of problems, dilemmas and conflicts that human beings may encounter in their lives.

Very often the dramatist has created his or her play around an idea or set of ideas that will be explored through the development of the drama. The audience can be made aware of themes in a number of ways.

- The dramatist can use the character to express certain ideas or views.
- The action of the play can involve the development of the theme(s).
- The setting might be important and contribute to thematic development.
- Stage directions can reveal attitudes or ideas.

Plays can have the power to provoke deep thought and personal reactions from members of the audience or readers.

In *Measure for Measure* by William Shakespeare, for example, the theme of 'morality' is explored in all kinds of ways. One aspect of this involves one of the characters, Isabella, being faced with a dilemma. The play is set in Vienna and the Duke has mysteriously left, leaving his deputy, Angelo, in charge. Morality in the city has become very lax over the years and Angelo has decided to enforce stringent laws to clean it up. Claudio, Isabella's brother, has been arrested and sentenced to death for getting his fiance, Juliet, pregnant. Isabella, who is about to enter a nunnery, has been to Angelo to plead for her brother's life. In the following scene she visits her brother in prison to tell him what has happened.

Measure for Measure, Act III, Scene i

CLAUDIO Now, sister, what's the comfort?

ISABELLA Why'
As all comforts are; most good, most good, indeed
Lord Angelo, having affairs to heaven,
Intends you for his swift ambassador,
Where you shall be an everlasting leiger.
Therefore, your best appointment make with speed;
To-morrow you set on,

CLAUDIO Is there no remedy?

1

ISABELLA None, but such remedy as, to save a head,
To cleave a heart in twain.

CLAUDIO But is there any?

ISABELLA Yes, brother, you may live:
There is a devilish mercy in the judge,
If you'll implore it, that will free your life,
But fetter you till death,

CLAUDIO Perpetual durance?

ISABELLA Ay, just; perpetual durance, a restraint,
Though all the world's vastidity you had,
To a determin'd scope.

CLAUDIO But in what nature?

ISABELLA In such a one as, you consenting to't,
Would bark your honour from that trunk you bear,
And leave you naked.

CLAUDIO Let me know the point.

ISABELLA O, I do fear thee, Claudio; and I quake,
Lest thou a feverous life shouldst entertain,
And six or seven winters more respect
Than a perpetual honour. Dar'st thou die?
The sense of death is most in apprehension;
And the poor beetle that we tread upon
In corporal sufferance finds a pang as great
As when a giant dies.

2

CLAUDIO Why give you me this shame?
Think you I can a resolution fetch
From flow'ry tenderness? If I must die,
I will encounter darkness as a bride
And hug it in mine arms.

ISABELLA There spake my brother; there my father's grave
Did utter forth a voice. Yes, thou must die:
Thou art too noble to conserve a life
In base appliances. This outward-sainted deputy,
Whose settled visage and deliberate word
Nips youth i'th' head, and follies doth enmew
As falcon doth the fowl, is yet a devil;
His filth within being cast, he would appear
A pond as deep as hell.

CLAUDIO The precise Angelo!

ISABELLA O, 'tis the cunning livery of hell
The damned'st body to invest and cover
In precise guards! Dost thou think, Claudio,
If I would yield him my virginity
Thou mightst be freed?

CLAUDIO O heavens! it cannot be.

ISABELLA Yes, he would give't thee, from this rank offence,
So to offend him still. This night's the time

That I should do what I abhor to name,
Or else thou diest to-morrow.

CLAUDIO Thou shall not do't.

3

ISABELLA O, were it but my life!
I'd throw it down for your deliverance
As frankly as a pin.

CLAUDIO Thanks, dear Isabel.

ISABELLA Be ready, Claudio, for your death to-morrow.

CLAUDIO Yes. Has he affections in him
That thus can make him bite the law by th' nose
When he would force it? Sure it is no sin;
Or of the deadly seven it is the least.

ISABELLA Which is the least?

CLAUDIO If it were damnable, he being so wise,
Why would he for the momentary trick
Be perdurably fin'd – O Isabel!

ISABELLA What says my brother?

CLAUDIO Death is a fearful thing.

ISABELLA And shamed life a hateful.

CLAUDIO Ay, but to die, and go we know not where;
To lie in cold obstruction, and to rot;
This sensible warm motion to become
A kneaded clod; and the delighted spirit
To bathe in fiery floods or to reside
In thrilling region of thick-ribbed ice;
To be imprison'd in the viewless winds,
And blown with restless violence round about
The pendent world; or to be worse than worst
Of those that lawless and incertain thought
Imagine howling – 'tis too horrible.
The weariest and most loathed worldly life
That age, ache, penury, and imprisonment,
Can lay on nature is a paradise
To what we fear of death.

4

ISABELLA Alas, alas!

CLAUDIO Sweet sister, let me live.
What sin you do to save a brother's life,
Nature dispenses with the deed so far
That it becomes a virtue.

5

ISABELLA O you beast!
O faithless coward! O dishonest wretch!
Wilt thou be made a man out of my vice?
Is't not a kind of incest to take life
From thine own sister's shame? What should I think?
Heaven shield my mother play'd my father fair!
For such a warped slip of wilderness
Ne'er issu'd from his blood. Take my defiance;
Die; perish. Might but my bending down
Reprieve thee from thy fate, it should proceed.
I'll pray a thousand prayers for thy death,
No word to save thee.

6

CLAUDIO Nay, hear me, Isabel,

ISABELLA O fie, fie, fie!
Thy sin's not accidental, but a trade.
Mercy to thee would prove itself a bawd;
'Tis best that thou diest quickly.

Commentary

1 Isabella does not tell her brother immediately.
2 She is unsure of Claudio's reaction.
3 Claudio does not want his sister to sacrifice herself for him.
4 He begins to change his mind.
5 He now wants her to do it to save him.
6 Isabella responds harshly to him.

Progress check

1 On what condition is Angelo prepared to free Claudio?

2 How has Isabella responded to Angelo's offer? What is your view on her decision?

3 Who do you feel the most sympathy for in this extract, Isabella or Claudio?

4 How do you respond to Claudio's behaviour?

5 What moral issues do you think Shakespeare is raising here?

1 On condition that Isabella gives her body to Angelo.
2 She has rejected it.
3 You must decide.
4 Again you must decide for yourself.
5 The question of Isabella's attitude to her chastity, Angelo's corruption and Claudio's attitude toward his sister's predicament.

> **KEY POINT**
>
> Most plays contain themes or issues that the dramatist explores and wants the audience to think about.

1.8 Soliloquies and asides

AQA A	U4
AQA B	U5
Edexcel	U5
OCR	U4
WJEC	U6
NICCEA	U6

Dramatists often make full use of various dramatic devices and it is likely that you will encounter both asides and soliloquies during the course of your studies.

In Shakespeare's *Othello* there is substantial use of both long and short asides. They reveal to the audience what is going on in the mind of the speaker. This is a particularly long aside from *Othello*. Iago watches his enemy, Cassio, take the hand of Othello's wife, Desdemona. Read it through carefully.

Othello Act II Scene i

IAGO *(Aside)* He takes her by the palm. Ay, well said, whisper. With as little web as this will I ensnare as great a fly as Cassio. Ay, smile upon her, do. I will gyve thee in thine own courtship. You say true, 'tis so indeed. If such tricks as these strip you out of your lieutenantry, it had been better you had not kissed your three fingers so oft, which now again you are most apt to play the sir in. Very good: well kissed, an excellent courtesy! 'Tis so indeed. Yet again your fingers to your lips? Would they were clyster-pipes for your sake!

The repeated use of asides also give us an insight into Othello's growing torment. For example, in the following extract Iago urges Othello to secretly observe his (Iago's) conversation with Cassio, to convince Othello (quite wrongly) that Cassio and Desdemona are having an affair. In fact, he and Cassio are talking about Bianca.

Othello Act IV, Scene i

OTHELLO *(Aside)* Look, how he laughs already!

IAGO I never knew a woman love man so.

CASSIO Alas, poor rogue! I think i'faith she loves me.

OTHELLO *(Aside)* Now he denies it faintly, and laughs it out.

IAGO Do you hear, Cassio?

OTHELLO *(Aside)* Now he importunes him to tell it o'er. Go to, well said, well said!

IAGO She gives it out that you shall marry her. Do you intend it?

CASSIO Ha, ha, ha!

OTHELLO *(Aside)* Do you triumph, Roman? Do you triumph?

CASSIO I marry her! What! A customer! Prithee bear some charity to my wit: do not think it so unwholesome. Ha, ha, ha!

OTHELLO *(Aside)* So, so, so, so: they laugh that win.

Progress check

1 What does the first aside reveal about Iago?
2 What do the other asides reveal to the audience?

Summary

The first aside reveals to the audience the wicked plan developing in Iago's mind and how he is going to turn Cassio's innocent affection for Desdemona against him. It gives a glimpse into his thoughts and the delight he takes in his evil. In the second extract the frequent asides act almost as a running commentary on the effect that Iago's words are having on Othello as his jealousy builds up.

Soliloquies, too, are used extensively to convey both information and inward emotion to the audience. In *King Lear*, for example, the wicked Edmund, the illegitimate son of Gloucester, who his father regards as a loving and dutiful son, reveals to the audience his real inner thoughts and feelings through a soliloquy.

King Lear, Act I, Scene ii

EDMUND Thou, Nature, art my goddess; to thy law
  My services are bound. Wherefore should I
  Stand in the plague of custom, and permit
  The curiosity of nations to deprive me,
  For that I am some twelve or fourteen moonshines
  Lag of a brother? Why bastard? Wherefore base?
  When my dimensions are as well compact,
  My mind as generous, and my shape as true,
  As honest madam's issue? Why brand they us
  With base? with baseness? bastardy? base, base?
Who in the lusty stealth of nature take
More composition and fierce quality
Than doth, within a dull, stale, tired bed,
Go to th'creating a whole tribe of fops,
Got 'tween asleep and wake? Well then,
Legitimate Edgar, I must have your land:
Our father's love is to the bastard Edmund
As to th'legitimate. Fine word, 'legitimate'!
Well, my legitimate, if this letter speed,
And my invention thrive, Edmund the base
Shall top th'legitimate – : I grow, I prosper;
Now, gods, stand up for bastards!

> Asides and soliloquies can be used by dramatists to enable characters to communicate what is in their minds or to comment on the action, giving the audience valuable information about what is happening. **KEY POINT**

Progress check

1 What does Edmund reveal to the audience through this soliloquy?
2 Look at the play you are studying and identify any soliloquies.

Make a list of each soliloquy in the play and for each one note down the following details:

(a) who is speaking

(b) the context of the soliloquy

(c) what is being said

(d) why the dramatist uses a soliloquy at that point in the drama.

1 Edmund reveals he intends to plot against his father and brother and that he resents being the illegitimate son.

1.9 Text and context

AQA A	U4, U6
AQA B	U5, U6
Edexcel	U4, U5, U6
OCR	U4
WJEC	U6
NICCEA	U6

Some examination boards test your knowledge of the context and background against which drama texts were written and performed. It is a good idea to know something about the dramatist who wrote the play or plays you are studying and about the historical period in which they lived and worked. This aspect of the examination will be dealt with in detail in chapter 5.

1.10 Approaches to your text

AQA A	U4
AQA B	U5
Edexcel	U5
OCR	U4
WJEC	U6
NICCEA	U6

There are a number of things you can do to help yourself prepare your drama text for the examination. Here are some suggestions:

- try to see a live performance of the play if at all possible
- watch as many video recordings, DVDs or films of different versions of the play – every performance is different
- make notes on the performance you have seen to help you to remember those important initial impressions
- read your drama text thoroughly
- listen to the play on audio tape
- go to the theatre as often as you can to see other plays in order to build up a sense of the nature of drama and the theatre.

Working from the text

If it is not possible to see a performance of the play there are still things you can do to help compensate for this. Here are some suggestions:

- work with others dramatising for yourselves sections or scenes from the text
- talk to others about how staging could be done
- imagine you are a director – plan carefully how you would stage a production of the play, the kind of actors you would cast, how you would bring your own interpretation out live on the stage, etc.
- use diagrams and drawings to work out sets, stage layout, props, etc. for selected scenes.

Some key areas

Think about relationships between the various elements of the play and how together they present a 'whole'. Here are some areas to think about:

- the **characters** – look at key speeches, shifts in focus, different ways of interpreting what they do and say
- look for various possible **meanings** in the play
- consider the **theatrical effects**
- think about the **pace and variety** of the action
- think about the **overall shape and structure** of the play and the impact that this could have on an audience.

> There are a great many things you can do to improve your chances of achieving a good result in your study of a drama text.

KEY POINT

Sample question and model answer

The following question is typical of the kind of question you could be asked on a play. In this case the dominant assessment objective that the question tests is AO4.

Above all, this question tests the candidate's ability to consider:

- different interpretations of texts by other readers (AO4)
- their own informed independent opinions (AO4).

It also, to a lesser extent, tests:

- knowledge and understanding of the text (AO2)
- ability to communicate that understanding clearly and coherently (AO1)
- exploration of the ways the writer's choices of form, structure and language inform meaning (AO3).

This is a closed book question.

Some critics feel that Sheridan has misjudged the entertainment value of Faulkland and Julia to such an extent that they become a distraction from the plot. Others feel that they are central to Sheridan's design and have an important role to play. What is your view of the function of these two characters in the drama?

Very often in plays one way in which the various characters are defined and developed is by comparing and contrasting them against other characters. This technique is particularly clear to see in 'The Rivals', especially with regard to the characters of Faulkland and Julia. Almost all their appearances throughout the play serve to emphasise particular aspects of their characters. Julia is seen as a woman of generous nature and tolerant disposition whereas Faulkland frequently exhibits an intolerance born of an insecurity which almost borders on jealousy in its intensity. She shows a steadiness and resolution and trust that contrast markedly with his wavering doubts and recriminations and constant questioning of her sincerity.

From the very first scene that they share together Sheridan makes this contrast between the two clear – she the sensible, level-headed and sincere young woman and he full of the self-indulgent sentimentality so effectively teased by Jack through the unwitting Acres earlier in the play. Faulkland is, however, fully aware of his short-comings as we can see through his self-reproval just before seeing Julia in Act III Scene ii –

> 'How mean does this captious, unsatisfied temper of
> mine appear to my cooler judgement ... I am ever
> ungenerously fretful, and madly capricious! I am
> conscious of it – yet I cannot correct myself!'
>
> (III.ii. 2–7)

Nevertheless, he is unable to stop himself upbraiding Julia almost immediately that she appears and her happiness at seeing Faulkland is quickly dampened by his outburst –

> 'I own to you that my joy at hearing of your health
> and arrival here, by your neighbour Acres, was somewhat
> damped, by his dwelling much on the high spirits you
> had enjoyed in Devonshire ... I should regard every
> mirthful moment in your absence as a treason to
> constancy: the mutual tear that steals down the cheek
> of parting lovers is a compact, that no smile shall
> live there till they meet again.'
>
> (III.ii. 27–35)

Margin notes:

Clear opening showing a focus on the question.

Develops introductory idea and supports idea with a quotation.

Spends too long through this section describing characters of Julia and Faulkland. Some over-long quotations here too.

Sample question and model answer (continued)

He goes on to question the integrity of her feelings for him showing clearly the extent of the romantic obsession that torments him and that Jack made fun of so much in Act II Scene ii. Julia's response is one intended to reassure Faulkland, to put his mind at rest and ease the unreasonable doubts that she knows he possesses as a part of his nature –

> 'Must I never cease to tax my Faulkland with this
> teasing, minute caprice? Can the idle reports of
> a silly boor weigh in your breast against my tried
> affection?'

> (III.ii. 36–38)

However, Julia cannot win against the wavering doubts that torment Faulkland; a point that she herself recognises more than anyone –

> 'I never can be happy in your absence. If I wear a
> countenance of content, it is to show that my mind
> holds no doubt of my Faulkland's truth. If I seemed
> sad, it were to make malice triumph; and say, that
> I had fixed my heart on one, who left me to lament
> his roving, and my own credulity'.

> (III.ii. 43–48)

Faulkland accepts her words and upbraids himself as being 'a brute' but as the scene progresses he moves between self-denigration and the constant questioning and doubting of Julia's constancy. In the end she can stand it no longer and breaks down in tears leaving Faulkland alone with his guilt and his doubts.

In the 'partner' scene to this one, Act V Scene i, Faulkland gives Julia her final test which succeeds only in driving them apart. In some ways this is a sombre and intense scene and the comedy in it is not immediately apparent. Instead of the lightness which characterises the greater part of this play we are faced, here, with the painful and moving emotions that Faulkland's feigned plight arouses in Julia.

This shows a clearer focus on the question.

One effect that the presence of Julia and Faulkland has on the play is to allow Sheridan to explore two very different characters: the commonsense steadfastness of Julia and the overly sentimental, brooding Faulkland. Their presence has a deepening effect on the play as Sheridan explores the interaction of these two characters.

Good ideas here developed further. The essay really begins to look at the function of the characters in the drama rather than simply saying what they are like and how they differ from each other.

As well as providing this kind of character contrast in the play, Julia and Faulkland also provide a contrast with the other pair of lovers, Jack and Lydia. In Act II Scene i we can see that Julia forms an immediate contrast to Lydia. We have just seen how immersed Lydia is in a world of romantic fantasy and this contrasts markedly with the commonsense attitude presented by Julia who clearly does not possess Lydia's over-worked romantic imagination. However, we can see that though not suffering the delusions of on overly-romantic imagination, Julia loves Faulkland deeply and defends him against the charges teasingly levelled against their relationship by Lydia. Despite the excuses with which Julia defends Faulkland's nature though, it is clear that she, like Lydia, will need to develop in the course of the play before her relationship can come to a satisfactory fruition. The effect overall of Julia's logical and serious defence of Faulkland in this scene serves to emphasise not only her own commonsense outlook but also to highlight the dreamy romanticism of Lydia.

Sample question and model answer (continued)

Just as the character of Julia creates a contrast with that of Lydia, so the character of Jack contrasts markedly with that of Faulkland. In Act II Scene i the fundamental difference between the two men is clearly seen. In Jack we see a lively young officer with a sharp wit and mischievous nature set against the melancholic, morose Faulkland. Faulkland's mood is immediately seen in his response to Jack's invitation to dine with him –

Good choice of quotation here to illustrate contrasts between Jack and Faulkland.

'Indeed I cannot: I am not in spirits to be of such a party'. (II.i.78.)

This provokes Jack to tease Faulkland about his attitude to love as he draws the distinction as he sees it between himself and Faulkland –

'Am not I a lover; aye, and a romantic one too? Yet do
I carry everywhere with me such a confounded farrago
of doubts, fears, hopes, wishes, and all the flimsy
furniture of a country miss's brain.'
(II.i.83–86)

However, Faulkland justifies the fears and doubts he feels by pointing to their difference of attitude –

Candidate begins to draw ideas together.

'Ah! Jack, your heart and soul are not, like mine, fixed
immutably only on one object. You throw for a large
stake, but losing – you could stake and throw again:
but I have set my sum of happiness on this cast, and
not to succeed, were to be stripped of all.'
(II.i.87–91)

In the end Faulkland's idealised, overly-sentimental, self-indulgent view of love leads him to this conclusion – that his entire future happiness, indeed, his very existence, depends on the success of his relationship with Julia. This idealised view of love also accounts for his view that there is a certain code of behaviour to which true lovers adhere. The fact that in his mind Julia fails to live up to this code is emphasised with the arrival of Acres and the subsequent teasing that Jack extracts from the situation. In this sense Faulkland suffers from a similar distortion of what 'love' is, as Lydia. Both, in their different ways suffer from a false and idealised view of love. Hers is overly-romantic and his overly-sentimental.

Effective conclusion which reinforces views discussed and sums up ideas.

Julia and Faulkland, then, have an important and central role to play in the drama. Faulkland allows Sheridan to focus some of the humour of the play on the vogue for 'sentimentality' that was current in the eighteenth century and so shows the shortcomings of a character who excessively dissects relationships and constantly questions motives. More than this, though, both Julia and Faulkland provide a contrast with Lydia and Jack and help to broaden the range and variety of characters in the play. In doing so they enrich and add depth to the plot overall.

Overall a good essay although the first part focuses too much on the describing of the characters of Julia and Faulkland rather than an analysis of their role in the play. The essay then begins to take off and there are some good, well-focused comments and ultimately an effective conclusion.

Exam practice and analysis

The following question tests AO5ii as the dominant objective:

- evaluate the significance of cultural, historical and other contextual influences upon literary texts and study.

This is an open book question.

'An impressive opening, a marvellous ending, and indifferent middle'.

Does this twentieth-century comment represent to you a fair summary of Doctor Faustus? Support your views by detailed illustration from the text.

Edexcel Specimen materials 2000

Here are some ideas to think about. They are taken from the mark scheme and relate to the Assessment Objectives for this question.

AO5ii   The question turns to a large extent on the issue of historical perspective; candidates are likely to be divided between those who consider the tension between the context in which the play was written and that from which the comment originated, and those who discern further levels and consider the importance of the context in which the play was set and in which they, as twenty-first-century readers (perhaps as distinct from spectators) with their own personal, cultural and religious perspective, approach it.

AO1   Quality of definition will be a significant discriminator here, with some candidates seeing 'impressive' and 'marvellous' simply as rather general superlatives, while others are likely to take them in their strongest possible sense as 'striking in impression' and 'awesome', in true contrast to 'indifferent'.

AO2ii   This question requires candidates to consider the play as a whole; some are likely to look at its beginning, middle and end in turn and in isolation, while others will set them in context and consider the structure of the play as a whole, examining how each of the three informs the other.

A03   Candidates are asked to analyse the text in detail; what will distinguish them is the extent to which their analysis is tailored to the terms of the quotation.

AO4   Reward for answers against this AO will depend on the quality of argument advanced, with some candidates simply giving uncritical acceptance to the proposition, while others will assess its validity part by part, and may well venture an alternative statement of their own as summary of the play.

Chapter 2

Poetry

The following topics are covered in this chapter:

- *Reading poetry*
- *Content and poetic voice*
- *Tone and mood*
- *Form and structure*

- *Rhyme and rhythm*
- *Imagery*
- *Approaching poetry*

2.1 Reading poetry

After studying this section you should be able to:

- recognise some of the features of poetry
- understand some of its purposes
- ask questions about a poem
- understand the different elements that make up a poem

LEARNING SUMMARY

AQA A	U4, U6
AQA B	U5
Edexcel	U5, U6
OCR	U4, U6
WJEC	U4, U6
NICCEA	U4

The study of poetry is a central element in all A2 courses and it does present particular challenges that are, perhaps, rather different from those posed by either drama or prose. It is certainly true that some poetry is only accessible to us if we do a certain amount of background reading and research. For example, some poetry contains archaic words that you need to look up, or it contains certain ideas or concepts that are alien to us today but which need to be understood in order to fully understand the poetry.

The question of what exactly poetry is – what makes it different from prose – is a question which many have asked. Certainly poetry can take many forms and poets can employ a wide range of different structures, techniques and styles when writing their poetry.

Although most poetry is written to be read by others it can also be a very private and personal medium that can evoke very individual responses from the reader. This means, of course, that our response to a poem may not be the same as someone else's response. On the other hand this does not mean that you can say just what you want about a poem. As with the other forms of literature that you study, your views need to be supported by close reference to the text itself.

Here are some features that a poem might have.

- Poetry can rhyme.
- Poetry can be organised in lines.
- Each line can begin with a capital letter.
- The poem can be organised in stanzas.
- The poem might have a regular rhythm.
- The poem might contain imagery.

On the other hand a poem need not necessarily have any of these features, which illustrates that poetry can be extremely varied in nature.

Progress check

Write down as many different kinds of poems that you can think of.
Here are some that you might have come across.

- Narrative poems that tell stories of various kinds.
- Poems that express emotions such as love.
- Poems that explore philosophical ideas.
- Poems that express spiritual or religious ideas.
- Poems that are humorous.
- Poems that deliberately use language in a way that doesn't make conventional sense, e.g. nonsense verse.

Poems then, can serve many purposes including to:

- amuse
- describe
- entertain
- express emotions
- narrate
- inform
- express grief or sadness
- celebrate
- commemorate
- philosophise.

The main thing to recognise is that every poem is an individual piece of work and that when reading a poem for the first time it is important to try to establish three key pieces of information about the poem. To do this you need to ask yourself the following questions:

What is the poet saying in this poem?

Why has the poem been written – what is the poet's purpose?

How does the poet uses language to express his or her views and achieve the desired effects?

Of course, a poem may have more than one purpose – the main thing is to be able to identify what the poet wants to achieve by writing the poem.

In order to express their ideas through poetry poets make various choices with regard to vocabulary, style, form, the use of imagery and other poetic features. A close examination of these features can provide useful clues as to what the poet's intentions are.

> Poetry can come in many different types and can have a wide range of purposes.
>
> **KEY POINT**

How poems work

In order to fully understand a poem and the ways in which it achieves its effects you have to understand the various elements which help to make it up. In most poems there are the key elements that combine to create the overall effect of the poem:

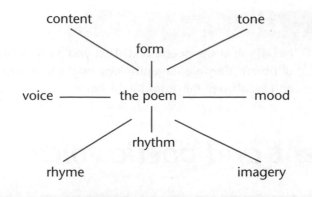

Progress check

Think about each of these elements of a poem. Write a brief note to explain what each of them means.

Here are some ideas:

Content: The content of a poem is, quite simply, what it is all about – the ideas, themes and storyline that it contains.

Form: This refers to the way in which the poem is structured or laid out. The key points here are **why** the poet has chosen a particular form and **what effect** is achieved through the use of that form.

Tone: The idea of tone can be closely linked with the 'voice' of the poem. There are many different kinds of tone a poet can employ.

Mood: The mood of the poem is closely linked to the tone but this refers more to the **atmosphere** that the poem creates.

Imagery: This is created by language being used in such a way as to help us to hear, see, taste or feel or generally understand **more clearly** and **vividly** what is being said.

Rhythm: Rhythm refers to the regular **beat** of the words of the poems. Often the rhythm pattern works on a line basis.

Rhyme: Rhyme occurs when the **sounds** of words written in the poem go together. This usually happens at the ends of lines although it does sometimes happen within lines when it is called 'internal rhyme'.

Voice: The voice, or poetic voice of a poem really identifies the 'speaker' of the poem. This could be the poet's own voice or it could be the voice of a character that the poet has invented.

Looking at these elements of a poem is simply a more detailed way of asking the questions that we have already mentioned –

What is the poem about?
Why was it written?
How has the poet chosen to write it?

Remember though, that all these elements interrelate and that the overall effect of the poem is dependent on these elements working together to produce a unified whole.

> The effect achieved by a poem is the result of a number of related features working together to produce the text.
>
> **KEY POINT**

Now look at the poetry texts that you are studying and think about what kind of poems they are (an anthology might have lots of different types of poems) and what their purposes might be.

2.2 Content and poetic voice

After studying this section you should be able to:

- *understand what is meant by the 'content' of poems*
- *understand what is meant by the 'poetic voice' of a poem*
- *relate these ideas to the poetry text that you are studying*

AQA A	U4, U6
AQA B	U6
Edexcel	U5, U6
OCR	U4, U6
NICCEA	U4

Basically the content of a poem is what it is all about – the ideas, themes and storyline that it contains. When examining a poem it is useful to begin by establishing a general outline of what it is about. This is sometimes referred to as the 'surface meaning' of the poem. Having an idea of this will give you a framework on which to build the more detailed and complex ideas that form as your analysis of the poem develops. Sometimes it is possible to respond to a poem without fully understanding every word or phrase and sometimes meaning 'evolves' as you continue to study a poem. However, having an initial idea or impression of what a poem is about, can be an important first step towards a fuller and more assured understanding.

When considering the content of a poem it is also important to identify the poetic voice of the poem. In other words decide who the 'speaker' of the poem is. In many cases the poetic voice may well be the poet's, but it may be that the words of the poem are 'spoken' through a character that the poet has created or a narrator figure other than the poet. This happens almost all the time in *The Canterbury Tales*, where usually a particular character is telling the tale. Chaucer (the writer) often then interrupts his character (his fictitious narrator) to address the reader. It can often happen in poems which are not so narrative-based too.

Identifying the speaker also helps to determine a number of other aspects of the poem such as tone, mood and the overall intention behind the poem. The poetic voice could be the poet's genuine voice expressing a heartfelt emotion or it could be the voice of a narrator expressing a view or feeling that the poet may or may not share.

At the beginning of this chapter we mentioned the idea that some poems need a certain amount of research or background knowledge in order to establish a full understanding of them. The following poem is a good example of this. It is short and the language it uses is relatively simple but you may find some aspects of it difficult to understand fully. It is written by the twentieth-century poet, Philip Larkin. Read it through carefully.

> ***Naturally the Foundation Will Pay Your Expenses***
> Hurrying to catch my Comet
>   One dark November day,
> Which soon would snatch me from it
>   To the sunshine of Bombay,
> I pondered pages Berkeley
>   Not three weeks since had heard,
> Perceiving Chatto darkly
>   Through the mirror of the third.

Crowds, colourless and careworn,
  Had made my taxi late,
Yet not till I was airborne
  Did I recall the date –
That day when Queen and Minister
  And Band of Guards and all
Still act their solemn-sinister
  Wreath-rubbish in Whitehall.

It used to make me throw up,
  These mawkish nursery games:
O when will England grow up?
  – But I outsoar the Thames,
And dwindle off down Auster
  To greet Professor Lal
(He once met Morgan Forster),
  My contact and my pal.

Philip Larkin

Progress check

Now look at the poem again.

1 Write a brief outline of what the poem is about (the content).
2 Who is the speaker of the poem?
3 What obstacles to understanding did you encounter when looking at the poem?

3 See below.
2 The lecturer.
1 A visiting lecturer flying out to India to deliver a lecture.

You probably understood the surface meaning of the poem in that it describes a lecturer who is flying out to India to give a lecture. You might have had some difficulty establishing the 'poetic voice' as this could be the poet himself speaking or it could be a character he has created.

A small amount of research, however, would make the whole thing much clearer. For example, you probably had trouble with some or all of these references:

  'I pondered pages Berkeley
    Not three weeks since had heard.'
  'Perceiving Chatto darkly
    Through the mirror of the Third.'
  'wreath-rubbish in Whitehall'
  'Mawkish'
  'down Auster'
  'Morgan Forster'

Here is some information that might help with an understanding of the content.

'Berkeley' refers to the University of California – the narrator looks through the pages of his lecture which he had given at that university less than three weeks before.

'Chatto' – this refers to the publisher, Chatto and Windus, who he thinks might publish the book he will write based on his lectures.

'The third' – a radio programme, now Radio Three. The narrator thinks he might be invited to give his lecture on radio.

'wreath-rubbish in Whitehall'. Remembrance Day parade.

'Mawkish' – sentimental in a feeble sickly kind of way.

'Auster' – a poetic name for the south wind.

'Morgan Forster' – this refers to the writer, E.M. Forster (1879–1970) the famous novelist and critic. Forster's books include *A Passage to India*, *Howard's End* and *A Room With A View*, amongst others.

Being aware of what these references mean will probably have helped a good deal in your understanding of the poem's content.

The poetic voice may be a little more difficult to establish but if you know anything at all about the poet Philip Larkin you will know he was a very private man who hated travelling abroad. It is not likely, therefore, that the jet-setting, ambitious lecturer of the poem is Larkin himself. The voice, therefore, must be that of a character or 'persona' that he has adopted. Once this is established it prompts the further question of what is Larkin's attitude to the character he has created? This then raises a series of other questions such as:

- What is the poet's attitude towards the poem's narrator?
- What does he think about his views (on the Remembrance Day Parade, for example)?
- Does he use the narrator to make some point of his own?
- Is Larkin's own 'voice' discernible behind the narrator's voice – is he mocking the 'character', for example?
- Does the tone of the poem help you with any of these questions? (See next section.)

> **KEY POINT**
>
> Background reading and research can help a great deal in establishing the meaning of some poems.

Progress check

Now look at the poetry text you are studying and choose one of the poems. Examine the poem to establish the surface meaning and the poetic voice.

2.3 Tone and mood

After studying this section you should be able to:

- *understand what is meant by tone and mood*
- *identify tone and mood in poems*
- *recognise the influence that tone and mood can have on poetry*

LEARNING SUMMARY

AQA A	U4, U6
AQA B	U5
Edexcel	U5, U6
OCR	U4, U6
WJEC	U4, U6
NICCEA	U4

The tone and mood that a poem creates can have a significant effect on the overall impact of the poem on the reader. As we have seen, a poem contains a 'voice' and like any voice it can project a certain tone that gives the listener (or reader) certain messages. Obviously there are many different kinds of tone. The tone might be angry or reflective, melancholy or joyful, bitter or ironic. Just as the tone of voice in which someone speaks tells us a great deal about the way they feel, so the tone of the 'poetic voice' tells us a great deal about how the poet or the narrator of the poem feels.

The mood of a poem is not quite the same thing as the tone although the two are very closely linked. When we refer to the mood of a poem we are really talking about the atmosphere that the poet creates in the poem.

When studying poetry it is important to recognise that it is not only the words that create the meaning and effect of the poem. The overall effect is achieved through a particular combination of all the various elements that we identified earlier. Part of this is the contribution made by tone and mood.

One way to try to help yourself establish the mood of a poem is to read it aloud. You can experiment with various readings, seeing which one you think best fits the particular poem. (Don't try this in an exam, of course.) The more practice you get at reading poems aloud and the more you are able to hear others read them, the better able you will be to 'hear' poems in your mind when you read them to yourself.

There are various ways in which tone and mood can be created. For example it can be created through:

- the loudness or softness of the voice speaking the poem
- the rhythm that is created
- the poet's choice of words
- the emphasis placed on particular words or phrases
- the breaks and pauses that the poet places in the poem.

Progress check

Read the following poems carefully. (Try reading them aloud as well as to yourself.) What kind of tone do you think is appropriate to each and what kind of mood does each poem create? How does each poet create a sense of tone and mood?

That Time of Year Thou Mayst in Me Behold

1 That time of year thou mayst in me behold
   When yellow leaves, or none, or few, do hang
2 Upon those boughs which shake against the cold,
   Bare ruined choirs where late the sweet birds sang.
3 In me thou see'st the twilight of such day
   As after sunset fadeth in the west,
4 Which by-and-by black night doth take away,
   Death's second self that seals up all in rest.
   In me thou see'st the glowing of such fire
5 That on the ashes of his youth doth lie,
   As the deathbed whereon it must expire,
6 Consumed with that which it was nourished by.
     This thou perceiv'st, which makes thy love more strong,
     To love that well which thou must leave ere long.

William Shakespeare

Engineers' Corner

7 Why isn't there an Engineers' Corner in Westminster Abbey?
   In Britain we've always made more fuss of a ballad than a blueprint ...
8 How many schoolchildren dream of becoming great engineers?

Advertisement placed in *The Times* by the Engineering Council.

We make more fuss of ballads than of blueprints –
That's why so many poets end up rich,
While engineers scrape by in cheerless garrets.
Who needs a bridge or dam? Who needs a ditch?

Whereas the person who can write a sonnet
Has got it made. It's always been the way,
For everybody knows that we need poems
And everybody reads them every day.

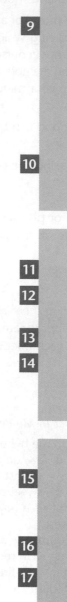

Yes, life is hard if you choose engineering –
You're sure to need another job as well;
9 You'll have to plan your projects in the evenings
Instead of going out. It must be hell.

While well-heeled poets ride around in Daimlers,
You'll burn the midnight oil to earn a crust,
With no hope of a statue in the Abbey,
With no hope, even, of a modest bust.

No wonder small boys dream of writing couplets
And spurn the bike, the lorry and the train.
10 There's far too much encouragement for poets –
That's why this country's going down the drain.

Wendy Cope

Ah! Sun-flower

11 Ah, Sun-flower! Weary of time,
Who countest the steps of the Sun,
12 Seeking after that sweet golden clime
Where the traveller's journey is done.

13 Where the Youth pined away with desire,
And the pale Virgin shrouded in snow,
14 Arise from their graves and aspire
Where my Sun-flower wishes to go.

William Blake

Adlestrop

15 Yes, I remember Adlestrop –
The name, because one afternoon
Of heat the express-train drew up there
Unwontedly. It was late June.

16 The steam hissed. Someone cleared his throat.
No one left and no one came
17 On the bare platform. What I saw
Was Adlestrop – only the name.

And willows, willow-herb, and grass,
And meadowsweet, and haycocks dry,
No whit less still and lonely fair
Than the high cloudlets in the sky.

18 And for that minute a blackbird sang
Close by, and round him, mistier,
19 Farther and farther, all the birds
Of Oxfordshire and Gloucestershire.

Edward Thomas

Commentary

1   Yellow leaves suggestive of death and decay.
2   Suggestive of winter followed up by 'cold'.
3   Twilight again – suggesting the end of things.
4   Sunset – another image of the end – the end of the day, this time.
5   After the fire – ashes.

Commentary (continued)

6 Death?
7 Rhyme scheme creates a sense of lightness.
8 Note the rhetorical questions.
9 Amusing, punchy line.
10 Light mocking tone.
11 Long vowel sounds give a tired feel.
12 'weary' – a tiredness.
13 'pined away' gives feeling of death.
14 followed up by 'Pale Virgin' shrouded in snow.
15 Hot, summer's day.
16 Onomatopoeic effect.
17 Little happening, quiet, deserted – adds to atmosphere.
18 The beauty of the bird-song.
19 Gives a sense of infinity, a timelessness to the poems.

Summary

The first poem links three topics, summer and winter, day and night and a burning fire and a dead one, in the sense that they are all transitions between one state and another. The passage of time is constantly referred to in this poem, and the final two lines focus the poem on the person to whom it is addressed – his lover. These last two lines enable the poet to change direction and create a kind of 'twist in the tail' ending to the poem. The tone created here is one of regret for how short a time we have to live and love and a wistfulness, perhaps even a melancholy, about the passing of time and wasted love.

The tone of Wendy Cope's poem is much lighter. She is writing with her tongue firmly in her cheek (although there is an underlying serious point about the poem if we choose to take it) and the rhyme scheme, rhythm and her choice of vocabulary and images combine to create a humourous poem, light in tone.

In the short poem by Blake the first stanza traces the daily movement of the sunflower as it follows the sun. Blake imagines that it does so out of a yearning for another, kinder world. The second stanza concerns two young lovers who yearned for a better world too but who died (the suggestion is of broken hearts). The mood, then is sad and melancholy and an atmosphere of regret, yearning and disappointment permeates the poem.

In 'Adlestrop' Thomas describes how his train stopped at a deserted country station one summer's day. The poem conveys the poet's response to the total scene through his memory. It is a memory which brings him happiness rather than sadness, though. Thomas succeeds in conveying the atmosphere of quietness, of the peacefulness of the natural scene and the steam train at the platform. A sense of nostalgia surrounds the experience.

> Tone and mood can exert an important influence on a poem and can be created in a variety of ways. Always be sensitive to tone and mood when reading a poem.   **KEY POINT**

Progress check

Now look at the poetry text you are studying. Pick three poems (use parts of one poem if you are studying a single long poem) and think about the tone and atmosphere the poet creates in them. Look at how a sense of a particular tone or atmosphere is created.

2.4 Form and structure

After studying this section you should be able to:

- *recognise different examples of form in poetry*
- *recognise the sonnet form*
- *discuss the effect of structure and form on poetry*

LEARNING SUMMARY

AQA A	U4, U6
AQA B	U5
Edexcel	U5, U6
OCR	U4, U6
WJEC	U4, U6
NICCEA	U4

Form and structure are two more important elements in poems that can contribute to the overall effect of a poem. We first need to establish what exactly is meant by the terms.

Form normally refers to the way in which the poem is actually written down on the page – in other words the kind of verse used (e.g. sonnet, blank verse, ode, etc.).

Structure normally refers to the way that the various ideas or emotions in a poem are arranged to form a coherent shape that satisfies the poet's purpose. Sometime it can mean the metrical pattern of the poem but it can also mean the order of ideas, etc.

In terms of form there are various formats that poems can take.

Here are some forms you might be familiar with:

- sonnet
- ode
- blank verse
- rhyming (heroic) couplets
- free verse
- quatrains
- lyrics.

Look up and make a note of the meaning of each of the above forms of poetry.

Now look at the following poem.

> ### The Four Ages of Man
>
> He with body waged a fight,
> But body won; it walks upright.
>
> Then he struggled with the heart;
> Innocence and peace depart.
>
> Then he struggled with the mind;
> His proud heart he left behind.
>
> Now his wars on God begins;
> At stroke of midnight God shall win.
>
> *William Butler Yeats (1865–1939)*

Look carefully at the form and structure of this poem. What do you notice about it?

Summary

'The Four Ages of Man'

This poem presents a coherent development reflected through the stanza form. It is written in rhyming couplets and each couplet forms a stanza. Each stanza presents an event and therefore has its own focus and each one contributes a little more to the poem's unifying theme of what it is to be human. The first stanza speaks of the body, the second the heart, the third the mind and the fourth the end of all three with the approach of death.

The sonnet

The sonnet form is particularly popular in English poetry and poets have written using this form for centuries. You may be studying a poet who wrote many sonnets, Shakespeare or Keats, for example. Some of the best-known poems in this language are written in this form. Basically a sonnet is a poem consisting of fourteen lines with a very structured rhyme scheme and a very definite rhythm pattern (usually iambic pentameter – see the section on Rhyme and rhythm). There are two main kinds of sonnet –

- **The Petrarchan** or **Italian sonnet** (named after the medieval Italian writer, Petrarch and
- The **Shakespearean** or **English sonnet**. The difference between the two lies basically in the structure. Here is the structure of the Italian Sonnet:

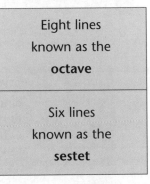

Eight lines
known as the
octave

Six lines
known as the
sestet

The rhyme scheme in this kind of sonnet can vary but generally the pattern is 'ABBAABBA CDECDE' or 'ABBAABBA CDCDCD'. In terms of structure, the octave sets out the theme or key idea of the poem and the sestet provides a response to it.

Here is the pattern for the English sonnet:

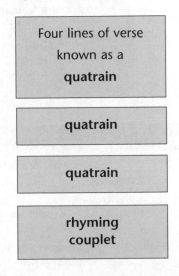

Four lines of verse
known as a
quatrain

quatrain

quatrain

rhyming couplet

The rhyme scheme of this kind of sonnet generally follows the pattern 'ABAB CDCD EFEF GG'. The theme or idea is developed through the quatrains and the concluding comment is provided through the final, rhyming couplet.

Read the following two sonnets.

On First Looking into Chapman's Homer

Much have I travell'd in the realms of gold,
  And many goodly states and kingdoms seen;
  Round many western islands have I been
Which bards in fealty to Apollo hold.
Oft of one wide expanse had I been told   5
  That deep-brow'd Homer ruled as his demesne;
  Yet did I never breathe its pure serene
Till I heard Chapman speak out loud and bold:
Then felt I like some watcher of the skies
  When a new planet swims into his ken;   10
Or like stout Cortez when with eagle eyes
  He star'd at the Pacific – and all his men
Look'd at each other with a wild surmise –
  Silent, upon a peak in Darien.

John Keats

Prayer

Some days, although we cannot pray, a prayer
utters itself. So, a woman will lift
her head from the sieve of her hands and stare
at the minims sung by a tree, a sudden gift.

Some nights, although we are faithless, the truth
enters our hearts, that small familiar pain;
then a man will stand stock-still, hearing his youth
in the distant Latin chanting of a train

Pray for us now. Grade I piano scales
console the lodger looking out across
a Midlands town. Then dusk, and someone calls
a child's name as though they named their loss.

Darkness outside. Inside, the radio's prayer –
Rockall. Malin. Dogger. Finisterre.

Carol Ann Duffy

Commentary

1 George Chapman – translated Homer's *Iliad* and *Odyssey*.
2 Well read.
3 Fealty – loyalty.
4 Apollo – Greek god of poetry and music.
5 Demesne – territory.
6 Ken – knowledge or perception.
7 Cortez – Spanish explorer.
8 Darien – an Isthmus in Central America.

Progress check

Which of these sonnets is an English sonnet and which an Italian? Why do you think the poet chose to write in sonnet form? What does the form add to the poem?

Summary

'On First Looking into Chapman's Homer' is by John Keats. He writes his sonnet in the Italian form – it is divided into two sections, the first group of eight lines (the octave) and the concluding group of six lines (the sestet). The poem concerns Keats's first experiences of looking at Chapman's translation of Homer's epic poems *The Iliad* and *The Odyssey*. The octave reveals Keats's previous reading of classical poetry, expressed as a journey through 'realms of gold'. The whole experience is described in ornate, 'poetic' language expressing lofty ideas of beauty.

In the sestet Keats changes direction to describe the impact of reading Chapman's Homer for the first time. He describes this experience through two images – sighting a new planet and discovering a new ocean. These last six lines use a simpler vocabulary and everyday language.

'Prayer' is a sonnet written by the modern poet Carol Ann Duffy and she adopts the Shakespearean sonnet form. The poem consists of three quatrains each with an ABAB rhyme scheme through which she builds up and develops her ideas to bring them to a conclusion in the rhyming couplet at the end. This rhyming couplet not only provides an unexpected ending to the poem but it gives the last line a feeling of finality.

> It is important to look at the form and structure of a poem as these elements can play an important part in shaping the poem's overall effect.
>
> **KEY POINT**

Progress check

Now look at the poems you are studying. Choose one or two and and try to determine what form the poet has used and why he or she has used that particular form.

2.5 Rhyme and rhythm

After studying this section you should be able to:

- *recognise rhyme schemes in poems*
- *appreciate the effect rhyme can have on a poem*
- *understand what rhythm in a poem is*
- *appreciate the effect rhythm can have on a poem*
- *apply this to the poetry text you are studying*

LEARNING SUMMARY

Rhyme

AQA A	U4, U6
AQA B	U5
Edexcel	U5, U6
OCR	U4, U6
WJEC	U4, U6
NICCEA	U4

The idea of rhyme in poetry is one that you are likely to be familiar with. In fact, the association between rhyme and poetry is so strong that some people still try to insist that poetry isn't 'proper' poetry unless it does rhyme. Although that isn't true, of course, rhyme can play an important part in contributing to the overall effect of the poem. The pattern of rhyme within a poem is called the rhyme scheme and is easy to work out. For example, look at John Donne's poem 'The Flea'.

The Flea

Mark but this flea, and mark in this,	A
How little that which thou deny'st me is;	A
Me it sucked first, and now sucks thee,	B
And in this flea, our two bloods mingled be;	B
Confess it, this cannot be said	C
A sin, or shame, or loss of maidenhead,	C
Yet this enjoys before it woo,	D
And pampered swells with one blood made of two,	D
And this, alas, is more than we would do.	D

Oh stay, three lives in one flea spare,
Where we almost, nay more than married are.
This flea is you and I, and this
Our marriage bed, and marriage temple is;
Though parents grudge, and you, we're met,
And cloistered in these living walls of jet.
   Though use make you apt to kill me,
   Let not to this, self murder added be,
   And sacrilege, three sins in killing three.

Cruel and sudden, hast thou since
Purpled thy nail, in blood of innocence?
In what could this flea guilty be,
Except in that drop which it sucked from thee?
Yet thou triumph'st, and say'st that thou
Find'st not thyself, nor me the weaker now;
   'Tis true, then learn how false, fears be;
   Just so much honour, when thou yield'st to me,
   Will waste, as this flea's death took life from thee.

John Donne

You will notice in this poem that the first line, which we will label 'A' rhymes with the second line so we will call this one 'A' too. Line three, which we will label 'B' rhymes with the fourth line which we will also call 'B'. The fifth line, which we will call C rhymes with the sixth line and then the last three lines of the first stanza all rhyme together so we will call them all D. The rhyme scheme of this poem, therefore is AABBCCDDD. You will find that this pattern is repeated in the remaining two stanzas of the poem

Of course, simply identifying a rhyme scheme is a pretty meaningless activity in itself. The important question comes after the rhyme scheme has been identified – what effect does the rhyme scheme have on the poem overall?

Progress check

Now look at 'The Flea' and write down any ideas you have on the effect that the rhyme schemes has. (It is worth reading aloud to get the full impact of the rhyme scheme.)

Summary

Here are some ideas that you might have noted.

- Each stanza is written in rhyming couplets ending with a triple rhyme. This give a sense of unity and completeness to each stanza. Each stanza works through a complete thought and then is rounded off.
- The way the rhyme scheme builds stanza by stanza as Donne gathers his

argument seems to add a sense of movement and momentum to the poem. He is, of course, trying to persuade his lady to sleep with him.

- The rhyme scheme also seems to give the poem a sense of something complete in its own right – his argument has been brought to an end, his case proven and there is no more to be said.

Sometimes a poet may use rhymes that occur within the line itself. In 'The Ancient Mariner', Coleridge uses this kind of rhyme –

> The fair breeze blew, the white foam flew,
> The furrow followed free;
> We were the first that ever burst
> Into that silent sea.

Here the rhyming of 'blew' and 'flew' combines with the effect of the alliteration to add emphasis to the sense of speed and movement of the ship.

On occasions, a rhyme can seem to be incomplete or inaccurate. It may be that the vowels in the words are not pronounced in the same way, for example love/move or trough/plough. These kind of rhymes are called eye rhymes or sight rhymes. Sometimes poets make the consonant or vowel different to create a half-rhyme. These are sometimes called slant rhymes or para-rhymes as well. Wilfred Owen was particularly fond of using this kind of rhyme.

> **KEY POINT**
>
> The rhyme scheme can be an important element in creating a poem's effect on the reader or listener.

Write down as many ideas as you can showing the effect a rhyme scheme can have on a poem.

Summary

Here are some of the effects that rhyme or half-rhyme can have on a poem.

- It can **emphasise** and **draw attention** to certain words.
- It can add a **musical quality** to a poem.
- It can create a deliberately **discordant effect**.
- It can **draw a poem's ideas together**.
- It can create an **incantatory** or **ritualistic effect**.
- Devices such as rhyming couplets can add a **sense of finality**.

Rhythm

Rhythm can also play an important part in the effect poems achieve. Nursery rhymes, which are probably the first kinds of poetry that you encountered, have very strong rhythms. It is the presence of these strong rhythm patterns that gives the rhymes such a strong appeal to children.

However, rhythms do not only appeal to children and a sense of rhythm can exert a powerful effect on any poem. A strong rhythm pattern can help to create mood in a poem and therefore influence its whole tone and atmosphere and its feeling of movement and life. Several factors can influence the rhythm.

The rhythm can be influenced by:

- **syllable stress**. Language possesses natural rhythms which we use every time we speak and pronounce words. Poets often make use of these natural stresses and in-built rhythm patterns to help contribute to the overall rhythmic effect.

- **emphatic stress**. Poets often deliberately place the emphasis on a particular word or part of the word in order to achieve a particular effect.
- **phrasing and punctuation**. The rhythm of poetry, along with other kinds of writing, can be influenced by other factors such as word order, length of phrases or the choice of punctuation marks, line and stanza breaks and use of repetition.
- **metre**. Poetic metre is the pattern of stressed and unstressed syllables in a line of poetry and as such is very closely linked to the idea of rhythm. These regular patterns of stressed and unstressed syllables are called metres. By analysing the metre, the reader can see how the poet is using the stress patterns within the language as part of the ways by which the meaning of the poem is conveyed. Variations in the pattern could mark changes in mood or tone or signify a change of direction in the movement of the poem.

> **KEY POINT**
>
> Rhythm can add an important dimension to a poem. Always look for the effects that it can create in a poem.

Progress check

Now look at the following poem, 'Daffodils' by William Wordsworth. Try to describe the effects created by both the rhyme and the rhythm of the poem.

Daffodils

1   I wandered lonely as a cloud
    That floats on high o'er vales and hills,
2   When all at once I saw a crowd,
    A host, of golden daffodils;
  Beside the lake, beneath the trees,
3   Fluttering and dancing in the breeze.

4   Continuous as the stars that shine
    And twinkle on the Milky Way,
  They stretched in never-ending line
    Along the margin of a bay:
  Ten thousand saw I at a glance,
5   Tossing their heads in sprightly dance.

  The waves beside them danced, but they
    Out-did the sparkling waves in glee:
6   A poet could not but be gay,
    In such a jocund company:
  I gazed – and gazed – but little thought
  What wealth the show to me had brought:

7   For oft, when on my couch I lie
    In vacant or in pensive mood,
  They flash upon that inward eye
    Which is the bliss of solitude;
  And then my heart with pleasure fills,
  And dances with the daffodils.

William Wordsworth

Commentary

1 Not loneliness but 'aloneness'.
2 Metaphor.
3 Metaphor.
4 Simile.
5 Personification.
6 Three stanzas describe the experience.
7 Final stanza showing its effect.

Summary

The regular lines (eight syllables per line consisting of four iambic feet) give an almost incantatory quality to the poem and imposes a pattern on the lines and the experience described. The whole poem is carefully regular – four stanzas, with regular line length, but it is perhaps the rhyme scheme that creates the greatest effect on the words. The ABABCC scheme gives each stanza a sense of completeness in itself as each stanza contains its own focal point given unity through the rhyme. The overall effect is to produce a sense of balance and harmony, reflecting the harmonious quality of nature and the comforting effect of the experience.

Progress check

Choose any of the poems that you are studying and write a short description showing the effect of rhyme and rhythm on your chosen poem.

2.6 Imagery

After studying this section you should be able to:

- recognise different types of imagery
- be aware of some of the effects that can be created through imagery
- apply these ideas to the text that you are studying

LEARNING SUMMARY

AQA A	U4, U6
AQA B	U5
Edexcel	U5, U6
OCR	U4, U6
WJEC	U4, U6
NICCEA	U4

Very often the effect a poem has on a reader will not simply consist of a response to what the poet has to say, but will draw on the reader's own intellectual and emotional experience. Imagery can be of central importance in creating this response within the reader.

The idea of imagery is a very simple one and, although it is used a good deal in poetic writing, it is of course found in other kinds of writing too. An image, quite simply, is words used in such a way as to create a picture in the mind of the reader so that ideas, feelings, description and so on are conveyed more clearly or vividly.

Images can work in several ways in the mind of the reader. On a simple level an image can be used literally to describe something. For example, in Wordsworth's 'Daffodils' (see page 54) the lines 'I saw a crowd / A host of golden daffodils, / Beside the lake, beneath the trees, / Fluttering and dancing in the breeze' create a literal image in our minds of the scene that Wordsworth wishes to describe. However, even here, in this apparently simple description, Wordsworth is using language metaphorically by describing the daffodils as 'dancing'.

Often images are non-literal or figurative: the thing being described is compared to something else with which it has something in common, to make the description more vivid to the reader. You will, no doubt, already be familiar with images, such as similes and metaphors, which work in this way.

> Imagery can make an important contribution to the overall effect of a poem.
>
> **KEY POINT**

Progress check

List and describe as many examples of figurative language as you can.

Summary

Here are some you might have thought of.

- **The simile**. Similes are easy to spot because they make the comparison quite clear, often by using the words 'as' or 'like'. For example, the lines 'continuous as the stars that shine / And twinkle on the Milky Way' simply but effectively convey a sense of the beauty of the scene and the sheer abundance of the daffodils.
- **The metaphor**. In some ways a metaphor is like a simile in that it too creates a comparison. However, it is less direct than the simile in that it does not use 'as' or 'like' to create the comparison. As we have seen Wordsworth metaphorically describes the daffodils as 'dancing'.
- **Personification**. Personification occurs when poets attribute an inanimate object or abstract idea with human qualities or actions. For example, in describing the daffodils as 'dancing', Wordsworth is making them sound as if they are people.
- **Aural imagery**. Some kinds of images rely not upon the pictures that they create in the mind of the reader but on the effect that they have on the ear, or a combination of both. **Alliteration** involves the repetition of the same consonant sound, usually at the beginning of each word, over several words together. Larkin uses this technique in 'Naturally the Foundation Will Pay Your Expenses' (see page 42), for example. It can be seen in phrases such as 'I pondered pages … Crowds, colourless and careworn … Still act their solemn-sinister …' and much of its impact lies in the effect that the repetition of the sounds creates on the reader's ear as well as the mind's eye. Another kind of aural device is **assonance**. This involves the repetition of a vowel sound to achieve a particular kind of effect. A third aural device is that of **onomatopoeia**. This refers to words that by their sound reflect their meaning. On a simple level words like 'bang' or 'thud' actually sound like the noises they describe.

It cannot be stressed enough, though, that there is little value in simply identifying these features – you will gain no marks at all, for example, for saying something like, 'the poet uses a good deal of alliteration in this poem'. Identifying imagery and the techniques whereby it is created is only of any value if you describe the **effect** that this use of language has on the poem and the reader.

> You must look at imagery in terms of what it does to the poem – what effect it has on the reader.
>
> **KEY POINT**

2.7 Approaching poetry

AQA A	U4, U6
AQA B	U5
Edexcel	U5, U6
OCR	U4, U6
WJEC	U4, U6
NICCEA	U4

Different kinds of poetry sometimes require different approaches. Some poems are short and contain relatively straightforward ideas which are easy to understand. On the other hand, you need to work really hard at some poems in order to come to an understanding of them. There might be a number of reasons for this. It could be because:

- they were written a long time ago when a different form of language was used. For example, in order to understand the poetry of Chaucer you need first to understand the Middle English in which he wrote his works. A poet like Milton uses references to mythology, the classical world or the Bible that you might need to research in order to appreciate fully what his poetry is saying.
- the ideas are complex, the ways the poet expresses ideas are obscure, or the content, style or structure of the poem is difficult. In this case you need to work hard to tease meaning from the poem. This is often the case with a poet like T.S. Eliot, for example. There may always be words, phrases and lines that are never fully understood. That might be just as the poet wanted it, of course.
- the poem may appear simple and use simple vocabulary but the ideas that it contains are deceptively complex. Much of the work of Philip Larkin is like this.

However, it is no good looking for a 'secret formula' that you can apply to any poem. Words and images that might be used in poems hold meanings, feelings and connotations which might provoke different responses in different people but this does not mean that 'anything goes' and that you can say exactly what you want about a poem. At A Level, the personal response is important but it is a personal response that will be informed by literary judgement and close analysis of the text. Prove your understanding of poetry generally.

Here are some ideas to help you improve that understanding.

- Read as much poetry as you can and become familiar with different types and styles.
- Think about the ideas in the poems that you read.
- Think about the way in which language is used in the poems that you read.
- Read poems aloud – sometimes this can help you to understand it more. Reading Chaucer aloud, for example, can help a good deal with your understanding of meaning.
- Ask questions – whenever you come across a new poem ask yourself questions about it. There are **three** key questions:
  - **what** is the poem about?
  - **how** is it written?
  - **why** has the poet chosen to write the poem in this way?
- Read around the work of an individual poet to help you understand his or her work more fully.
- Find out as much biographical detail about the poet as you can – this can sometimes throw light on the poetry.
- Understand the historical, social and political context within which the poet produced their work – for example, knowing something about the history of the troubles in Northern Ireland can help you understand some of the poems of Seamus Heaney.

Sample question and model answer

This question tests the candidate's ability to consider:

- knowledge and understanding of the text (AO2)
- ability to communicate that understanding clearly and coherently (AO1)
- exploration of the ways the writer's choices of form, structure and language inform meaning (AO3)
- evaluate the significance of cultural, historical and other contextual influences upon literary texts and study (AO5ii).

Allow one hour for this question.

Read the following poem through carefully. Analyse the ways in which Raleigh explores and presents his thoughts here. You should refer to:

- **the content and meaning of the poem**
- **its tone and mood**
- **its structure and form**
- **the use of imagery and its effect**
- **the use of rhyme and rhythm.**

On the Life of Man
What is our life? a play of passion,
Our mirth the music of division,
Our mothers' wombs the tiring houses be,
Where we are dressed for this short comedy,
Heaven the judicious sharp spectator is,
That sits and marks who still doth act amiss,
Our graves that hide us from the searching sun,
Are like drawn curtains when the play is done,
Thus march we playing to our latest test,
Only we die in earnest, that's no jest.

Student response

Basically this is a poem concerned with life, and ultimately, death. Raleigh begins the poem by asking a question – 'What is life?' This immediately sets our minds to work and prepares us for the subsequent lines in which Raleigh puts forward a possible way in which life can be considered. He illustrates this view of life by a series of images and ideas, moving from one image into the next.

Immediately after his opening question he starts his answer, and introduces the central image which is maintained throughout the poem – the image by which he compares life to a theatrical play – 'a play of passion'. In this initial image the word 'passion' must be considered to be important. Raleigh does not consider life to be merely a 'play', but a 'play of passion'. The word 'passion' transforms what could have been a more shallow, perhaps somewhat flat image, into one of much more power. Life is composed of 'passions', differing in kind, and varying in degree and intensity and so this one word relates the whole image much more positively to the idea of life.

From here Raleigh moves into his next image – 'Our mirth the music of division,' maintaining the comparison between life and a play. A play has various interludes and divisions in which music is often played or sung. The music can serve to change the mood of a play, or perhaps as a little light relief for the audience. In the same way life is broken up by 'mirth' which can intermittently lighten the 'play of passion' bringing a little light relief into an often serious life.

Clear focus on the poem.

Detailed analytical approach.

Close focus on language, imagery and its effect.

Sample question and model answer (continued)

In the next two lines Raleigh goes on to broaden his comparison of life to a play. As actors are prepared for the stage in the 'tiring house' so we are 'dressed for this short comedy' of life in our mother's womb. The 'tiring house' is the part of the theatre where the actors are made ready for their appearance on the stage. Raleigh uses this as a metaphor to describe the function of the womb – the place where a human is made ready for his emergence into the world. It may be noticed that in this metaphor Raleigh speaks of life as a 'short comedy'. We must bear in mind, however, that to the Elizabethans a comedy was not necessarily something in a light-hearted vein, in fact usually a 'comedy' had a good deal of seriousness in it. The term 'comedy' was applied merely to indicate that the play did not end in tragedy.

Develops ideas and pursues the imagery, discussing fully its effect on the poem.

The poem continues –

> 'Heaven the judicious sharp spectator is,
> that sits and marks who still doth act amiss.'

Textual support well chosen.

Here Raleigh is using a very visual image to describe something which can never be seen. This adds to the power of this image because he succeeds in conveying an impression of the intangible in terms of the tangible. We can readily visualise the theatre-goer looking down on the stage with a critical awareness of what is taking place below and this is how Raleigh sees 'heaven' – watching the world for those 'who doth act amiss'. Raleigh has here introduced a religious undertone, but this is not developed in any way. Although the poem is concerned with life, it does not give an impression of being concerned in any major sense with religion.

Contains logical, clear progression developing ideas and making perceptive comments.

The poem progresses to the next idea –

> 'Our graves that hide us from the searching sun,
> Are like the drawn curtains when the play is done.'

Raleigh here likens death to the end of the performance. This simile is particularly lucid, while still maintaining the central image of the theatre. The grave, where we all end our days, is compared to the 'curtains' that are drawn at the end of a play. As the curtains shut out the light and darken the stage so our graves 'hide us from the searching sun'.

Good analysis.

> 'Thus march we playing to our latest rest
> Only we die in earnest, that's no jest.'

Even in these final lines, which bring the poem to a satisfactory conclusion, the idea of the theatre is still present. However, these lines contain a more serious note as Raleigh, having draped the general idea of life and death heavily in metaphor, brings the reader back to reality with the actual inevitability of death that faces us all. The last three words end the poem with a finality that rejects the lighter tone of the previous lines, leaving no more to be said.

Awareness of the poem as a piece which has an effect on the reader.

In this ten-line poem the rhyme scheme is AA, BB, CC, DD, EE. This simple scheme consisting of rhyming couplets suits the poem well as, apart from the first two lines, each of the images is developed in two lines, both lines linked with the rhyming words. The rhyme scheme, therefore, divides the poem up into the individual ideas and accompanying images.

Technical detail but this is again related to effect.

The metre is made up of a ten-syllable line organised in iambic pentameter. This, together with the rigid rhyme scheme, gives an impression of compactness of form and Raleigh succeeds in fitting his ideas tightly and neatly into this balanced framework. His thoughts are clearly developed through concise and simple images which work towards their ultimate conclusion.

Overall a strong piece of work which gives a detailed analysis of the poem and makes some perceptive and relevant observations on it. A confident approach which reveals a student with ideas and perception.

Exam practice and analysis

The following question tests AO5ii as the dominant objective:
- evaluate the significance of cultural, historical and other contextual influences upon literary texts and study.

Other assessment objectives that are tested are:
- AO1 communicate clearly the knowledge, understanding and insight appropriate to literary study
- AO2ii respond with knowledge and understanding to literary texts of different types and periods
- AO3 show detailed understanding of the ways in which writers' choices of form, structure and language shape meanings
- AO4 articulate independent opinions and judgements informed by different interpretations of literary texts by other readers.

This is an open book question.

Do you agree that on the basis of your study of Caribbean verse, 'what interests poets is the same the world over'?

Edexcel Specimen material 2000

Here are some ideas to think about. They are taken from the mark scheme and relate to the Assessment Objectives for this question.

AO5ii In asking candidates in effect to consider the extent to which poetry in general and Caribbean verse in particular transcends the bounds of place and culture, the question requires them to assess the importance of geographical/cultural/ethnic context in shaping poetry and possible responses to it; some candidates are likely simply to side-step this issue, while others may well seek to emphasise the existence of both regional and universal dimensions in poetry of all cultures and in reactions to it.

AO1 Interpretation of 'interests' will be key here, with some candidates taking it to mean simply subject-matter, while others will see it as embracing technical concerns as well.

AO2ii Candidates are likely to be divided here between those who focus only on the universal themes treated in this anthology and on the common elements of the verse they have studied, and those who look at similarities and differences and examine both the regional and universal aspects of their chosen verse, considering these in terms both of subject matter and technique.

AO3 At the top of the range candidates are likely to consider not only individual examples of technique but also different approaches to poetry as a whole.

AO4 In assessing the validity of the proposition, some candidates are likely to give it their unqualified agreement, while others are likely to distinguish between subject-matter and more purely poetic concerns, between Caribbean poets, and between Caribbean and other poems.

Chapter 3

Prose

The following topics are covered in this chapter:

- *Studying a novel*
- *Opening pages*
- *Narrative viewpoint*
- *Characters and their development*
- *Setting and atmosphere*
- *Studying short stories*
- *Studying non-fiction*

If you have completed your studies at AS Level you will have already studied one prose text. As part of your A2 course you will be required to study one further prose text. In terms of set texts, the majority of prose texts set for study are novels although some specifications present options which include short stories and non-fiction works. Depending which specification you are following it is also possible that you will encounter extracts from non-fiction as well as fiction prose texts as part of your synoptic unit.

3.1 Studying a novel

After studying this section you should be able to:

- *understand ways of thinking about a novel*
- *understand some different aspects of study*
- *have some ideas of ways of studying your text*

LEARNING SUMMARY

AQA A	U5
AQA B	U4
Edexcel	U4, U6
OCR	U5, U6
WJEC	U5
NICCEA	U5

The first thing to note is that novels, like other forms of writing, come in many forms and you need to adapt your approach to suit the kind of text it is. For example, you might be studying a pre-1900 work by someone like Dickens or Hardy, where for the most part, the writers portray life-like characters in realistic settings. On the other hand you might be studying a twentieth-century novel which does not follow realistic conventions of plot or character.

One thing that you can do to help yourself undertake and make sense of your novel is to develop strategies for approaching them and identify the most important things to pay attention to.

There are two main ways of looking at the novel:

1 You can look at the 'content' of the book – the world that the novel describes and creates – almost as if it were a real world. You may feel you can enter into this world and see the characters and events as real and find that you develop feelings about them such as liking or pity or hatred. Looking at your novel from this position you are likely to discuss the characters as if they were real people able to choose their actions and words for themselves.

2 The second way that you can look at your novel is to see it as a 'text' – as a creation of the author. The characters are not real people but they are creations of the author designed to perform specific functions in the text. The author uses them and manipulates them to create particular effects and they only exist through the words on the page.

The first of these attitudes may be how you approach a novel when reading purely for pleasure and this may well be the attitude that you begin with when studying a novel. As your study increases in depth, however, you will move much more towards the second attitude. This requires the much more detached and analytic approach that examiners look for at A Level. This analytic viewpoint is essential. **Remember: you always need to know how the text is written as well as what it says.**

When studying your novel there are a number of aspects that you need to know well. In one way or another most of the exam questions you encounter will be linked to one or other of them:

- **an overview**. You need a clear understanding of the plot and how it is structured
- **narrative viewpoint**: who tells the story? This then leads to the question, WHY? Why has the writer chosen to use this viewpoint?
- **character**: questions sometimes focus on the ways in which writers create and present their characters and the functions they perform in the text
- **language and style**: the distinctive qualities in the writer's choice of language and the ways in which they use it to create their effects
- **the setting of the novel**: questions can relate to the kind of setting the novel has and the ways in which the writer uses language to create a sense of setting and atmosphere
- **the context in which the novel was written**: questions could focus on the historical context, the social and political context or the personal context of the writer and the ways in which these factors influenced the shaping of the novel
- **the kind of novelist that you are studying**: knowing something about the writer might help with your understanding of the text.

> You need to examine the novel you are studying analytically as a 'text' created by the writer.
>
> **KEY POINT**

Progress check

Think about the above list of features in relation to the novel you are studying. Make brief notes on each point.

Novels, especially of the kind set for A Level study, are usually substantial texts and it is important that you become very familiar with the one you are studying. You need to know what happens and where to find the details that you might want to locate quickly. Here are some ways that will help you become familiar with your novel.

- **Read the novel through quickly** before you begin to study it. This will give you an overview of what it is about and help you to see the details of plot, structure and character.
- **Do some research on the novel.** Find out about the author, where he or she lived, the historical context in which they wrote. Knowing something about the historical and social conventions of the time can help with your understanding of the text. Also, some boards focus on the prose text to test knowledge of context.
- **Keep a notebook or file** for your work on each text. Keep separate sections for aspects such as character, setting, themes, narrative viewpoint. As you study the book write down your observations on each of these aspects making a note of important quotations, etc.
- If you are studying the text for a closed book exam it can be useful to **annotate your text** using marginal notes or underlining or sidelining important sections. If you are studying for an open book exam, remember, you are not free to annotate your texts as you wish. In this case highlighting, underlining and annotations that do not amount to more than cross referencing and/or the glossing of individual words or phrases are allowed. Annotations that go beyond this are not allowed. You should consult the particular specification you are following for details.

There are several things you can do to help you study your text.

Progress check

Plan how you are going to approach the study of your novel.

Types of novel

Like other kinds of writing, novels come in all kinds of different forms. Some are relatively short with few characters and quite simple plots and some are very complex with many characters and layers to the plot. Novels can also vary very much in terms of the subject matter they deal with and how they deal with it. Here are some forms of novel you might come across.

- 'Social novels' that deal with themes to do with social issues. These kinds of novels usually have a message to convey to the reader. Much writing by D.H. Lawrence comments on social issues and issues relating to the ways that human beings relate to each other.
- **Picaresque novels** follow a central character on a journey during which various adventures or incidents take place. *Moll Flanders* by Daniel Defoe is an example of this kind of novel.
- **Fictional biography** which focuses on the life and developments of one particular character is another kind of novel, such as Dickens's *David Copperfield.*
- **Historical novels** deal with events set in the past such as Barry Unsworth's *Sacred Hunger* or *Hawksmoor* by Peter Ackroyd.
- **Humorous novels.** Many novels contain elements of humour. Much of Jane Austen's writing could be said to be humorous, or novels such as *Captain Corelli's Mandolin* by Louis de Bernières or *Catch 22* by Joseph Heller.
- **Tragedies.** Some novels deal with tragic themes such as Emily Brontë's *Wuthering Heights*, Thomas Hardy's *The Return of the Native* or *Petals of Blood* by Ngugi wa Thiong'o.
- **Futuristic novels** which are set in some future time such as Orwell's *Nineteen Eighty-Four* or Huxley's *Brave New World*. Very often in this kind of novel the writer uses the futuristic setting or theme to make some social comment on the society of the day.

There are many different kinds of novels. Be aware of the kind of novel you are studying.

Progress check

Think about the novel you are studying and decide what kind of novel you think it is. Remember, though, that often novels do not fit snugly into one category. Think also about the purpose that the writer of your novel had in writing the text.

3.2 Opening pages

After studying this section you should be able to:

LEARNING SUMMARY

- understand the importance of the opening pages of a novel
- identify some of the important features of the opening pages
- apply these ideas to the text you are studying

AQA A	U5
AQA B	U4
Edexcel	U4, U6
OCR	U5, U6
WJEC	U5
NICCEA	U5

The opening pages of a novel are particularly important and often the first few pages tell us a good deal about the novel itself. In these opening pages the writer tries to capture our attention so that we want to read on. He or she will probably also present us with some important characters, themes or situations in these pages.

For example, read the following two openings.

1.

1 It was nine-thirty on Christmas Eve. As I crossed the long entrance hall of Monk's Piece on my way from the dining room, where we had just enjoyed the first of the happy, festive meals, towards the drawing room and the fire around which my family were now assembled, I paused and then, as I often do in the course of an evening, went to the front door, opened it and stepped outside.

2 I have always liked to take a breath of the evening, to smell the air, whether it is sweetly scented and balmy with the flowers of midsummer, pungent with the bonfires and leaf-mould of autumn, or crackling cold from frost and snow. I like to look about me at the sky above my head, whether there are moon and stars or utter blackness, and into the darkness ahead of me; I like to listen for the cries of nocturnal creatures and the moaning rise and fall of the wind, or the pattering of rain in the orchard trees, I enjoy the rush of air towards me up the hill from the flat pastures of the river valley.

3 Tonight, I smelled at once, and with a lightening heart, that there had been a change in the weather. All the previous week, we had had rain, thin, chilling rain and a mist that lay low about the house and over the countryside. From the windows, the view stretched no farther than a yard or two down the garden. It was wretched weather, never seeming to come fully light, and raw, too. There had been no pleasure in walking, the visibility was too poor for any shooting and the dogs were permanently morose and muddy. Inside the house, the lamps were lit throughout the day and the walls of larder, outhouse and cellar oozed damp and smelled sour, the fires sputtered and smoked, burning dismally low.

4 My spirits have for many years now been excessively affected by the ways of the weather, and I confess that, had it not been for the air of cheerfulness and bustle that prevailed in the rest of the house, I should have been quite cast down in gloom and lethargy, unable to enjoy the flavour of life as I should like and irritated by my own susceptibility. But Esmé is merely stung by inclement weather into a spirited defiance, and so the preparations for our Christmas holiday had this year been more than usually extensive and vigorous.

5 I took a step or two out from under the shadow of the house so that I could see around me in the moonlight. Monk's Piece stands at the summit of land that rises gently up for some four hundred feet from where the little River Nee traces its winding way in a north to south direction across this fertile, and sheltered, part of the country. Below us are pastures, interspersed with small clumps of mixed, broad leaf woodland. But at our backs for several square miles it is a quite different area of rough scrub and heathland, a patch of wildness in the midst of well-farmed country. We are but two miles from a good-sized village, seven from the principal market town, yet there is an air of remoteness and isolation which makes us feel ourselves to be much further from civilization.

from The Woman in Black *by Susan Hill*

Commentary

1 This is a ghost story and 'Christmas Eve' gives the beginning a specific location in time. Also there is the connection between Christmas and the traditional ghost story.
2 Hill sets up lot of contrasts here. What is their effect?
3 Note the image of cold, rain, mist, dismal weather – the graphic details such as 'oozed damp', 'smelled sour'.
4 The narrator reveals something of his own susceptibility to melancholy.
5 Note how Hill evokes a sense of isolation – a removal from civilisation.

2.

1 'Now, what I want is Facts. Teach these boys and girls nothing but Facts. Facts alone are wanted in life. Plant nothing else, and root out everything else. You can only form the minds of reasoning animals upon Facts; nothing else will ever be of any service to them. This is the principle on which I bring up my own children, and this is the principle on which I bring up these children. Stick to Facts, sir!'

2 The scene was a plain, bare, monotonous vault of a schoolroom, and the speaker's square forefinger emphasized his observations by underscoring every sentence with a line on the schoolmaster's sleeve. The emphasis was helped by the speaker's square wall of a forehead, which had his eyebrows for its base, while his eyes found commodious cellarage in two dark caves, overshadowed by the wall. The emphasis **3** was helped by the speaker's mouth, which was wide, thin, and hard set. The emphasis was helped by the speaker's voice, which was inflexible, dry, and dictatorial. The emphasis was helped by the speaker's hair, which bristled on the skirts of his bald head, a plantation of firs to keep the wind from its shining surface, all covered with knobs, like the crust of a plum pie, as if the head had scarcely warehouse-room for the hard facts stored inside. The speaker's obstinate carriage, square coat, square legs, square shoulders – nay, his very neckcloth, trained to take **4** him by the throat with an unaccommodating grasp, like a stubborn fact, as it was – all helped the emphasis. 'In this life, we want nothing but Facts, sir; nothing but Facts!' The speaker, and the schoolmaster, and the third grown person present, all backed a little, and swept with their eyes the inclined plane of little vessels then and there arranged in order, ready to have imperial gallons of facts poured into them **5** until they were full to the brim.

from Hard Times *by Charles Dickens*

Commentary

1 Emphasis placed on 'Facts' suggests a lack of emphasis attached to imagination.
2 Notice the bareness, plainness and monotony of the schoolroom. Even the speaker's finger is 'square' and his forehead a 'square wall'.
3 Note the description of his mouth. What kind of impression of him as a character does this give?
4 How do you respond to the description of the speaker?
5 What is the effect of this image of 'little vessels'?

Progress check

Is the narrator in the first or the third person? What character (including the narrators) are introduced? What do you learn about them?

Now think carefully about these openings and consider the following points:

• What **situation** is being presented?
• What kind of **atmosphere** is created?
• Are things **explained** to you or are you **plunged into the middle** of the story?

- What do you notice about the writer's style? Take note of the vocabulary, imagery, sentence structure used.
- How does the writer arouse your interest and make you want to read on?

Summary

The extract from *The Woman in Black* is written in the first person which gives the piece a more personal feel to it – as though the narrator is addressing you personally. Hill sets the scene quite specifically – we are told it is Christmas Eve, for example, but despite this festive season, this scene seems to contain an air of solitude and melancholy. It is night time and the vocabulary used reinforces this sense of darkness and there is the suggestion of death and cold – 'outhouse and cellar oozed damp and smelled sour', 'fires … burning dismally low' and this physical setting of the narrator's house reinforces the sense of isolation.

The extract from *Hard Times* is quite different in character. It is written in the third person and we are launched straight into the story. In fact a lesson is in progress and the novel opens with the schoolmaster's words being spoken to his class. Dickens then goes on to describe the scene in detail. Notice how he gives an impression of monotony with the emphasis on squareness, and a level-headed solidity that has no room for imagination. Descriptions like that of the speaker's mouth as being 'thin, and hard set' and his voice being 'inflexible, dry and dictatorial' tell us something of his character. There is also humour in his physical description such as his bald head being like the 'crust of a plum pie'. At the end of the extract it is clear that we are in a schoolroom and we are left in little doubt as to what kind of schoolroom it is.

> The opening of a novel is very important and the first few pages give a lot of clues as to the kind of book you are dealing with.
>
> **KEY POINT**

Progress check

Now look at the novel you are studying and read the opening section through very carefully. Make notes on what you learn from these opening pages.

3.3 Narrative viewpoint

After studying this section you should be able to:

- *understand the importance of narrative viewpoint*
- *identify different types of narrative viewpoints*
- *appreciate the effect viewpoint can have on a narrative*

LEARNING SUMMARY

AQA A	U5
AQA B	U4
Edexcel	U4, U6
OCR	U5, U6
WJEC	U5
NICCEA	U5

In the previous two extracts, Susan Hill was writing in the first person while Charles Dickens had chosen to write his narrative in the third person. Both forms of narrative have their advantages and disadvantages and each hold various possibilities for the writer.

Progress check

Have another look at the first two extracts and note down what effect each narrative viewpoint has.

Here are some ideas you might have considered:

First person

- the author takes on the role of a character
- the story is told from the 'inside'
- the narrator appears to address you directly
- this increases the illusion that the story is 'real'
- this view is more limited because we can only 'see' things through the narrator's eyes
- we do not know what is going on inside other people's heads.

Third person

- the narrator becomes almost 'god-like' in that they see and hear everything – a kind of 'fly on the wall' approach. This is sometimes called the omniscient (all-knowing) narrator
- the narrator can tell us of events that happen in different places at different times
- we are told how different characters feel
- we are often told what they are thinking
- the narrator is more detached and can make comments on the characters, perhaps mocking them or making positive or negative judgements on them.

Sometimes a writer may choose to make the narrator of the story quite clearly a character in that story. The writer might even choose to have more than one narrator. For example, Emily Brontë uses this technique in *Wuthering Heights*.

Now look carefully at the following three short extracts.

- Decide on the narrative viewpoint of each piece.
- What effect does each have on the narrative?
- What do you learn about the narrator(s) in each extract?
- How is information conveyed to you?

1.

'I see the house at Wuthering Heights has "Earnshaw" carved over the front door. Are they an old family?'

'Very old, sir; and Hareton is the last of them, as our Miss Cathy is of us – I mean, of the Lintons. Have you been to Wuthering Heights? I beg pardon for asking: but I should like to hear how she is.'

'Mrs. Heathcliff? she looked very well, and very handsome; yet, I think, not very happy.'

'Oh dear, I don't wonder! And how did you like the master?'

'A rough fellow, rather, Mrs. Dean. Is not that his character?'

'Rough as a saw-edge, and hard as whinstone. The less you meddle with him the better.'

'He must have had some ups and downs in life to make him such a churl. Do you know anything of his history?'

'It's a cuckoo's, sir – I know all about it: except where he was born, and who were his parents, and how he got his money, at first. And Hareton has been cast out like an unfledged dunnock! The unfortunate lad is the only one in all this parish that does not guess how he has been cheated.'

'Well, Mrs, Dean, it will be a charitable deed to tell me something of my neighbours: I feel I shall not rest, if I go to bed; so be good enough to sit and chat an hour.'

'Oh, certainly, sir! I'll just fetch a little sewing, and then I'll sit as long as you please. But you've caught cold: I saw you shivering, and you must have some gruel to drive it out.'

The worthy woman bustled off, and I crouched nearer the fire; my head felt hot, and the rest of me chill: moreover I was excited, almost to a pitch of foolishness, through my nerves and brain. This caused me to feel, not uncomfortable, but rather fearful (as I am still) of serious effects from the incidents of to-day and yesterday. She returned presently, bringing a smoking basin and a basket of work; and, having placed the former on the hob, drew in her seat, evidently pleased to find me so companionable.

2 Before I came to live here, she commenced – waiting no further invitation to her story – I was almost always at Wuthering Heights; because my mother had nursed Mr. Hindley Earnshaw, that was Hareton's father, and I got used to playing with the children: I ran errands too, and helped to make hay, and hung about the farm ready for anything that anybody would set me to. One fine summer morning – it was the beginning of harvest, I remember – Mr. Earnshaw, the old master, came downstairs, dressed for a journey; and after he had told Joseph what was to be done during the day, he turned to Hindley, and Cathy, and me – for I sat eating my porridge with them – and he said. speaking to his son, 'Now, my bonny man, I'm going to Liverpool to-day, what shall I bring you? You may choose what you like: only let it be little, for I shall walk there and back: sixty miles each way, that is a long spell!' Hindley named a fiddle, and then he asked Miss Cathy; she was hardly six years old, but she could ride any horse in the stable, and she chose a whip. He did not forget me: for he had a kind heart though he was rather severe sometimes. He promised to bring me a pocketful of apples and pears, and then he kissed his children good-bye and set off.

from Wuthering Heights *by Emily Brontë*

Commentary

1 Mr Lockwood speaks these opening words. He is renting a property near Wuthering Heights and he has recently been to pay a neighbourly call on Heathcliff. He begins by narrating the story and then asks Nellie Dean to tell him about Heathcliff and the others at Wuthering Heights.
2 Nellie Dean takes over the narration of the story.

2.

1 It was eleven o'clock before the family were all in bed, and two o'clock next morning was the latest hour for starting with the beehives if they were to be delivered to the retailers in Casterbridge before the Saturday market began, the way thither lying by bad roads over a distance of between twenty and thirty miles, and the horse and waggon being of the slowest. At half-past one Mrs Durbeyfield came into the large bedroom where Tess and all her little brothers and sisters slept.

'The poor man can't go,' she said to her eldest daughter, whose great eyes had opened the moment her mother's hand touched the door.

Tess sat up in bed, lost in a vague interspace between a dream and this information.

'But somebody must go,' she replied. 'It is late for the hives already. Swarming will soon be over for the year; and if we put off taking 'em till next week's market the call for 'em will be past, and they'll be thrown on our hands.'

Mrs Durbeyfield looked unequal to the emergency. 'Some young feller, perhaps, would go? One of them who were so much after dancing with 'ee yesterday,' she presently suggested.

'O no – I wouldn't have it for the world!' declared Tess proudly. 'And letting everybody know the reason – such a thing to be ashamed of! I think *I* could go if Abraham could go with me to keep me company.'

2 Her mother at length agreed to this arrangement. Little Abraham was aroused from his deep sleep in a corner of the same apartment, and made to put on his clothes while still mentally in the other world. Meanwhile Tess had hastily dressed herself; and the twain, lighting a lantern, went out to the stable. The rickety little waggon was already laden, and the girl led out the horse Prince, only a degree less rickety than the vehicle.

3 The poor creature looked wonderingly round at the night, at the lantern, at their two figures, as if he could not believe that at that hour, when every living thing was intended to be in shelter and at rest, he was called upon to go out and labour. They put a stock of candle-ends into the lantern, hung the latter to the off-side of the load, and directed the horse onward, walking at his shoulder at first during the uphill parts of the way, in order not to overload an animal of so little vigour. To cheer themselves as well as they could, they made an artificial morning with the lantern, some bread and butter, and their own conversation, the real morning being far from come. Abraham, as he more fully awoke (for he had moved in a sort of trance so far), began to talk of the strange shapes assumed by the various dark objects against the sky; of this tree that looked like a raging tiger springing from a lair; of that which resembled a giant's head.

from Tess of the D'Urbervilles *by Thomas Hardy*

Commentary

1 Much description is given through the narration.
2 Note how we see into characters' minds.
3 The narrator even seems to see into the mind of the animal.

3.

1 Tonight, I find myself here in a guest house in the city of Salisbury. The first day of my trip is now completed, and all in all, I must say I am quite satisfied. This expedition began this morning almost an hour later than I had planned, despite my having completed my packing and loaded the Ford with all necessary items well before eight o'clock. What with Mrs Clements and the girls also gone for the week, I suppose I was very conscious of the fact that once I departed, Darlington Hall would stand empty for probably the first time this century – perhaps for the first time since the day it was built. It was an odd feeling and perhaps accounts for why I delayed my departure so long, wandering around the house many times over, checking one last time that all was in order.

2 It is hard to explain my feelings once I did finally set off. For the first twenty minutes or so of motoring, I cannot say I was seized by any excitement or anticipation at all. This was due, no doubt, to the fact that though I motored further and further from the house, I continued to find myself in surroundings with which I had at least a passing acquaintance. Now I had always supposed I had travelled very little, restricted as I am by my responsibilities in the house, but of course, over time, one does make various excursions for one professional reason or another, and it would seem I have become much more acquainted with those neighbouring districts than I had realized. For as I say, as I motored on in the **3** sunshine towards the Berkshire border, I continued to be surprised by the familiarity of the country around me. But then eventually the surroundings grew unrecognizable and I knew I had gone beyond all previous boundaries. I have heard people describe the moment, when setting sail in a ship, when one finally loses sight of the land. I imagine the experience of unease mixed with exhilaration often described in connection with this moment is very similar to what I felt in the Ford as the surroundings grew strange around me. This occurred just after I took a turning and found myself on a road curving around the edge of a hill. I could sense the steep drop to my left, though I could not see it due to the trees and thick foliage that lined the roadside. The feeling swept over me that I had truly left Darlington Hall behind, and I must confess I did feel a slight sense of alarm – a sense aggravated by the feeling that I was perhaps not on the correct road at all, but speeding off in totally the wrong direction into a wilderness. It was only the feeling of a moment, but it caused me to slow down. And even when I had assured myself I was on the right road, I felt compelled to stop the car a moment to take stock, as it were.

from The Remains of the Day *by Kazuo Ishiguro*

Commentary

1 The narrator explains what is in his mind.
2 The character seems very restrained and controlled. Why might this be?
3 Look carefully at this description. Think about the impression this creates of the man.

Summary

The unusual thing about the *Wuthering Heights* extract is that, although the story is told in the third person, there are in fact two narrators. Mr Lockwood begins the narrative but this is taken over later by Nellie Dean. In fact, if you are studying this novel, you will know that there are also other narrators at different points too. One of the effects that this multi-narrator approach has is to allow us to see things from different perspectives – each narrator brings their own perspective to the story. It also allows Brontë to unfold all these elements of the plot in a natural way as well as providing a variety of narrative voice. In this first extract it is clear that Lockwood has had a bad experience at Wuthering Heights and knows nothing of the history of the family. Nellie on the other hand, is an old family retainer who has a wealth of knowledge about Wuthering Heights that she is only too willing to share with him. The majority of this information is conveyed to us through the dialogue between the two of them.

The second extract, from *Tess of the D'Urbervilles*, is written in the third person. The 'omniscient' narrator can tell us that when Tess sat up in bed she was 'lost in an interspace between a dream and this information'. He is also able to tell us what goes through the horse's mind when he is woken. This narrative perspective gives us a detailed view of what is happening and the information is conveyed to us through a combination of dialogue and narrative description.

The third extract, from *The Remains of the Day* by Kazuo Ishiguro, is written in the first person which give a more intimate feel to the narrative. It seems as if the character is speaking to us directly. It is made even more intimate because the character is telling us what is in his mind. Because the narrative is in the first person all the information we have is that given by the character himself. We can gather that he worked at Darlington Hall and that he had been responsible for the running of it (he is, in fact, the butler) but he has now left to go on a trip. The hall is left completely empty and he feels a sense of unease about this. The fact that he has travelled so little is a sign of his commitment to his job. The tone is very restrained and almost formal, as you might expect from a butler used to the formality of mannered society.

> The narrative viewpoint from which a novel is written has an important effect on the way that the story is told.

KEY POINT

Progress check

Look at the text you are studying and determine whether it is written in the first or third person. Make brief notes on what effect this has on the narrative.

3.4 Characters and their development

| After studying this section you should be able to: |

- *recognise ways in which writers can create characters*
- *understand some of the functions of characters in a narrative*
- *understand some of the ways in which writers can reveal characters to their readers*

AQA A	U5
AQA B	U4
Edexcel	U4, U6
OCR	U5, U6
WJEC	U5
NICCEA	U5

When reading a novel, much of the interest lies in the characters whom we meet. Don't forget, though, that although the writer is trying hard to convince us that they are real, we must not forget, as students of literature, that they are creations of the writer. We need to be analytical in our approach and be able to see how language has been used to create and present them and to understand the role they perform in the narrative.

In a novel, characters are revealed to us in a number of ways.

Progress check

Think about any novel that you have read and write down two ways in which you learned about characters.

Here are some of the ways that characters are revealed to us:

- through the description of them given to us by the narrator
- through the dialogue of the novel – in other words by what they say and what others say about them
- the thoughts and feelings that they have
- how they behave and react to other characters
- through the writer's use of imagery and symbols. Characters may be described using similes or metaphors, or be associated symbolically with a colour or element. Heathcliffe, in *Wuthering Heights*, for example, is often linked with fire and with the colour black.

Progress check

Here are some introductory character sketches from Charles Dickens's *Hard Times*, D.H. Lawrence's *Sons and Lovers* and Jane Austen's *Pride and Prejudice*. Read them through carefully and make notes on the following:

1 What do you learn about each character from the author's description?
2 Are you just given factual information or do you learn anything about the character's 'inner life'?
3 What particular words or phrases strike you as effective in each description?
4 Does the author seem to have a particular attitude towards the character?

1.

Why, Mr Bounderby was as near being Mr Gradgrind's bosom friend, as a man perfectly devoid of sentiment can approach that spiritual relationship towards another man perfectly devoid of sentiment. So near was Mr Bounderby – or, if the reader should prefer it, so far off.

He was a rich man: banker, merchant, manufacturer, and what not. A big, loud man, with a stare and a metallic laugh. A man made out of a coarse material, which seemed to have been stretched to make so much of him. A man with a great puffed head and forehead, swelled veins in his temples, and such a strained skin to his face that it seemed to hold his eyes open and lift his eyebrows up. A man with a pervading appearance on him of being inflated like a balloon, and ready to start. A man who could never sufficiently vaunt himself a self-made man. A man who was always proclaiming, through that brassy speaking-trumpet of a voice of his, his old ignorance and his old poverty. A man who was the Bully of humility.

A year or two younger than his eminently practical friend, Mr Bounderby looked older; his seven or eight and forty might have had the seven or eight added to it again, without surprising anybody. He had not much hair. One might have fancied he had talked it off; and that what was left, all standing up in disorder, was in that condition from being constantly blown about by his windy boastfulness.

from Hard Times *by Charles Dickens*

2.

PAUL WOULD be built like his mother, slightly and rather small. His fair hair went reddish, and then dark brown; his eyes were grey. He was a pale, quiet child, with eyes that seemed to listen, and with a full, dropping underlip.

As a rule he seemed old for his years. He was so conscious of what other people felt, particularly his mother. When she fretted he understood, and could have no peace. His soul seemed always attentive to her.

As he grew older he became stronger. William was too far removed from him to accept him as a companion. So the smaller boy belonged at first almost entirely to Annie. She was a tom-boy and a 'flybie-skybie', as her mother called her. But she was intensely fond of her second brother. So Paul was towed round at the heels of Annie, sharing her game. She raced wildly at lerky with the other young wild-cats of the Bottoms. And always Paul flew beside her, living her share of the game, having as yet no part of his own. He was quiet and not noticeable. But his sister adored him. He always seemed to care for things if she wanted him to.

from Sons and Lovers *by D.H. Lawrence*

3.

Between him and Darcy there was a very steady friendship, in spite of a great opposition of character – Bingley was endeared to Darcy by the easiness, openness, ductility of his temper, though no disposition could offer a greater contrast to his own, and though with his own he never appeared dissatisfied. On the strength of Darcy's regard Bingley had the firmest reliance, and of his judgment the highest opinion. In understanding Darcy was the superior. Bingley was by no means deficient, but Darcy was clever. He was at the same time haughty, reserved, and fastidious, and his manners, though well bred, were not inviting. In that respect his friend had greatly the advantage. Bingley was sure of being liked wherever he appeared, Darcy was continually giving offence.

The manner in which they spoke of the Meryton assembly was sufficiently characteristic. Bingley had never met with pleasanter people or prettier girls in his life; everybody had been most kind and attentive to him, there had been no formality, no stiffness, he had soon felt acquainted with all the room; and as to

Miss Bennet, he could not conceive an angel more beautiful. Darcy, on the contrary, had seen a collection of people in whom there was little beauty and no fashion, for none of whom he had felt the smallest interest, and from none received either attention or pleasure. Miss Bennet he acknowledged to be pretty, but she smiled too much.

from Pride and Prejudice *by Jane Austen*

Commentary

1 What impression is created by Bounderby.
2 Which members of the family does Lawrence link Paul with?
3 What differences between Darcy and Bingley are highlighted here?

Summary

In the first extract Bounderby is very much defined by his physical appearance although we are given other details about him too. For example, we are told that he is a man 'devoid of sentiment'. We are also told that he is rich. Dickens's description of him as being like a balloon gives the impression of someone far too full of his own importance which is confirmed by reference to his 'brassy voice' and 'windy boastfulness'. It seems clear from the tone and content of Dickens's description that he is not presenting a character he wanted to appeal to his reader, rather one who represented values with which he himself had no sympathy.

In the second extract it is clear that Paul is very much associated with his mother and with his older sister. The references to him being 'pale' and 'quiet' 'with eyes that seemed to listen' and having 'a full, dropping underlip' give the impression of a rather sad, thoughtful child. He is perhaps physically not very strong and we are told 'he seemed old for his years'. He is very close to his sister and he seems sensitive and caring about her. All these details are conveyed to us through the third-person narration.

In the third extract Darcy is described as an intelligent man, more intelligent than Bingley, in fact, but unlike Bingley we are told that he was often 'haughty and reserved'. Austen uses their very different reactions to the people they have met to highlight the difference between the two, often using very subtle hints such as Darcy's view of Miss Bennet who – 'he acknowledged to be pretty, but she smiled too much'.

> We learn about characters in many different ways and writers can create and present them in many different ways.
>
> **KEY POINT**

Progress check

Now look at the text you are studying and make a list of the central characters. For each character make brief notes on how the writer reveals details about them to the reader.

Development of character

Now let's look at character in more detail. Very often, in an exam question, you are asked to look at the ways in which a character is presented and how they relate to other characters or change and develop throughout the course of the novel.

Read the following extract carefully. It is from D.H. Lawrence's *Sons and Lovers* and describes how the young Gertrude Coppard had met the man she was to marry, Walter Morel.

1 When she was twenty-three years old, she met, at a Christmas party, a young man from the Erewash Valley. Morel was then twenty-seven years old. He was well set-up, erect, and very smart. He had wavy black hair that shone again, and a vigorous black beard that had never been shaved. His cheeks were ruddy, and his red, moist mouth was noticeable because he laughed so often. And so heartily. He had that rare thing, a **2** rich ringing laugh. Gertrude Coppard had watched him, fascinated. He was so full of colour and animation, his voice ran so easily into comic grotesque, he was so ready and so pleasant with everybody. Her own father had a rich fund of humour, but it was satiric. This man's was different: soft, non-intellectual, warm, a kind of gambolling.

She herself was opposite. She had a curious, receptive mind, which found much pleasure and amusement in listening to other folk. She was clever in leading folk on to talk. She loved ideas and was considered very intellectual. What she liked most of all was an argument on religion or philosophy or politics with some educated man. This she did not often enjoy. So she always had people tell her about themselves, finding her pleasure so.

3 In her person she was rather small and delicate, with a large brow, and dropping bunches of brown silk curls. Her blue eyes were very straight, honest, and searching. She had the beautiful hands of the Coppards. Her dress was always subdued. She wore dark blue silk, with a peculiar silver chain of silver scallops. This, and a heavy brooch of twisted gold, was her only ornament. She was still perfectly intact, deeply religious, and full of beautiful candour.

Walter Morel seemed melted away before her. She was to the miner that thing of mystery and fascination, a lady. When she spoke to him, it was with a southern pronunciation and a purity of English which thrilled him to hear. She watched him. He danced well, as if it were natural and joyous in him to dance. His grandfather was a French refugee who had married an English barmaid – if it had been a marriage. Gertrude Coppard watched the young miner as he danced, a certain subtle exultation like glamour in his movement, and his face the flower of his body, ruddy, with tumbled black hair, and laughing alike whatever partner he bowed above. She thought him rather wonderful, never having met anyone like him. Her father was to her the type of all men. And George Coppard, proud in his bearing, handsome, and rather bitter; who preferred theology in reading, and who drew near in sympathy only to one man, the Apostle Paul; who was harsh in government, and in familiarity ironic; who ignored all sensuous pleasure; – he was very different from the miner. Gertrude herself was rather contemptuous of dancing; she had not the slightest inclination towards that accomplishment, and had never learned even a Roger de Coverley. She was a puritan, like her father, high-minded, and really stern. Therefore the dusky, golden softness of this man's sensuous flame of life, that flowed off his flesh like the flame from a candle, not baffled and gripped into incandescence by thought and spirit as her life was, seemed to her something wonderful, beyond her.

He came and bowed above her. A warmth radiated through her as if she had drunk wine.

'Now do come and have this one wi' me,' he said caressively. 'It's easy, you know. I'm pining to see you dance.'

4 She had told him before she could not dance. She glanced at his humility and smiled. Her smile was very beautiful. It moved the man so that he forgot everything.

'No, I won't dance,' she said softly. Her words came clean and ringing.

Not knowing what he was doing – he often did the right thing by instinct – he sat beside her, inclining reverentially.

'But you mustn't miss your dance,' she reproved.

'Nay, I don't want to dance that – it's not one as I care about.'

'Yet you invited me to it.'

He laughed very heartily at this.

'I never thought o' that. Tha'rt not long in taking the curl out of me.'

It was her turn to laugh quickly.

'You don't look as if you'd come much uncurled,' she said.

'I'm like a pig's tail, I curl because I canna help it,' he laughed, rather boisterously.

'And you are a miner!' she exclaimed in surprise.

'Yes. I went down when I was ten.'

She looked at him in wondering dismay.

'When you were ten! And wasn't it very hard?' she asked.

'You soon get used to it. You live like th' mice, an' you pop out at night to see what's going on.'

'It makes me feel blind,' she frowned.

'Like a moudiwarp! he laughed. 'Yi, an' there's some chaps as does go round like moudiwarps.' He thrust his face forward in the blind, snout-like way of a mole, seeming to sniff and peer for direction.

from Sons and Lovers by D.H. Lawrence

Commentary

1 Notice the vocabulary 'erect', 'vigorous', 'ruddy'.
2 What is the significance of the laugh.
3 How does this description of Gertrude contrast with that of Morel?
4 Notice Morel's dialect speech form, whereas Gertrude speaks in standard English? Why does Lawrence do this?

Progress check

Study the passage closely and then answer the following questions.

1 How do you learn about the characters of Gertrude and Morel?
2 What kind of imagery or ideas does Lawrence associate with each of the characters?
3 What is revealed about each of the characters through the dialogue?
4 What indications are here that they may not be a very well matched couple?

Summary

In the extract Lawrence very carefully defends his characters. Morel is described very much through his physical appearance, his 'vigorous' beard, his 'ruddy' cheeks and his 'red' mouth giving an impression of life and vitality and fire. His 'rich, ringing laugh' adds to the picture of a sensuous and attractive man. Lawrence tells us that Gertrude is the opposite of this man and he describes her through her mind and intellect. Where he does use physical description with Gertrude it is linked with her character. For example, her 'blue eyes were very straight and honest and searching', 'her dress was always subdued'. Lawrence accentuates the difference between them through the dialogue. Morel speaks in the broad Nottinghamshire dialect of the miner whereas Gertrude speaks in the standard English of the educated lady. Nevertheless she is drawn to him in the same way as opposites are said to attract. She has never encountered a man like him before and she is fascinated by him. However, there are signs that a relationship between them would be destined to failure because the attraction is very much based on the physical but underneath they have quite different characters, and Lawrence is very clear to highlight these differences.

> It is important to look at the ways in which characters are presented and the ways in which they interact with each other. The author often uses these aspect to convey information to the audience.

KEY POINT

Progress check

Now look at the characters in the text that you are studying. Choose THREE of these characters and examine the ways in which the writer presents them to the reader.

3.5 Setting and atmosphere

After studying this section you should be able to:

LEARNING SUMMARY

- *understand the importance of setting in a novel*
- *recognise some of the ways that writers can create settings and a sense of place*
- *see how the setting of a novel can be an important influence on other aspects of the narrative*

AQA A	U5
AQA B	U4
Edexcel	U4, U6
OCR	U5, U6
WJEC	U5
NICCEA	U5

The setting of a novel can be an important element and can be closely related to the development of the plot. Setting can be much more than a simple 'backdrop' against which the action takes place and often can be closely bound up with the characters themselves. For example, in Jane Austen's novel, *Emma,* the action is set in Highbury which is described as 'a large and populous village almost amounting to a town'. The main storyline of the novel concerns the social status of the various families in Highbury. Although Austen gives little description of the setting, because her main focus is on the social interaction between the various characters, she does occasionally give a glimpse of the surroundings. In this short extract, for example, she gives us the description of the grounds of Donwell Abbey, the home of Mr Knightley.

> It was hot; and after walking some time over the gardens in a scattered, dispersed way, scarcely any three together, they insensibly followed one another to the delicious shade of a broad short avenue of limes, which stretching beyond the garden at an equal distance from the river, seemed the finish of the pleasure grounds. – It led to not nothing but a view at the end over a low stone wall with high pillars, which seemed intended, in their erection, to give the appearance of an approach to the house, which never had been there. Disputable, however, as might be the taste of such a termination, it was in itself a charming walk, and the view which closed it extremely pretty. – The considerable slope, at nearly the foot of which the Abbey stood gradually acquired a steeper form beyond its grounds; and at half a mile distant was a bank of considerable abruptness and grandeur, well clothed with wood; – and at the bottom of this bank, favourably placed and sheltered, rose the Abbey-Mill Farm, with meadows in front, and the river making a close and handsome curve around it.
>
> It was a sweet view – sweet to the eye and the mind. English verdure, English culture, English comfort, seen under a sun bright without being oppressive.
>
> *from* Emma *by Jane Austen*

Progress check

Look carefully at this description.

1 What does the physical situation of the Abbey compared with Abbey-Mill Farm tell you?
2 What is your overall impression of the description?
3 What sort of man do you think would would own the Abbey?

In other novels the setting can play a much more significant role. In Hardy's *The Return of the Native*, for example, the story is set against the imposing background of Egdon Heath. The presence of this wild and untamed heath exerts such an influence on the action in terms of mood and atmosphere that some critics have described it as almost becoming a character in itself. Hardy gives a good deal of attention to creating a sense of the heath's wildness, as in this description with which the novel opens:

A SATURDAY afternoon in November was approaching the time of twilight, and the vast tract of unenclosed wild known as Egdon Heath embrowned itself moment by moment. Overhead the hollow stretch of whitish cloud shutting out the sky was as a tent which had the whole heath for its floor.

The heaven being spread with this pallid screen and the earth with the darkest vegetation, their meeting-line at the horizon was clearly marked. In such contrast the heath wore the appearance of an instalment of night which had taken up its place before its astronomical hour was come: darkness had to a great extent arrived hereon, while day stood distinct in the sky. Looking upwards, a furze-cutter would have been inclined to continue work; looking down, he would have decided to finish his faggot and go home. The distant rims of the world and of the firmament seemed to be a division in time no less than a division in matter. The face of the heath by its mere complexion added half an hour to evening; it could in like manner retard the dawn, sadden noon, anticipate the frowning of storms scarcely generated, and intensify the opacity of a moonless midnight to a cause of shaking and dread.

In fact, precisely at this transitional point of its nightly roll into darkness the great and particular glory of the Egdon waste began, and nobody could be said to understand the heath who had not been there at such a time. It could best be felt when it could not clearly be seen, its complete effect and explanation lying in this and the succeeding hours before the next dawn: then, and only then, did it tell its true tale. The spot was, indeed, a near relation of night, and when night showed itself an apparent tendency to gravitate together could be perceived in its shades and the scene. The sombre stretch of rounds and hollows seemed to rise and meet the evening gloom in pure sympathy, the heath exhaling darkness as rapidly as the heavens precipitated it. And so the obscurity in the air and the obscurity in the land closed together in a black fraternization towards which each advance half-way.

From The Return of the Native *by Thomas Hardy*

Progress check

Look at the passage carefully.

1 What kind of language does Hardy use to describe the heath?
2 What imagery does he use and what effects does it create?
3 What kind of mood and atmosphere are associated with the heath?
4 What is your overall impression of the heath?

The setting and atmosphere that the writer creates can be important elements in the novel. Be aware of the kind of settings used, the differing moods and atmospheres created and how the writer creates them.

Progress check

Now look at the novel you are studying. Make notes on the setting or settings that the writer creates. What kind of atmosphere is created in the novel?

3.6 Studying short stories

After studying this section you should be able to:

- *think about ways in which you can approach the reading of short stories*
- *think about ways you can prepare yourself for writing about short stories*
- *consider some of the particular features of short stories*

AQA A	U5
AQA B	U4
Edexcel	U4, U6
OCR	U5, U6
WJEC	U5
NICCEA	U5

You may be studying a collection of short stories as one of your prose texts. If you are, then it is important to recognise that most of what has been dealt with so far in this chapter also applies to the short story too. However, it is also important to recognise that although the novel and the short story share the same prose medium the short story has its own artistic methods which can be quite different from those of the novel. Such differences as exist between these two genres are very often in scale rather than in kind. If a novel can deal with the growth of a character, trace changes in thought, follow changes in fortune and so forth, a short story can too.

Here are some features of short stories that you should bear in mind.

- Very often a short story focuses on a single character in a single situation rather than tracing a range of characters through a variety of situations and phases of development as novels often do.
- Often the focus for the story is the point at which the central character(s) undergo some event or experience that presents a significant moment in their personal development. It can be seen as a 'moment of truth' in which something or some perception, large or small, changes within the character.
- Not all short stories reach some kind of climax, though. Some stories may give a kind of 'snapshot' of a period of time or an experience, for example 'a day in the life of'.
- Some stories end inconclusively, leaving the reader with feelings of uncertainty, while other kinds of story do not seem to have a discernible plot at all.
- Sometimes the reader might feel completely baffled by what they have read and might tentatively explore a range of possible interpretations in his or her head. This may, of course, have been exactly the response that the writer intended.

Overall, then, because by their very nature, short stories are 'short', they tend to focus on fewer characters than novels because there is simply not the time or space to develop a large cast of characters. Again, because of the shortness, they often have a fairly short time-scale.

Short stories possess many of the features of the novel but they are very much a separate genre. Be aware of the particular features and strengths of the short-story form.

Progress check

Look at the short story text you are studying.
What kind of stories are they?
How do they differ from novels that you have read?

3.7 Studying non-fiction

After studying this section you should be able to:

- recognise different types of non-fiction prose texts
- consider the variety and aims of prose non-fiction
- think about where you might encounter non-fiction prose on your course

LEARNING SUMMARY

AQA A	U6
AQA B	U6
Edexcel	U4
OCR	U5, U6
WJEC	U5
NICCEA	U5

There are two possible ways in which you might encounter non-fiction prose texts on the A2 course. You might:

- study a prose text that is non-fiction, such as Brittain's *Testament of Youth*
- encounter extracts from prose texts as part of your synoptic assessment.

Prose texts can take many different forms but very often many of the techniques of the novelist are also the techniques of the non-fiction writer and so much of what has been discussed so far in this chapter is applicable to non-fiction writing too. For example, non-fiction writers often write about characters and although their characters really existed they still need to re-create them in words. Similarly, they often describe scenes and settings, create moods and atmospheres and their texts often contain themes, ideas or messages that the writer wants to convey to the reader. Some texts, of course, also combine factual information with that which comes from the imagination of the writer. When studying prose texts, our approach is not necessarily any different from when we study novels, or even drama or poetry.

We still need to ask the key questions of:

- what is this text about?
- how has the author chosen to write about it?
- what is the purpose in writing it?

Here are some forms of non-fiction writing you might encounter:

- the essay
- autobiographical or biographical writing
- diaries
- documentaries
- journalism.

Now look at the following extract. It is taken from *Testament of Youth*, the autobiography of Vera Brittain. She left Oxford University in 1916 and volunteered to go to France as a VAD (Voluntary Aid Detachment). Here she describes her arrival at a camp hospital at Etaples.

A heavy shower had only just ceased as I arrived at Etaples with three other V.A.D.s ordered to the same hospital, and the roads were liquid with such mud as only wartime France could produce after a few days of rain.

Leaving our camp-kit to be picked up by an ambulance, we squelched through the littered, grimy square and along a narrow, straggling street where the sole repositories for household rubbish appeared to be the pavement and the gutter. We finally emerged into open country and the huge area of camps, in which, at one time or another, practically every soldier in the British Army was dumped to await further orders for a still less agreeable destination. The main railway line from Boulogne to Paris ran between the hospitals and the distant sea, and amongst the camps, and along the sides of the road to Camiers, the humped sandhills bristled with tufts of spiky grass.

The noise of the distant guns was a sense rather than a sound; sometimes a quiver shook the earth, a vibration trembled upon the wind, when I could actually hear nothing. But that sense made any feeling of complete peace impossible; in the atmosphere was always the tenseness, the restlessness, the slight rustling, that comes before an earthquake or with imminent thunder. The glamour of the place was even more compelling, though less delirious, than the enchantment of Malta's beauty; it could not be banished though one feared and resisted it, knowing that it had to be bought at the cost of loss and frustration. France was the scene of titanic, illimitable death, and for this very reason it had become the heart of the fiercest living ever known to any generation. Nothing was permanent; everyone and everything was always on the move; friendships were temporary, appointments were temporary, life itself was the most temporary of all. Never, in any time or place, had been so appropriate the lament of 'James Lee's Wife';

To draw one beauty into our heart's core,
And keep it changeless! Such our claim;
So answered, - Never more!

Whenever I think of the War to-day, it is not as summer but always as winter; always as cold and darkness and discomfort, and an intermittent warmth of exhilarating excitement which made us irrationally exult in all three. Its permanent symbol, for me, is a candle stuck in the neck of a bottle, the tiny flame flickering in an ice-cold draught, yet creating a miniature illusion of light against an opaque infinity of blackness.

from Testament of Youth *by Vera Brittain*

Progress check

Look at the extract carefully and answer the following questions:

1 What techniques does Brittain use to give the reader an impression of her surroundings?
2 Do her methods have anything in common with those of the novelist?
3 Are there any differences?

Summary

Brittain uses vivid and detailed description to give the reader an impression of her surroundings. Note how she brings in the various senses to strengthen the impression of the place – 'The noise of the distant guns was a sense rather than a sound; sometimes a quiver shook the earth, a vibration trembled upon the wind, when I could actually hear nothing'. Clearly she is using here the same techniques as a novelist would to set the scene and create a sense of atmosphere. As far as this extract is concerned there are no differences between her writing and that of a novelist or short-story writer. We know that Brittain was writing from first-hand experience here but it could equally be a piece of prose written in the first person and created purely from the writer's imagination.

> The techniques of the non-fiction writer can have many things in common with those of the novelist or short-story writer.

KEY POINT

Progress check

If you are studying a non-fiction text answer the following questions:

1 What kind of non-fiction text is it?
2 In what ways are the writing techniques used similar to those of the novelist?
3 In what ways are they different?

Text and context

Some examination boards test your knowledge of the context and background against which prose texts were written and performed. It is a good idea to know something about the writer who wrote the prose text you are studying and about the historical period in which they lived and worked. This aspect of the examination will be dealt with in detail in Chapter 5.

Approaches to your text

There are a number of things you can do to help yourself prepare your prose text for the examination. Here are some suggestions.

- Make sure that you have read your text several times and know your way around it in detail – don't skimp that final read before the exam.
- If there is a film, DVD or video recording of your text it is worth watching it. Remember, though, the storylines are often altered for film or television so make sure you are aware of this. In the exam you should be writing about the text, not the film.
- Make notes on your impressions right from the first reading. You may change your mind later but those initial impressions can be important.

Some key areas

Think about relationships between the various elements of the text and how together they present a 'whole'. Here are some areas to think about and make notes on.

- **Characterisation**: information about how we learn about characters; indications of characters changing or developing; significant new information about a character; views on what the writer is trying to achieve in the presentation of character; look at key speeches, look for shifts in focus, different ways of interpreting what they do and say.
- **Themes**: look for various possible 'meanings' in the text; the development of any themes; introduction of new thematic elements; moral problems or issues raised for the characters or the reader.
- **Narrative technique**: the ways in which the writer manipulates the narrative; narrative voice and perspective; narrative intrusion or comment; think about the pace and variety of the action.
- **Structure**: think about the overall shape and structure of the text and the impact that this could have on the reader.
- **Tone**: is it familiar or formal, personal or impersonal? Who is being addressed?
- **Language use**: look at the vocabulary and syntax; is imagery or symbolism used? If so, what is its effect?
- **Speech and dialogue**: what kind of speech is used, direct or indirect? Do characters speak for themselves or does the narrator intrude or comment? Is the dialogue realistic? What function does it perform – development of character, plot, themes, introduction of a dramatic element?
- **Setting and description**: what is significant about where the action takes place? How is the setting described?
- **Your own response.**

Sample question and model answer

The following question is typical of the kind of question you could be asked on a novel. In this case the dominant assessment objective that the question tests is AO3
* exploration of the ways the writer's choices of form, structure and language inform meaning (AO3).

Above all, this question tests the candidate's ability to consider:
* their understanding of the ways in which writers' choices of form, structure and language shape meaning (AO3)
* their own informed independent opinions (AO4).

It also, to a lesser extent tests:
* knowledge and understanding of the text (AO2)
* ability to communicate that understanding clearly and coherently (AO1)
* the use of appropriate terminology and accurate and coherent written expression (AO1).

Through a detailed examination of three examples discuss Lawrence's use of symbolism in *Sons and Lovers*.

In *Sons and Lovers* Lawrence expresses the central themes of the novel in two ways. First of all the ideas of the book are described through various episodes – what has been referred to as the 'narrative logic' of the book. These ideas, however, are also expressed in another way involving the use of imagery and symbolism. This use of imagery in a symbolic role often not only supplements the narrative but actually replaces it.

> *Essay begins by focusing on the question directly.*

Perhaps a key reason why Lawrence uses symbolism so much to express his ideas is that he needs to relate not only what happens in his story but also how people feel. The symbolic image provides him with a means of doing this that allows the reader to relate the metaphor to reality – to relate the actions and behaviours of characters in the novel to the world at large. In other words they create a bridge between the world of fiction presented by the novel and the individual world of the reader by providing the reader with a set of ideas that he or she can relate to.

> *Provides a rationale for the use of symbolism.*

An example of this use of symbolic imagery comes early in the novel. At the end of the first chapter, Mrs Morel, pregnant with Paul, is forced from the house and out into the night by her drunken husband. Immediately the scene changes from the heat of the violent clash between husband and wife as Mrs Morel finds herself alone in the cold moonlight. This experience assumes a symbolic significance as her 'inflamed soul' is bathed in the cool, white light. As she stands in the garden she becomes aware of the child within her –

> *Gives first example – aptly chosen. The symbolic significance is enlarged upon, supported by well chosen quotation.*

> 'She walked down the garden path, trembling in every limb, while the child boiled within her.'

Her mind runs over the quarrel as – .

> 'mechanically she went over the last scene, then over it again, certain phrases, certain moments coming each time like a brand red-hot down on her soul.'

Her mind cannot rest and worries deliriously over events. In her distressed state she wanders into the side garden and then the front, without really being aware of where she is, but then she becomes aware of the tall white lilies 'reeling in the moonlight' and the air is 'charged with their perfume, as with a presence.' In one sense the 'reeling' lilies symbolically parallel her own reeling state of mind and the turmoil in her soul caused by the disturbing and traumatic conflict with her husband. She put her hand into the 'white bin' of the flowers and 'drank a deep draught of the scent' which has an almost intoxicating effect on her –

Sample question and model answer (continued)

> 'Except for a slight feeling of sickness, and her consciousness in the child, herself melted out of the scent into the shiny, pale air. After a time the child, too, melted with her in the mixing-pot of moonlight, and she rested with the hills and the lilies and houses, all swum together in a kind of swoon.'

When she finally regains entry to the house her face is smeared with the yellow dust of the lilies' pollen and the whole experience has, in a symbolic sense, marked a 'fertilisation of her soul' in which a bond is formed between herself and the unborn child within her womb.

A second instance of the use of symbolic language is cited and examined in some detail, again there is good, well-chosen textual support.

Flowers are also at the centre of two further passages in which Lawrence conveys a symbolic meaning in the novel. Firstly, Miriam's feelings about flowers reveal a good deal about her character. When she and Paul walk in the wood in the dusk she is eager to show him a wild-rose bush she had discovered. The bush is clearly of significance to Miriam, 'she knew it was wonderful' and yet to spiritually make it hers she knows that Paul must see it too. When she finds the bush she moves forward to the flowers 'and touched them in worship'.

It is, however, this very tendency of Miriam's to imbue the roses with a spiritual connotation that marks the difference between her and Paul – a difference that will eventually end their relationship. For Paul, the flowers are redolent of life, 'they seem as if they walk like butterflies, and shake themselves,' but for Miriam they represent something more ethereal, something spiritual – the embodiment of her virginity in the 'white, virgin scent'.

Paul, though, feels imprisoned by Miriam's spiritual awe and their parting emphasises the difference between them. Miriam 'walked home slowly, feeling her soul satisfied with the holiness of the night' but Paul revels in the freedom he feels on breaking free of Miriam –

> 'And as soon as he was out of the wood, in the free open meadow, where he could breathe, he started to run as fast as he could. It was like a delicious delirium in his veins.'

For Miriam, then, the flowers represent something spiritual and intangible whereas for Paul the flowers are the embodiment of life.

A third, nicely contrasted, example is given. This is examined in less detail than the others but nevertheless the comments are relevant and perceptive.

In his relationship with Clara, however, flowers assume a rather different symbolic meaning. In the scene where Paul and Clara make love for the first time the passion of Clara is symbolically reflected in the scattering of scarlet carnation petals –

> 'When he arose, he, looking on the ground all the time, saw suddenly sprinkled on the black, wet beech-roots many scarlet carnation petals, like splashed drops of blood; and red, small splashes fell down from her bosom, streaming down her dress to her feet.'

The red of the flowers suggests the passion of the relationship, a thing full of life contrasted with the white 'virgin scent' of Miriam's ivory roses. The way they scatter themselves is reminiscent of a kind of confetti, giving a sort of confirmation to the relationship.

A short but relevant conclusion rounds the essay off effectively. Overall this is a very good essay that shows focus on the question, understanding of the author's choice of form and structure and the way in which he uses language to inform meaning.

It is through the richness of the symbolism that Lawrence gives the novel its full meaning and significance. The variety of symbolic motifs that he uses in the novel allows Lawrence to create meaning beyond the purely surface meaning and so more fully explore and give expression to his central theme of human relationships.

Exam practice and analysis

The following question tests AO1 as the dominant assessment objective – to communicate clearly the knowledge, understanding and insight appropriate to literary study. However, all the other assessment objectives are addressed too (with the exception of the comparison element of 2ii).

Louis De Bernières: *Captain Corelli's Mandolin*

Captain Corelli's Mandolin covers a period of fifty years of political, social and geographical upheaval. How successful do you think it is as a 'history' of this period?

OCR Specimen Material 2000

Here are some ideas to think about. They are taken from the mark scheme, and relate to the Assessment Objectives for this question.

The task clearly asks for a personal judgement on a central but perhaps not obvious question about the book (AO4); candidates also need to consider what impact evaluating the novel in terms of its historical and literary contexts has on their view of the book's effectiveness (AO5ii).

Answers that are penetrating and original would show:

AO1   assured presentation of cogent arguments, using appropriate terminology.

AO4   independent opinions on the success of *Captain Corelli's Mandolin* as a 'history', with a sophisticated sense of what this might mean, and judgements of its merits assessed in other terms, formed by their own reading of the novel and informed by different interpretations by other readers.

AO5ii   a real appreciation of the influence of historical perspectives on their reading of the novel, noting characteristic attitudes of the context in which the novel was written (London, 1994) and in which it is set (Cephallonia, 1941–1990s) and commenting on the possible tension between these two and between these and their own present-day and other perspectives (gender, political, cultural).

Chapter 4

Comparing texts

The following topics are covered in this chapter:

- *Comparing texts and A2*
- *Approaching the comparison*
- *Comparing poems*
- *Comparing full-length texts*
- *Types of exam question*

4.1 Comparing texts and A2

AQA A	U5
AQA B	U6
Edexcel	U6
OCR	U6
WJEC	U5
NICCEA	U6

Another of the features of the A2 course which is different from the AS is that at A2 Level you will be required to compare texts as part of your assessment. This is outlined in Assessment Objective 2ii which says that you should

> respond with knowledge and understanding to literary texts of different types and periods, exploring and commenting on relationships and comparisons between literary texts.

Most specifications offer pairs of texts for study although some specifications do offer an element of choice here. In terms of the 'different period' element of the Assessment Objective, this is generally taken to be not less than thirty years. In order for a text to be of a different type, though, it may still be of the same genre. For example, a chronological novel and a non-chronological novel are texts of different types; a naturalistic play and an absurdist play are of different types.

Here are some of the things you will need to do:

- **communicate** clearly
- be prepared to **comment on specific sections** of text and **widen your comments** to the whole of both texts with reference to the way language is used
- be prepared to answer on **thematic, generic, developmental** and **stylistic links** and comparisons in the texts.
- comment on **relationships and comparison**
- discuss the ways **form, structure and language shape meaning**
- **evaluate** contents.

This chapter therefore focuses on the central areas which you have already studied through the prose, poetry and drama units of this book. You will need to use the skills you have developed through your study of texts at AS Level. Which pairing you study will probably depend on which your teacher or lecturer chooses or which have been selected for your study modules.

4.2 Approaching the comparison

After studying this section you should be able to:

- *recognise what is involved in comparing texts*
- *understand some strategies that you can adopt for comparison*

LEARNING SUMMARY

AQA A	U5
AQA B	U6
Edexcel	U6
OCR	U6
WJEC	U5
NICCEA	U6

Before you can really get to grips with the comparison, of course, you must read and study each of the texts, looking at all the relevant features that we have discussed in earlier units. When you have developed a sound knowledge of the two texts that you are studying you will need to begin to think carefully about them as a pair. Writing comparatively about two texts is inevitably a more complex process than writing about a single one. Sometimes, particularly under pressure in an exam, it may seem easier to write first about one text and then about the other, perhaps linking them in the final paragraph. However, this is not really comparative writing and this approach rarely produces a satisfactory result or one which will achieve a high mark.

Of course, as you have been reading and studying them it is likely that you will have been noting links, similarities or differences between them, but in order to compare them fully it is useful to have some kind of framework which will help structure your thoughts and your work.

The following model is one way in which you could approach your comparative study

1 Establish the major links between texts first of all – make sure that you are clear about similarities and differences between them in terms of characters, themes or situations.
2 Go on to look at specific details:
   • the **settings** of the texts
   • the **writers' attitudes** to the subject or theme
   • the **narrative viewpoint**
   • the **structure** of the texts
   • the **tone** of the writing
   • the use of **imagery**
   • **vocabulary**
   • **other stylistic features**.

When you have done this, go on to consider the differences or contrasts between the texts.

Here is a more detailed plan for you to use when thinking about your texts:

Comparative areas and issues

• Characters
• Themes
• Linguistic features
• Dramatic techniques
• Historical context
• Social context

Analysis and explanation

Identification of central contextual frameworks and structural features

• General historical context within which each text was written.
• Social structure within which each text is set.
• Comparison of the overall structure of each text.

Description and comparison of the features of each text

• Comparison of the **characters** in each text – their roles, their significance within the scheme of the text, their function in relationship with other areas such as the development of theme.
• **Thematic** links within the text.

Language – a comparison of the ways in which language is used in each text, e.g.:

• Soliloquies
• 'Comic' scenes
• Imagery
• Rhetorical features
• Pace
• Tone.

Narrative or poetic or dramatic techniques, effects and meanings:

- Effects created in each text
- The techniques used to create these effects
- Relationships between effects, themes and characters
- The creation of 'meaning'.

Different levels of analysis:

- Different views of the texts
- Different interpretations of characters, themes and meanings
- Audience/reader response.

Evaluation

Consideration of the success of each text:

- in terms of the various ideas and features described above
- as a piece of narrative, poetry or drama
- as a comment on the themes presented.

> Approach your comparison systematically, looking at a range of features of both texts.
>
> **KEY POINT**

Progress check

Now think about the pair of texts that you are studying. Using the methods described above draw up a plan of how you are going to approach your comparative study of these texts. Make sure that you think about details such as which themes you are going to deal with, the characters, the use of language, etc.

4.3 Comparing poems

After studying this section you should be able to:

LEARNING SUMMARY

- *see how poems can be compared*
- *recognise some strategies that you could apply in your own work for comparing poems*

AQA A	U5
AQA B	U6
Edexcel	U6
OCR	U6
WJEC	U5
NICCEA	U6

You may be asked to compare poetry texts. It can help your analysis if you organise your ideas in the form of a table.

Progress check

Read the following poems through carefully and make notes on each poem. Combine your findings in the form of a table.

Ode on a Grecian Urn

1 Thou still unravish'd bride of quietness,
Thou foster-child of silence and slow time,
2 Sylvan historian, who canst thus express
A flowery tale more sweetly than our rhyme:
What leaf-fring'd legend haunts about thy shape
Of deities or mortals, or of both,
3 In Tempe or the dales of Arcady?
4 What men or gods are these? What maidens loth?
5 What mad pursuit? What struggle to escape?
What pipes and timbrels? What wild ecstasy?

6 Heard melodies are sweet, but those unheard
Are sweeter; therefore, ye soft pipes, play on;
Not to the sensual ear, but, more endear'd,
Pipe to the spirit ditties of no tone:
7 Fair youth, beneath the trees, thou canst not leave
Thy song, nor ever can those trees be bare;
Bold Lover, never, never canst thou kiss,
Though winning near the goal – yet, do not grieve;
She cannot fade, though thou hast not thy bliss,
For ever wilt thou love, and she be fair!

Ah, happy, happy boughs! that cannot shed
Your leaves, nor ever bid the Spring adieu;
And, happy melodist, unwearied,
For ever piping songs for ever new;
More happy love! more happy, happy love!
For ever warm and still to be enjoy'd,
For ever panting, and for ever young;
All breathing human passion far above,
That leaves a heart high-sorrowful and cloy'd,
A burning forehead, and a parching tongue.

Who are these coming to the sacrifice?
To what green altar, O mysterious priest,
Lead'st thou that heifer lowing at the skies,
And all her silken flanks with garlands drest?
What little town by river or sea shore,
Or mountain-built with peaceful citadel,
Is emptied of this folk, this pious morn?
And, little town, thy streets for evermore
Will silent be; and not a soul to tell
Why thou art desolate, can e'er return.

8 O Attic shape! Fair attitude! with brede
9 Of marble men and maidens overwrought,
With forest branches and the trodden weed;
10 Thou, silent form, dost tease us out of thought
11 As doth eternity: Cold Pastoral!
When old age shall this generation waste,
Thou shalt remain, in midst of other woe
Than ours, a friend to man, to whom thou say'st,
'Beauty is truth, truth beauty,' – that is all
ye know on earth, and all ye need to know.

John Keats

The Prelude

Book 1 (1850)

And in the frosty season, when the sun
Was set, and visible for many a mile
The cottage windows blazed through twilight gloom,
I heeded not their summons: happy time
It was indeed for all of us – for me
It was a time of rapture! Clear and loud
The village clock tolled six, – I wheeled about,
Proud and exulting like an untired horse
That cares not for his home. All shod with steel,
We hissed along the polished ice in games
Confederate, imitative of the chase
And woodland pleasures, – the resounding horn,
The pack loud chiming, and the hunted hare.
So through the darkness and the cold we flew,
And not a voice was idle; with the din,
Smitten, the precipices rang aloud;
The leafless trees and every icy crag
Tinkled like iron; while far distant hills
Into the tumult sent an alien sound
Of melancholy not unnoticed, while the stars
Eastward were sparkling clear, and in the west
The orange sky of evening died away.

William Wordsworth

Commentary

1   Still: can be read as an adjective meaning 'not moving' or an adverb meaning 'so far.'

2   Sylvan historian – the urn is being addressed here as the storyteller which presents events through the pictures on it. Sylvan means 'woodland' or is another way of describing the country, the rural nature of the scenes depicted on the urn.

3   Tempe – a valley in Greece renowned for its landscape.

4   Arcady – Arcadia – an area of Greece which was home to the shepherds – an earthly paradise.

5   Loth – reluctant.

6   Timbrels – tambourines.

7   Ditties of no tone – tunes that cannot be heard by humans.

8   Attic – i.e. from Athens.

9   Brede – decorative border.

10   The images are laid on the surface of the urn.

11   Pastoral – idealised rural life.

Summary

Here are some suggestions:

	Keats	Wordsworth
Subject	Thoughts inspired by looking at the design on a Grecian Urn.	An experience remembered from childhood.
Speaker/situation	First person, the poet describes what comes into his imagination when looking at the design on the urn.	First person, the poet describes the experience of skating on a frozen lake.
Form	Written as an ode with five ten-line stanzas. Rhymes.	An extract from a longer poem. No stanzas. No rhyme.
Ideas/messages	The first stanza creates a word picture. The second examines the 'unheard' pipes, the youth, the lover, the permanence and thus the impossibility of change in the representation. The third compares the representation to nature, music and love. Stanza four examines the other figures on the urn and the final stanza reiterates Keats's central idea that 'Beauty is Truth'.	A vivid description of the scene as an almost spiritual experience. The imagery creates a strong sense of time and place and exultation.
Tone/atmosphere	The poem has a meditative tone as the poet ponders on abstract ideas.	The tone is one of excitement, vitality, movement and life.
Imagery	The poem uses the imagery of the urn and the scene which he almost brings to life.	The images reflect the natural scene, the image of the wheeling horse, the frozen hills.
Vocabulary	Words such as 'love', 'beauty', 'happiness', 'truth' suggest that he is dealing with deep and important issues.	'Rapture', 'wheeled', 'exulting', capture the sense of movement and joy.
Rhyme, rhythm and sound effects	The rhyme scheme gives a pattern and cohesion to the carefully ordered and developed thoughts.	The freedom of the verse reflects the freedom the poet feels. The rhythm gives a sense of movement.

> These are very basic notes, of course. When you do this with the texts that you are studying you will need a much deeper analysis.
>
> **KEY POINT**

Progress check

Now look at the following two poems. Compare and contrast them and make notes on your ideas.

The Ecchoing Green

The Sun does arise
And make happy the skies,
The merry bells ring
To welcome the Spring,
The sky-lark and thrush,
The birds of the bush,
Sing louder around
To the bells' chearful sound,
While our sports shall be seen
On the Ecchoing Green.

Old John with white hair
Does laugh away care,
Sitting under the oak
Among the old folk.
They laugh at our play,
And soon they all say:
'Such, such were the joys
When we all, girls & boys,
In our youth-time were seen.
On the Ecchoing Green.'

Till the little ones, weary,
No more can be merry;
The sun does descend,
And our sports have an end.
Round the laps of their mothers
Many sisters and brothers,
Like birds in their nest,
Are ready for rest,
And sport no more seen
On the darkening Green.

William Blake

Proverbial Ballade

Fine words won't turn the icing pink;
A wild rose has no employees;
Who boils his socks will make them shrink
Who catches cold is sure to sneeze.
Who has two legs must wash two knees;
Who breaks the egg will find the yolk;
Who locks his door will need his keys –
So say I and so say the folk.

You can't shave with a tiddlywink,
Nor make red wine from garden peas,
Nor show a blindworm how to blink,
Nor teach an old racoon Chinese.
The juiciest orange feels the squeeze;
Who spends his portion will be broke;
Who has no milk can make no cheese –
So say I and so say the folk.

He makes no blot who has no ink,
Nor gathers honey who keeps no bees.
The ship that does not float will sink;
Who'd travel far must cross the seas.
Lone wolves are seldom seen in threes;
A conker ne'er becomes an oak;
Rome wasn't built by chimpanzees –
So say I and so say the folk.

Wendy Cope

Progress check

If you are studying poetry as part of your comparative study then try this technique on some of the poems you are studying.

4.4 Comparing full-length texts

After studying this section you should be able to:

- *understand what is involved in comparing full-length texts*
- *develop strategies for approaching the comparison of full-length texts*

AQA A	U5
AQA B	U6
Edexcel	U6
OCR	U6
WJEC	U5
NICCEA	U6

As with other texts, the first thing that you must do when comparing novels is to establish what they are about. Look for a common theme between them. Once you are clear about the broad connections you then need to look for more detailed similarities and differences. It is also a good idea to find passages and quotations from the text that illustrate your ideas.

In exams, when you are asked to compare two texts you are sometimes given an extract from each as a starting point to work from. Look at the following question, for example:

Look at the opening pages of *The Remains of the Day* by Kazuo Ishiguro and *A Room with a View* by E.M. Forster. Compare the techniques that each writer uses to begin his novel.

It seems increasingly likely that I really will undertake the expedition that has been preoccupying my imagination now for some days. An expedition, I should say, which I will undertake alone, in the comfort of Mr Farraday's Ford; an expedition which, as I foresee it, will take me through much of the finest countryside of England to the West Country, and may keep me away from Darlington Hall for as much as five or six days. The idea of such a journey came about, I should point out, from a most kind suggestion put to me by Mr Farraday himself one afternoon almost a fortnight ago, when I had been dusting the portraits in the library. In fact, as I recall, I was up on the step-ladder dusting the portrait of Viscount Wetherby when my employer had entered carrying a few volumes which he presumably wished returned to the shelves. On seeing my person, he took the opportunity to inform me that he had just that moment finalized plans to return to the United States for a period of five weeks between August and September. Having made this announcement, my employer put his volumes down on a table, seated himself on the *chaise-longue*, and stretched out his legs. It was then gazing up at me, that he said:

'You realize, Stevens, I don't expect you to be locked up here in this house all the time I'm away. Why don't you take the car and drive off somewhere for a few days? You look like you could make good use of a break.'

Coming out of the blue as it did, I did not quite know how to reply to such a suggestion. I recall thanking him for his consideration, but quite probably I said nothing very definite for my employer went on:

'I'm serious, Stevens. I really think you should take a break. I'll foot the bill for the gas. You fellows, you're always locked up in these big houses helping out, how do you ever get to see around this beautiful country of yours?'

This was not the first time my employer had raised such a question; indeed, it seems to be something which genuinely troubles him. On this occasion, in fact, a reply of sorts did occur to me as I stood up there on the ladder; a reply to the effect that those of our profession, although we did not see a great deal of the country in the sense of touring the countryside and visiting picturesque sites, did actually 'see' more of England than most, placed as we were in houses where the greatest ladies and gentlemen of the land gathered. Of course, I could not have expressed this view to Mr Farraday without embarking upon what might have seemed a presumptuous speech. I thus contented myself by saying simply:

'It has been my privilege to see the best of England over the years, sir, within these very walls.'

Mr Farraday did not seem to understand this statement, for he merely went on: 'I mean it, Stevens. It's wrong that a man can't get to see around his own country. Take my advice, get out the house for a few days.'

As you might expect, I did not take Mr Farraday's suggestion at all seriously that afternoon, regarding it as just another instance of an American gentleman's unfamiliarity with what was and what was not commonly done in England. The fact that my attitude to this same suggestion underwent a change over the following days – indeed, that the notion of a trip to the West Country took an ever-increasing hold on my thoughts – is no doubt substantially attributable to – and why should I hide it? – the arrival of Miss Kenton's letter, her first in almost seven years if one discounts the Christmas cards. But let me make it immediately clear what I mean by this; what I mean to say is that Miss Kenton's letter set off a certain chain of ideas to do with professional matters here at Darlington Hall, and I would underline that it was a preoccupation with these very same professional matters that led me to consider anew my employer's kindly meant suggestion.

from The Remains of the Day *by Kazuo Ishiguro*

'The Signora had no business to do it,' said Miss Bartlett, 'no business at all. She promised us south rooms with a view close together, instead of which here are north rooms, looking into a courtyard, and a long way apart. Oh. Lucy!'

'And a Cockney, besides!' said Lucy, who had been farther saddened by the Signora's unexpected accent. 'It might be London.' She looked at the two rows of English people who were sitting at the table; at the row of white bottles of water and red bottles of wine that ran between the English people; at the portraits of the late Queen and the late Poet Laureate that hung behind the English people heavily framed; at the notice of the English church (Rev. Cuthbert Eager, M. A. Oxon.), that was the only other decoration on the wall. 'Charlotte, don't you feel, too, that we might be in London? I can hardly believe that all kinds of other things are just outside. I suppose it is one's being so tired.'

'This meat has surely been used for soup,' said Miss Bartlett, laying down her fork.

'I want so to see the Arno. The rooms the Signora promised us in her letter would have looked over the Arno. The Signora had no business to do it at all. Oh, it is a shame.'

'Any nook does for me,' Miss Bartlett continued; 'but it does seem hard that you shouldn't have a view.'

Lucy felt that she had been selfish. 'Charlotte, you mustn't spoil me: of course, you must look over the Arno, too. I meant that. The first vacant room in the front–'

'You must have it,' said Miss Bartlett, part of whose travelling expenses were paid by Lucy's mother – a piece of generosity to which she made many a tactful allusion. 'No, no. You must have it.'

'I insist on it. Your mother would never forgive me, Lucy.' 'She would never forgive *me*.'

The ladies' voices grew animated, and – if the sad truth be owned – a little peevish. They were tired, and under the guise of unselfishness they wrangled. Some of their neighbours interchanged glances, and one of them – one of the ill-bred people whom one does meet abroad – leant forward over the table and actually intruded into their argument. He said:

'I have a view, I have a view.'

Miss Bartlett was startled. Generally at a pension people looked them over for a day or two before speaking, and often did not find out that they would 'do' till they had gone. She knew that the intruder was ill-bred, even before she glanced at him. He was an old man, of heavy build, with a fair, shaven face and large eyes. There was something childish in those eyes, though it was not the childishness of senility. What exactly it was Miss Bartlett did not stop to consider, for her glance passed on to his clothes. These did not attract her. He was probably trying to become acquainted with them before they got into the swim. So she assumed a dazed expression when he spoke to her, and then said: 'A view? Oh, a view! How delightful a view is!'

from A Room with a View *by E.M. Forster*

Progress check

Look carefully at the two passages. What differences and/or similarities do you find in these passages? You should look at **style**, **language** and **content** in your answer.

Summary

Here are some ideas that you might have noted.

Similarities

- Both passages focus on a kind of 'social etiquette'.
- Both are concerned to some degree with a 'class consciousness'.
- The language contains elements of formality.
- Both writers use an event to create interest and make the reader want to read on to find out what will happen.

Differences

- The first passage is written in the first person and the second one is in the third person.
- In the second passage the narrator is reporting events to us whereas in the first one we see events as they happen.
- The second passage seems to be concerned with the rather snobbish attitudes of Miss Bartlett, whereas in the first passage, the narrator, Stevens, is a butler and is aware of his place in the hierarchy. His employer does not seem to exhibit snobbish attitudes, though.

4.5 Types of exam question

After studying this section you should be able to:

- *identify different question types that you might encounter in the exam*
- *understand what you need to do to answer these questions*

LEARNING SUMMARY

AQA A	U5
AQA B	U6
Edexcel	U6
OCR	U6
WJEC	U5
NICCEA	U6

In the examination there are two basic question types that you will come across.

- Questions that will ask you something that will involve you in comparing both texts. This kind of question is likely to be quite open-ended and wide-ranging in nature and will possibly require you to assess each whole text in your answer.
- Questions that start by drawing your attention to a particular part of each text and then ask you to compare certain aspects of the given sections. Sometimes this kind of question can invite you to bring in other areas of the novels too in your answer but it might focus exclusively on the sections indicated. Read the question carefully and watch out for this.

In the exam you get two questions on these texts and you have to answer ONE of them.

Using *Nineteen Eighty-Four* and *Brave New World* as texts, here are some examples of question types.

The first type of question

1 Do these two novels have any relevant message for today's reader about the future of our society?

2 What aspects have interested you most in your reading of *Brave New World* and *Nineteen Eighty-Four*?

3 How has your study of *Brave New World* and *Nineteen Eighty-Four* extended your understanding of the nature of anti-utopian literature?

4 Compare the ways in which Orwell and Huxley present their characters in *Nineteen Eighty-Four* and *Brave New World*.

5 Write about the distinctive features of each novel, commenting on how effective you have found each book in terms of warning of the dangers of totalitarianism.

The second type of question draws you to a particular part of the text. This kind of question is likely to ask you to write more specifically on some aspects of the parts of the text that have been indicated to you.

Here is an example of that second type of question.

Remind yourself of the opening section of *Nineteen Eighty-Four*, from the beginning to the section ending 'WAR IS PEACE FREEDOM IS SLAVERY IGNORANCE IS STRENGTH'.

Now remind yourself of the opening section of *Brave New World* from the beginning to the section ending 'to undergo Bokanovsky's process.'

How effective do you find these as openings to the novels? You should comment on each writer's style, the effects they wanted to create from the opening pages of their novel and the overall impressions you are given of the kind of world they are describing.

Sample question and model answer

The main Assessment Objective tested here is AO2ii to:
- respond with knowledge and understanding to literary texts of different types and periods, exploring and commenting on relationships and comparison between literary texts.

This question also tests the candidate's ability to consider:
- knowledge and understanding of the text (AO2)
- ability to communicate that understanding clearly and coherently (AO1)
- exploration of the ways the writer's choices of form, structure and language inform meaning (AO3).

Allow one and a half hours for this question.

Compare and contrast the openings of the two novels and evaluate the effectiveness of each.

1.

A squat grey building of only thirty-four storeys. Over the main entrance the words, CENTRAL LONDON HATCHERY AND CONDITIONING CENTRE, and, in a shield, the World State's motto, COMMUNITY, IDENTITY, STABILITY.

The enormous room on the ground floor faced towards the north. Cold for all the summer beyond the panes, for all the tropical heat of the room itself, a harsh thin light glared through the windows, hungrily seeking some draped lay figure, some pallid shape of academic goose-flesh, but finding only the glass and nickel and bleakly shining porcelain of a laboratory. Wintriness responded to wintriness. The overalls of the workers were white, their hands gloved with a pale corpse-coloured rubber. The light was frozen, dead, a ghost. Only from the yellow barrels of the microscopes did it borrow a certain rich and living substance, lying along the polished tubes like butter, streak after luscious streak in long recession down the work tables.

'And this,' said the Director opening the door, 'is the Fertilizing Room.'

Bent over their instruments, three hundred Fertilizers were plunged, as the Director of Hatcheries and Conditioning entered the room, in the scarcely breathing silence, the absentminded, soliloquizing hum or whistle, of absorbed concentration. A troop of newly arrived students, very young, pink and callow, followed nervously, rather abjectly, at the Director's heels. Each of them carried a note-book, in which, whenever the great man spoke, he desperately scribbled. Straight from the horse's mouth. It was a rare privilege. The DHC for Central London always made a point of personally conducting his new students round the various departments.

Just to give you a general idea,' he would explain to them. For of course some sort of general idea they must have, if they were to do their work intelligently – though as little of one, if they were to be good and happy members of society, as possible. For particulars, as everyone knows, make for virtue and happiness; generalities are intellectually necessary evils. Not philosophers, but fret-sawyers and stamp collectors compose the backbone of society.

'Tomorrow,' he would add, smiling at them with a slightly menacing geniality, 'you'll be settling down to serious work. You won't have time for generalities. Meanwhile ...'

Meanwhile, it was a privilege. Straight from the horse's mouth into the note-book. The boys scribbled like mad.

Tall and rather thin but upright, the Director advanced into the room. He had a long chin and big, rather prominent teeth, just covered, when he was not talking, by his full, floridly curved lips. Old, young? Thirty? fifty? fifty-five? It was hard to say. And anyhow the question didn't arise; in this year of stability, A.F. 632, it didn't occur to you to ask it.

'I shall begin at the beginning,' said the DHC, and the more zealous students recorded his intention in their notebooks: *Begin at the beginning*. 'These,' he waved his hand, 'are

Sample question and model answer (continued)

the incubators.' And opening an insulated door he showed them racks upon racks of numbered test-tubes. 'The week's supply of ova. Kept,' he explained, 'at blood heat; whereas the male gametes,' and here he opened another door, 'they have to be kept at thirty-five instead of thirty-seven. Full blood heat sterilizes.' Rams wrapped in thermogene beget no lambs.

Still leaning against the incubators he gave them, while the pencils scurried illegibly across the pages, a brief description of the modem fertilizing process; spoke first, of course, of its surgical introduction – 'the operation undergone voluntarily for the good of Society, not to mention the fact that it carries a bonus amounting to six months' salary'; continued with some account of the technique for preserving the excised ovary alive and actively developing; passed on to a consideration of optimum temperature, salinity, viscosity; referred to the liquor in which the detached and ripened eggs were kept; and, leading his charges to the work tables, actually showed them how the liquor was drawn off from the test-tubes; how it was let out drop by drop on to the specially warmed slides of the microscopes; how the eggs which it contained were inspected for abnormalities, counted and transferred to a porous receptacle; how (and he now took them to watch the operation) this receptacle was immersed in a warm bouillon containing free-swimming spermatozoa – at a minimum concentration of one hundred thousand per cubic centimetre, he insisted; and how, after ten minutes, the container was lifted out of the liquor and its contents re-examined; how, if any of the eggs remained unfertilized, it was again immersed, and, if necessary, yet again; how the fertilized ova went back to the incubators; where the Alphas and Betas remained until definitely bottled; while the Gammas, Deltas and Epsilons were brought out again, after only thirty-six hours, to undergo Bokanovsky's Process.

from Brave New World *by Aldous Huxley*

2.

It was a bright cold day in April, and the clocks were striking thirteen. Winston Smith, his chin nuzzled into his breast in an effort to escape the vile wind, slipped quickly through the glass doors of Victory Mansions, though not quickly enough to prevent a swirl of gritty dust from entering along with him.

The hallway smelt of boiled cabbage and old rag mats. At one end of it a coloured poster, too large for indoor display, had been tacked to the wall. It depicted simply an enormous face, more than a metre wide: the face of a man of about forty-five, with a heavy black moustache and ruggedly handsome features. Winston made for the stairs. It was no use trying the lift. Even at the best of times it was seldom working, and at present the electric current was cut off during daylight hours. It was part of the economy drive in preparation for Hate Week. The flat was seven flights up, and Winston, who was thirty-nine and had a varicose ulcer above his right ankle, went slowly, resting several times on the way. On each landing, opposite the lift shaft, the poster with the enormous face gazed from the wall. It was one of those pictures which are so contrived that the eyes follow you about when you move. BIG BROTHER IS WATCHING YOU, the caption beneath it ran.

Inside the flat a fruity voice was reading out a list of figures which had something to do with the production of pig-iron. The voice came from an oblong metal plaque like a dulled mirror which formed part of the surface of the right-hand wall. Winston turned a switch and the voice sank somewhat, though the words were still distinguishable. The instrument (the telescreen, it was called) could be dimmed, but there was no way of shutting it off completely. He moved over to the window: a smallish, frail figure, the meagreness of his body merely emphasised by the blue overalls which were the uniform of the Party. His hair was very fair, his face naturally sanguine, his skin roughened by coarse soap and blunt razor blades and the cold of the winter that had just ended.

Outside, even through the shut window-pane, the world looked cold. Down in the street little eddies of wind were whirling dust and torn paper into spirals, and though

Sample question and model answer (continued)

the sun was shining and the sky a harsh blue, there seemed to be no colour in anything, except the posters that were plastered everywhere. The black-moustachio'd face gazed down from every commanding corner. There was one on the house-front immediately opposite. BIG BROTHER IS WATCHING YOU, the caption said, while the dark eyes looked deep into Winston's own. Down at street level another poster, torn at one corner, flapped fitfully in the wind, alternately covering and uncovering the single word INGSOC. In the far distance a helicopter skimmed down between the roofs, hovered for an instant like a bluebottle, and darted away again with a curving flight. It was the police patrol, snooping into people's windows. The patrols did not matter, however. Only the Thought Police mattered.

Behind Winston's back the voice from the telescreen was still babbling away about pig-iron and the overfulfilment of the Ninth Three-Year Plan. The telescreen received and transmitted simultaneously. Any sound that Winston made, above the level of a very low whisper, would be picked up by it; moreover, so long as he remained within the field of vision which the metal plaque commanded, he could be seen as well as heard. There was of course no way of knowing whether you were being watched at any given moment. How often, or on what system, the Thought Police plugged in on any individual wire was guesswork. It was conceivable that they watched everybody all the time. But at any rate they could plug into your wire whenever they wanted to. You had to live – did live, from the habit that became instinct – in the assumption that every sound you made was overheard, and, except in darkness, every movement scrutinised.

Winston kept his back turned to the telescreen. It was safer; though, as he well knew, even a back can be revealing. A kilometre away the Ministry of Truth, his place of work, towered vast and white above the grimy landscape. This, he thought with a sort of vague distaste – this was London, chief city of Air-strip One, itself the third most populous of the provinces of Oceania. He tried to squeeze out some childhood memory that should tell him whether London had always been quite like this. Were there always these vistas of rotting nineteenth-century houses, their sides shored up with baulks of timber, their windows patched with cardboard and their roofs with corrugated iron, their crazy garden walls sagging in all directions? And the bombed sites where the plaster dust swirled in the air and the willowherb straggled over the heaps of rubble; and the places where the bombs had cleared a larger patch and there had sprung up sordid colonies of wooden dwellings like chicken-houses? But it was no use, he could not remember: nothing remained of his childhood except a series of bright-lit tableaux, occurring against no background and mostly unintelligible.

The Ministry of Truth – Minitrue, in Newspeak – was startlingly different from any other object in sight. It was an enormous pyramidal structure of glittering white concrete, soaring up, terrace after terrace, three hundred metres into the air. From where Winston stood it was just possible to read, picked out on its white face in elegant lettering, the three slogans of the Party:

> WAR IS PEACE
> FREEDOM IS SLAVERY
> IGNORANCE IS STRENGTH.

from Nineteen Eighty-Four *by George Orwell*

Student Response

Although both these novels are set in a future time, in worlds very different to that of our own time, they also present a very different view of the futures they portray. These differences are very apparent right from the start of the novels. *Brave New World*, with its description of the 'Central London Hatchery and Conditioning Centre' gives us the sense of a science-led society. The scale and importance of the building is revealed through the ironic understatement of the opening sentence – 'A squat, grey building of only thirty-four storeys'.

Introduction deals with both passages.

Sample question and model answer (continued)

Focus on the language of the passage – uses reference to text.	There follows a paragraph which describes the enormous room on the ground floor that we are taken into by the third-person narrator. The scene created has an atmosphere of coldness, despite the fact that we are told the room had 'tropical heat'. The room has the bleakness of a laboratory created by the 'glass and nickel and bleakly shining porcelain ... the light was frozen, dead as a ghost'.
	The narrative continues with the Director speaking. We learn that he is the director of the establishment and that he is showing a group of students around the hatchery. It is clear that he is a man of some importance as the students pay attention to his words and make notes as he goes along.
Switches to *Nineteen Eighty-Four* – again there is focus on the ways in which language is use to create atmosphere.	There is no such 'scientific-based' opening to *Nineteen Eighty-Four*, although Orwell does immediately catch the reader's attention with the rather strange 'It was a bright clear day in April, and the clocks were striking thirteen'. Far from the clinical world of science, though, the overwhelming feel from this opening is one of dirt, dust and grit blown around by a cold and uncomfortable wind. We are immediately, in the second sentence, introduced to the character who is to be the focal point of the novel, Winston Smith. It soon becomes clear that this is no 'hi-tech' world of test tubes and
Draws valid contrasts between the openings.	laboratories – it is a world where Winston's hallway smells of 'boiled cabbage and old rag mats'. In the second paragraph, though, we are introduced to one of the huge posters of the man we are soon to become familiar with and know as 'Big Brother'.
Provides evidence to back up comments.	Further details confirm the down-at-heel world that Winston inhabits – the lift doesn't work, the electricity is cut during daylight hours and the standard of living seems poor. Orwell also drops in various details at this stage, which, as yet, are not explained but which will later be given a significance. The reference to 'Hate Week', for example, and the fact that Winston has a varicose ulcer on his leg. We are also introduced to a key
Perceptive comment on mottos and slogans.	slogan here – 'Big Brother is Watching You'. Huxley also gives us a motto early on – in the case of *Brave New World* this is 'Community, Identity, Stability.' Both these mottos later can be seen to be thematically linked and of central importance to their respective novels.
Returns to *Brave New World* – the emphasis on the scientific content.	The narrative of *Brave New World* continues with the Director's tour. Through his explanation we learn about the incubation process, the scientific jargon giving us details of 'optimum temperature, salinity, viscosity' and so on. He describes the details of eggs inspected for abnormalities, their transfer to 'a porous receptacle', its immersion 'in a warm bouillon containing free-swimming spermatozoa – at a minimum concentration of one hundred thousand per cubic centimetre'. The final words of the extract continue the pseudo-scientific language talking of Alphas, Betas, Gammas, Deltas and Epsilons and a process which we only know at this stage as 'Bokanovsky's Process'.
Contrasts drawn with *Nineteen Eighty-Four*.	Orwell's description of Winston's flat does have a hint of the 'futuristic' in the telescreen through which his every move can be monitored, giving an added dimension to the phrase 'Big Brother is Watching You'. However, everything else about the world that Winston inhabits seems austere and lacking in any of the comforts of life –
Effective quotation to support the points.	'the meagreness of his body merely emphasised by the blue overalls which were the uniform of the Party. His hair was very fair, his face naturally sanguine, his skin roughened by the coarse soap and blunt razor blades and the cold of the winter that had just ended.'

Sample question and model answer (continued)

Again there is emphasis on the cold, dusty, dirty world, even though the sun was shining the sky was a 'harsh blue', 'there seemed to be no colour in anything'. The sense of being watched is emphasised further by more references to Big Brother, being watched and the police helicopter, one of the patrols of the 'Thought Police'. This reference isn't explained immediately either but the idea it provokes is an ominous one. Further unfamiliar terms are introduced by Orwell – 'Ninth Three-Year Plan', 'Ingsoc,' 'Air-strip One', 'The Ministry of Truth – Minitrue', and 'Newspeak'. This is clearly not our world, a fact emphasised by the three slogans of the Party which consist of a puzzling contradiction –

> 'War is Peace
> Freedom is Slavery
> Ignorance is Strength.'

In their different ways both these openings are effective and create an impression of what is to be developed further in each novel. In some ways, the opening of Huxley's novel seems to be more conventionally 'futuristic' or 'science'-based whereas there are aspects of Orwell's novel which seem to be set more in the past than the future – the poor living conditions, for example. Having said this, there are a number of alien and futuristic references that capture the reader's imagination. In this respect it could be argued that the opening raises more question marks and contradictions in the reader's imagination, thus making it the more effective opening.

Again a sense of detail used. The idea of creation of tension emerging.

Good summing up of ideas drawing the threads together.

Overall this is a good answer in which the student makes a real attempt to integrate comments on the two novels. She does not just write about one novel and then the other but has tried to genuinely compare the two.

Exam practice and analysis

The following question tests AO5ii as the dominant objective:

- evaluate the significance of cultural, historical and other contextual influences upon literary texts and study.

Other assessment objectives that are also tested are:

- AO1 communicate clearly the knowledge, understanding and insight appropriate to literary study
- AO3 show detailed understanding of the ways in which writers' choices of form, structure and language shape meanings.

This is an open book question.

Allow one and a half hours to answer the question.

Forster: *A Room with a View*

Ishiguro: *The Remains of the Day*

Compare and contrast the presentation of the main father and son relationship in both of these texts (i.e. the Emersons; Stevens and his father). You should start your consideration with a careful reading of the opening chapter in *A Room with a View* and 'Day One Evening – Salisbury' in *The Remains of the Day*.

WJEC Specimen Material 2000

Some points to note.

- You are steered towards the opening sections to begin with but you are not necessarily required to restrict your answer to these parts of the text.
- A good answer will point to a number of similarities in the relationships and the way they are presented.
- But there are a number of points that separate them too.
- A good answer will also show an awareness of the differences in the period in which the two texts were written.

Chapter 5

Texts in context

The following topics are covered in this chapter:

- *What is context?*
- *Contexts to consider*
- *The writer's biography*
- *Other works*
- *Historical, social and political contexts*
- *Genre, style and literary period*
- *Language*
- *Readings of the text by other readers*
- *The text as part of a larger work*

5.1 What is context?

After studying this section you should be able to:

- understand what is meant by 'context' in terms of the exam
- understand why it is important
- see context in the light of the texts that you are studying
- recognise where it will be tested in your course

AQA A	U4, U6
AQA B	U4, U5, U6
Edexcel	U4, U5, U6
OCR	U4, U5, U6
WJEC	U6
NICCEA	U5, U6

One of the differences between the study of English Literature at AS Level and its study at A2 Level is that A2 Level Assessment Objective 5ii states that the examination will assess a candidate's ability to evaluate the significance of cultural, historical and other contextual influences upon literary texts and study.

We need to begin by asking what is meant by 'contextual influences'.

These influences could include aspects such as:

- the context of period or era including **significant social, historical, political and cultural processes**
- the context of the work in terms of the **writer's biography** or their **environment and social surrounding**
- the **language** context, including relevant episodes in the use and development of literary language, colloquial language use or dialect styles and so on
- the different context of a work established by its **reception over time**, including the recognition that works have different meanings and effects in different periods (note here the connection with AO4) and the awareness of different critical responses.

If you have already studied the course at AS Level then you will already have come across the idea of 'contexts' but your awareness of it will have been simpler than that required at A2 Level. At A2 Level you should be exploring context as well as text and be evaluating its significance as a shaping influence on the creation of the text.

> Contextual influences can be an important factor determining the type of text a writer produces. You will need to explore and evaluate these issues as part of your A2 course.

KEY POINT

Where will it be tested?

Exactly where it will be tested in your course depends on the particular specification you are following. Here is a breakdown of where AO5ii is tested by different boards so that you can identify exactly which text(s) this aspect will be tested on.

AQA A   Unit 4 The Poetry Section
Unit 6 The Synoptic Module

AQA B   Unit 4 Comparing Texts (coursework)
Unit 5 The pre-1880 Drama Text
Unit 6 Exploring Texts (synoptic module)

OCR   Unit 4 (2710) Poetry and Drama pre-1900
Unit 5 (2711/2712) Prose (post-1914) coursework or exam
Unit 6 (2713) Comparative and Contextual Study (double weighting) (synoptic assessment)

Edexcel   Unit 4 Modern Prose
Unit 5 Poetry and drama
Unit 6 Synoptic module

WJEC   Unit 6 (E Lit 6) Drama (pre-1770) and linked material. This is the only module in which this assessment objective is tested (synoptic module)

NICCEA   Unit 5 Twentieth-century Prose
Unit 6 Drama synoptic.

What about different interpretations by other readers?

As the idea of different interpretations of texts by other readers is often linked to the contextual influences which give rise to a text, it is useful to see where you will be tested on this objective too. You will notice some overlap in some specifications.

Here is a breakdown of where different boards test AO4 – to articulate independent opinions and judgements, informed by different interpretations.

AQA A   Unit 4 Drama question
Unit 5
Unit 6

AQA B   Unit 4 Comparison
Unit 5 The Poetry question
Unit 6 Synoptic

OCR   Unit 4 Poetry and Drama Pre-1900
Unit 5 Prose (post-1914)
Unit 6 Synoptic module

Edexcel   Unit 4 Modern prose
Unit 5 Poetry and Drama
Unit 6 Synoptic

WJEC   Unit 4 Poetry pre-1900
Unit 6 Drama pre-1770

NICCEA   Unit 5 Twentieth-century Prose (5% of weighting)
Unit 6 Drama Synoptic

Why study context?

When we study a novel, a poem or a play or any other piece of writing we usually focus primarily on the text itself. All our efforts go into analysing the text itself and we spend little time looking at the historical, cultural or other influences that help to create the kind of text we are studying. However, no text has ever been produced in a vacuum. All texts are the product of a whole variety of factors that influence both the ways in which writers write and the ways in which readers read a text. Studying and learning about these background influences can provide us with information that can increase our understanding and appreciation of the text.

Through this kind of work we can see the text in a wider context which in itself can enhance or even change the perspective that we have of the work itself.

> Studying the contextual influences which gave rise to a text can provide information that will help us to understand and appreciate the meaning and significance of that text.

KEY POINT

The following example illustrates how even a small amount of contextual knowledge can inform and perhaps even change your response to a text.

Read the following poem carefully:

> My prime of youth is but a frost of cares;
>   My feast of joy is but a dish of pain;
> My crop of corn is but a field of tares;
>   And all my good is but vain hope of gain:
> The day is past, and yet I saw no sun;
> And now I live, and now my life is done.
>
> My tale was heard, and yet it was not told;
>   My fruit is fall'n, and yet my leaves are green;
> My youth is spent, and yet I am not old;
>   I saw the world, and yet I was not seen:
> My thread is cut, and yet it is not spun;
> And now I live, and now my life is done.
>
> I sought my death, and found it in my womb;
>   I looked for life, and saw it was a shade;
> I trod the earth, and knew it was my tomb;
>   And now I die, and now I was but made;
> My glass is full, and now my glass is run;
> And now I live, and now my life is done.

Progress check

Make notes on your interpretation of the poem. Here are some questions that might help.

Who is the narrator?
What state of mind does the writer appear to be in?
What does he have to say through his poem?

Summary

The poem seems to be about death. The narrator is a young person who is lamenting the fact that although he still had so much life to look forward to, his life, for some reason, is at an end.

Our interpretation so far is quite general. However, a little background knowledge of the context which gave rise to the writing of this poem can improve our understanding of it considerably. Now read the following information concerning the context within which this poem was written.

The poem is entitled 'Elegy For Himself' (an elegy is a poem that laments or mourns something and is usually sad or reflective in nature) and was written by Chidiock Tichborne (1558?–86). Both Tichborne and his father were devout Catholics. At this time, the Protestant Queen Elizabeth was on the throne and Catholics were held under much suspicion. In 1583 Tichborne was interrogated by the authorities about importing 'popish relics' when he had returned from abroad where he had travelled without permission. In 1586 he became involved in the Babington Plot which was a conspiracy to assassinate Queen Elizabeth and replace her with her Catholic cousin Mary (Queen of Scots). The plot was bungled, however, and the conspirators arrested. Tichborne was amongst them and he was hanged on 20 September 1586. He is said to have written this poem whilst imprisoned in the Tower of London the night before his execution.

Progress check

Having read the background to this poem make a list of the ways in which this information has informed or even changed your response to the poem.

Summary

Here are some ways the contextual information might have informed your response.

- On a historical level, this poem is clearly the product of an Elizabethan writer with all the political aspects that that period involves.
- On an analytical level, the knowledge that Tichborne was shortly to be executed helps you make sense of phrases like 'dish of pain', 'now my life is done', 'My youth is spent, and yet I am not old'.
- On an emotional level, this knowledge adds an intensity to the poem. You can imagine this young man, in his cell the night before his execution, writing this poem. You can imagine his feelings and his grief at the thought of the life that he will not live.

> Even a small amount of contextual information can have a significant impact on your perception of a text.

KEY POINT

5.2 Contexts to consider

LEARNING SUMMARY

After studying this section you should be able to:

- *understand the kinds of contexts that you might study*
- *see how they can help you understand the texts you are studying*

AQA A	U4, U6
AQA B	U4, U5, U6
Edexcel	U4, U5, U6
OCR	U4, U5, U6
WJEC	U6
NICCEA	U5, U6

When studying literature at A Level you are expected to learn to recognise and comment on aspects of context that are relevant to the text you are studying. At AS Level you simply had to show an awareness of these but at A2 Level you are expected to show a deeper understanding of their significance. The first thing to understand, though, is to recognise what kinds of things you need to consider in order to place a text that you are studying 'in context'.

Here are some things that you can consider:

- the **biography** of the writer
- the **other works** the writer has produced
- the **historical period** the text was written in
- the **place** in which it was written
- the **genre** chosen or **literary style** of the period
- the ways in which **language** was used at the time the text was written

- how our reading of the text can be influenced by the way **other readers**, both at the time the text was written and since, have interpreted or received the text
- the position of the text as a **part of a larger work**.

In the following section we will look at these areas in more detail using some practical examples.

5.3 The writer's biography

After studying this section you should be able to:

- *understand the value of learning about a writer's biography*
- *see how this knowledge can help you understand the texts you are studying*

LEARNING SUMMARY

AQA A	U4, U6
AQA B	U4, U5, U6
Edexcel	U4, U5, U6
OCR	U4, U5, U6
WJEC	U6
NICCEA	U5, U6

Knowledge of the lives of the writers of the texts we study can be both interesting and enjoyable but more than this, it can shed valuable light on the text we are studying. In fact, it can be difficult to make sense of some writing at all unless we know something of the writer's life and views. On the other hand, some critics believe that a text should stand alone, independent of any biographical details about the author. Others insist that we should learn as much as we can about a writer in order to understand their work as fully as possible. In many ways both these views hold some truth and to a large extent it depends on the work itself how valuable biographical knowledge is.

The following poem by William Wordsworth stands alone as a poem, but some biographical knowledge of the author can help us towards a fuller understanding of this text.

Read the poem through carefully.

Elegaic Stanzas

Suggested by a Picture of Peele Castle in a Storm painted by Sir George Beaumont

I was thy Neighbour once, thou rugged Pile!
Four summer weeks I dwelt in sight of thee:
I saw thee every day; and all the while
Thy Form was sleeping on a glassy sea.

So pure the sky, so quiet was the air!
So like, so very like, was day to day!
Whene'er I look'd, thy Image still was there;
It trembled, but it never pass'd away.

How perfect was the calm! it seem'd no sleep;
No mood, which season takes away, or brings:
I could have fancied that the mighty Deep
Was even the gentlest of all gentle Things.

Ah! THEN, if mine had been the Painter's hand,
To express what then I saw; and add the gleam,
The light that never was, on sea or land,
The consecration, and the Poet's dream;

I would have planted thee, thou hoary Pile!
Amid a world how different from this!
Beside a sea that could not cease to smile;
On tranquil land, beneath a sky of bliss;

Thou shouldst have seem'd a treasure-house, a mine
Of peaceful years; a chronicle of heaven;—

Of all the sunbeams that did ever shine
The very sweetest had to thee been given.

A Picture had it been of lasting case,
Elysian quiet, without toil or strife;
No motion but the moving tide, a breeze,
Or merely silent Nature's breathing life

Such, in the fond delusion of my heart,
Such Picture would I at that time have made:
And seen the soul of truth in every part;
A faith, a trust, that could not be betray'd.

So once it would have been,—'tis so no more;
I have submitted to a new control:
A power is gone, which nothing can restore;
A deep distress hath humaniz'd my Soul.

Not for a moment could I now behold
A smiling sea and he what I have been.
The feeling of my loss will ne'er be old.
This, which I know, I speak with mind serene.

Then, Beaumont, Friend! who would have been the Friend
If he had lived, of Him whom I deplore,
This Work of thine I blame not, but commend;
This sea is anger, and that dismal shore.

Oh 'tis a passionate Work!—yet wise and well:
Well chosen is the spirit that is here;
That Hulk which labours in the deadly swell,
This rueful sky, this pageantry of fear!

And this huge Castle, standing here sublime,
I love to see the look with which it braves,
Cased in the unfeeling armour of old time,
The light'ning, the fierce wind, and trampling waves.

Farewell, farewell the Heart that lives alone,
Hous'd in a dream, at distance from the Kind!
Such happiness, wherever it be known,
Is to be pitied; for 'tis surely blind.

But welcome fortitude, and patient chear,
And frequent sights of what is to be born!
Such sights, or worse, as are before me here. —
Not without hope we suffer and we mourn.

William Wordsworth

Progress check

1 What is the poem about?
2 What does it reveal about the poet's view of life?

Summary

1 The subject matter is that of Sir George Beaumont's painting depicting Peele Castle in a storm. In the first half of the poem (lines 1–32) Wordsworth tells us that he once visited the castle in calm weather. Had he been a painter, at that time he would not have produced a painting like Beaumont's but he would have painted the sea in a tranquil and calm mood. He now sees that these youthful ideas were deluded. In the second part of the poem he feels that he is no longer a dreaming poet and he sees that the depiction of the castle in a

storm represents reality – Beaumont's picture represents a true image of human life.

2 He rejects his former views and recognises the realities of life. He adopts a stoical view and resolves to endure in patience the harshness of life.

Now read the following biographical details.

The change of view reflected in this poem reflects a more fundamental change of view in Wordsworth's philosophy. He had been greatly affected by the death of his brother John. John was captain of the merchant ship the *Earl of Abergavenny* and was drowned when the ship was wrecked in Weymouth Bay in a storm on 5 February, 1805. Peele Castle is near Barrow-in-Furness in Cumbria and Wordsworth had stayed near there in a period of calm summer weather in 1794. In 1806 he visited Sir George Beaumont and saw his painting of the castle. The poem depicts the shift in Wordsworth's attitude to life by comparing his original impressions of the castle with his response twelve years later to Beaumont's painting.

> **KEY POINT**
>
> Find out as much as you can about the biography of the writers you are studying.

Progress check

Now look at the text(s) you are studying and on which you will need to evaluate contextual influences. Find out as much as you can about the life of the writer of each text.

5.4 Other works

After studying this section you should be able to:

- recognise the value of being aware of other works that the writer has produced
- see if there are any common themes, philosophies, ideas explored, etc. in the texts they have written
- apply these ideas to the specific texts that you are studying

LEARNING SUMMARY

AQA A	U4, U6
AQA B	U4, U5, U6
Edexcel	U4, U5, U6
OCR	U4, U5, U6
WJEC	U6
NICCEA	U5, U6

It can be important to know not only about the lives of the writers that you are studying but also about the other works that they have written. If you know something about the other works of the writer, and better still, if you have read any of them, you will be in a better position to draw conclusions about the text you are studying. For example, you will be able to determine whether or not the text you are studying is typical of the work of that writer or not. You might also be able to tell whether the author has particular themes that they explore through their books. For example, if you are studying D.H. Lawrence's *The Rainbow* then you would find that a knowledge of some of his other writing such as *Sons and Lovers* and *Women in Love* would help you to see how he explores similar themes across several texts. You will also be able to see where the particular text you are studying stands in the context of the writer's other works.

One of the areas that Lawrence felt passionately about was education and how, very often, it failed those it was meant to educate. (He was a teacher himself for a while and so had first-hand experience.) Many of his writings contain elements to do with the theme of education. The following two pieces are examples of these. The first is taken from his novel *The Rainbow* where Ursula Brangwen has recently taken up a teaching post. The second is a poem written by Lawrence.

Read the two pieces through very carefully.

Ursula felt her heart faint inside her. Why must she grasp all this, why must she force learning on fifty-five reluctant children, having all the time an ugly, rude jealousy behind her, ready to throw her to the mercy of the herd of children, who would like to rend her as a weaker representative of authority. A great dread of her task possessed her. She saw Mr Brunt, Miss Harby, Miss Schofield, all the school-teachers, drudging unwillingly at the graceless task of compelling many children into one disciplined, mechanical set, reducing the whole set to an automatic state of obedience and attention, and then of commanding their acceptance of various pieces of knowledge. The first great task was to reduce sixty children to one state of mind, or being. This state must be produced automatically, through the will of the teacher, and the will of the whole school authority, imposed upon the will of the children. The point was that the headmaster and the teachers should have one will in authority, which should bring the will of the children into accord. But the headmaster was narrow and exclusive. The will of the teachers could not agree with his, their separate wills refused to be so subordinated. So there was a state of anarchy, leaving the final judgement to the children themselves, which authority should exist.

So there existed a set of separate wills, each straining itself to the utmost to exert its own authority. Children will never naturally acquiesce to sitting in a class and submitting to knowledge. They must be compelled by a stronger, wiser will. Against which will they must always strive to revolt. So that the first great effort of every teacher of a large class must be to bring the will of the children into accordance with his own will. And this he can only do by an abnegation of his personal self, and an application of a system of laws, for the purpose of achieving a certain calculable result, the imparting of certain knowledge. Whereas Ursula thought she was going to become the first wise teacher by making the whole business personal, and using no compulsion. She believed entirely in her own personality.

So that she was in a very deep mess. In the first place she was offering to a class a relationship which only one or two of the children were sensitive enough to appreciate, so that the mass were left outsiders, therefore against her. Secondly, she was placing herself in passive antagonism to the one fixed authority of Mr Harby, so that the scholars could more safely harry her. She did not know, but her instinct gradually warned her. She was tortured by the voice of Mr Brunt. On it went, jarring, harsh, full of hate, but so monotonous, it nearly drove her mad: always the same set, harsh monotony. The man was become a mechanism working on and on and on. But the personal man was in subdued friction all the time. It was horrible – all hate! Must she be like this? She could feel the ghastly necessity. She must become the same – put away the personal self, become an instrument, an abstraction, working upon a certain material, the class, to achieve a set purpose of making them know so much each day. And she could not submit. Yet gradually she felt the invincible iron closing upon her. The sun was being blocked out. Often when she went out at playtime and saw a luminous blue sky with changing clouds, it seemed just a fantasy, like a piece of painted scenery. Her heart was so black and tangled in the teaching, her personal self was shut in prison, abolished, she was subjugate to a bad, destructive will. How then could the sky be shining? There was no sky, there was no luminous atmosphere of out-of-doors. Only the inside of the school was real – hard, concrete, real and vicious.

from The Rainbow *by D.H. Lawrence*

Last Lesson of the Afternoon

When will the bell ring, and end this weariness?
How long have they tugged the leash, and strained apart,
My pack of unruly hounds! I cannot start
Them again on a quarry of knowledge they hate to hunt,
I can haul them and urge them no more.

No longer now can I endure the brunt
Of the books that lie out on the desks; a full threescore
Of several insults of blotted pages, and scrawl
Of slovenly work that they have offered me.
I am sick, and what on earth is the good of it all?
What good to them or me, I cannot see!

So, shall I take
My last dear fuel of life to heap on my soul
And kindle my will to a flame that shall consume
Their dross of indifference; and take the toll
Of their insults in punishment? – I will not! –

I will not waste my soul and my strength for this.
What do I care for all that they do amiss!
What is the point of this teaching of mine, and of this
Learning of theirs? It all goes down the same abyss.

What does it matter to me if they can write
A description of a dog, or if they can't?
What is the point? To us both, it is all my aunt!
And yet I'm supposed to care, with all my might.

I do not, and will not; they won't and they don't;
    and that's all!
I shall keep my strength for myself; they can keep
    theirs as well.
Why should we beat our heads against the wall
Of each other? I shall sit and wait for the bell.

D.H. Lawrence

Progress check

1 What view of education do these two pieces express?
2 How are these views conveyed to the reader?
3 What similarities and/or differences do you see between them?

Summary

1 Both of them express a strong dissatisfaction with the system as it exists. Ursula finds the idea of producing mass uniformity amongst her pupils undesirable but on the other hand she senses the negativity of the youngsters to the ideas of restriction and enforced learning. Lawrence's poem expresses much the same view except that there is more a sense of someone who has tried and failed and given up the struggle. It has become a case of self-preservation for the poet.

2 Both the extract from *The Rainbow* and the poem use a good deal of imagery to convey the ideas. Much of the imagery relates to personal development (or lack of it) and the 'inner-self'.

3 In the extract from *The Rainbow* there is the sense that Ursula finds the whole process unsatisfactory and disappointing – quite different from what she had

expected but she is still involved with her pupils. She is still part of the struggle. In the poem there is very much the feeling of a teacher who has given up. He has resigned himself to the fact that he cannot win this struggle and so has withdrawn from it out of a sense of self-preservation.

> A knowledge of other texts an author has written can be useful to help you set the text you are studying in context.

Progress check

Find out as much as you can about other works by the writer of the text(s) you are studying. If you haven't the time to read them, then read summaries of them. Watch out for favourite or typical themes running through the writer's works. Is the text you are studying typical of the works of that writer?

5.5 Historical, social and political contexts

After studying this section you should be able to:

- *recognise the significance of historical, social and political contexts*
- *understand how a knowledge of these can help you understand the texts you are studying*

AQA A	U4, U6
AQA B	U4, U5, U6
Edexcel	U4, U5, U6
OCR	U4, U5, U6
WJEC	U6
NICCEA	U5, U6

Some knowledge of the historical background of a text and of the social and political climate of the time can help you to make sense of some aspects of the writing. Different times, places and cultures have their own style and conventions and even variations in language.

Historical context

The following extract is taken from the beginning of the play *Dr Faustus* by Christopher Marlowe and was written in the latter part of the sixteenth century.

Read the extract through carefully.

> **Dr Faustus, Act I, Scene i**
>
> *Faustus in his study*
>
> **FAUSTUS** Settle thy studies, Faustus, and begin
> To sound the depth of that thou wilt profess;
> Having commenc'd, be a divine in show,
> 1 Yet level at the end of every art,
> And live and die in Aristotle's works.
> Sweet Analytics, 'tis thou hast ravish'd me!
> 2 *Bene disserere est finis logices.*
> Is to dispute well logic's chiefest end?
> Affords this art no greater miracle?
> Then read no more, thou hast attain'd that end;
> A greater subject fitteth Faustus' wit.
> 3 Bid *on kai me on* farewell, Galen come,

Seeing *ubi desinit philosophus, ibi incipit medicus.*

4

Be a physician, Faustus, heap up gold,
And be eterniz'd for some wondrous cure.
Summum bonum medicinae sanitas,

5

The end of physic is our body's health.
Why, Faustus, hast thou not attain'd that end?
Is not thy common talk sound aphorisms?
Are not thy bills hung up as monuments,
Whereby whole cities have escap'd the plague
And thousand desperate maladies been cur'd?
Yet art thou still but Faustus, and a man.
Couldst thou make men to live eternally
Or being dead raise them to life again,
Then this profession were to be esteem'd.

6

Physic, farewell! Where is Justinian?

7

Si una eademque res legatur duobus, alter rem, alter valorem rei, etc.
A petty case of paltry legacies!

8

Exhereditare filium non potest pater, nisi—
Such is the subject of the Institute
And universal body of the law.
This study fits a mercenary drudge
Who aims at nothing but external trash,
Too servile and illiberal for me.
When all is done, divinity is best.

9

Jerome's Bible, Faustus, view it well.

10

Stipendium peccati mors est. Ha! *Stipendium, etc.* The reward

11

of sin is death: that's hard. *Si peccasse negamus, fallimur, et nulla est in nobis veritas.* If we say that we have no sin, we deceive ourselves, and there's no truth in us. Why, then, belike we must sin, and so consequently die.
Ay, we must die an everlasting death.
What doctrine call you this? *che sara, sara*:
What will be, shall be! Divinity, adieu!
These metaphysics of magicians
And necromantic books are heavenly;
Lines, circles, letters, and characters:
Ay, these are those that Faustus most desires.
O, what a world of profit and delight,
Of power, of honour, of omnipotence,
Is promis'd to the studious artisan!

12

All things that move between the quiet poles
Shall be at my command: emperors and kings
Are but obey'd in their several provinces,
Nor can they raise the wind or rend the clouds;
But his dominion that exceeds in this
Stretcheth as far as doth the mind of man:

13

A sound magician is a demi-god;
Here tire, my brains, to get a deity.

Commentary

1   Ancient Greek philosopher
2   'to argue well is the goal of logic'
3   'being and not being' – a traditional subject for philosophical debate
4   'where philosophy ends, the physician begins'
5   'the ultimate goal of medicine is health'
6   Roman Emporer who codified Roman law – used as a textbook by law students
7   'If one and the same thing is left to two people, one should receive the thing, the other should receive the value of the thing.'
8   'a father may not disinherit his son unless…'
9   fourth century A.D. monk and scholar
10 'the payment for sin is death'
11 'we deceive ourselves if we say that we do not sin, and there is no truth in us.'
12 North and South Poles
13 To become a god

Progress check

1   What is Faustus doing in this extract?
2   What difficulties have you encountered in establishing meaning here?

Summary

1   In this extract Faustus is listing all the great authors he has read, all of whom now seem useless to him.
2   There are probably a number of things that you found difficult here:
    - The actual language used by Faustus is different from modern-day English and therefore the meaning is not always clear.
    - Many of the references he uses, such as to necromantic books, Jerome's Bible, etc. need explanation in order to fully understand what is meant.
    - The frequent use of Latin phrases also tends to obscure meaning.

> The main point here is that the historical period in which the text was written is very different from our own time. In order to fully understand all the references and language a certain amount of research needs to be done.
>
> **KEY POINT**

Social and political context

Works written in more recent times may be written in language similar to our own but perhaps contain social or political ideas of the time.

Charles Dickens, for example, often used his novels as a vehicle for social criticism. The following extract is taken from his novel, *Hard Times*.

Read it through carefully.

> Coketown, to which Messrs Bounderby and Gradgrind now walked, was a triumph of fact; it had no greater taint of fancy in it than Mrs Gradrind herself. Let us strike the key-note, Coketown, before pursuing our tune.
>
> It was a town of red brick, or of brick that would have been red if the smoke and ashes had allowed it; but, as matters stood it was a town of unnatural red and black like the painted face of a savage. It was a town of machinery and tall chimneys, out of which interminable serpents of smoke trailed themselves for ever

and ever, and never got uncoiled. It had a black canal in it, and a river that ran purple with ill-smelling dye, and vast piles of buildings full of windows where there was a rattling and a trembling all day long, and where the piston of the steam-engine worked monotonously up and down, like the head of an elephant in a state of melancholy madness. It contained several large streets all very like one another, and many small streets still more like one another, inhabited by people equally like one another, who all went in and out at the same hours, with the same sound upon the pavements, to do the same work, and to whom every day was the same as yesterday and tomorrow, and every year the counterpart of the last and the next.

These attributes of Coketown were in the main inseparable from the work by which it was sustained; against them were to be set off, comforts of life which found their way all over the world, and elegancies of life which made, we will not ask how much of the fine lady, who could scarcely bear to hear the place mentioned. The rest of its features were voluntary, and they were these.

You saw nothing in Coketown but what was severely workful. If the members of a religious persuasion built a chapel there – as the members of eighteen religious persuasions had done – they made it a pious warehouse of red brick, with sometimes (but this only in highly ornamented examples) a bell in a bird-cage on the top of it. The solitary exception was the New Church; a stuccoed edifice with a square steeple over the door, terminating in four short pinnacles like florid wooden legs. All the public inscriptions in the town were painted alike, in severe characters of black and white. The jail might have been the infirmary, the infirmary might have been the jail, the town-hall might have been either, or both, or anything else, for everything that appeared to the contrary in the graces of their construction. Fact, fact, fact, everywhere in the immaterial. The M'Choakumchild school was all fact, and the school of design was all fact, and the relations between the lying-in hospital and the cemetery, and what you couldn't state in figures, or show to be purchaseable in the cheapest market and saleable in the dearest, was not, and never should be, world without end, Amen.

from Hard Times *by Charles Dickens*

Progress check

Dickens seems to be making a social comment here. What point do you think he is making?

Summary

Dickens seems to be saying that Coketown is a place which is driven by the industrial processes that sustain it. It lacks feeling and imagination and this has been carried into every aspect of the place. The children learn 'FACTS' and the name of the teacher, Mr M'Choakumchild, sums up the effect that he has on the children he teaches. Dickens's point is that industrialisation has produced a society that is lacking in human warmth and feeling.

Cultural context

'Place' can also be an important element. Many modern British writers can trace their roots to other countries and other cultures. Some of this is what we call 'post-colonial' writing and many British writers originated in countries that were former colonies such as the West Indies, India, several African states, Canada, Australia and New Zealand. Very often such writers set their work within a particular cultural context which can have a significant bearing on their work. Examples of such writers that you might study at A Level are Maya Angelou, Toni Morrison and Alice

Walker who write from the context of the American South with its legacy of slavery, Margaret Atwood from a Canadian background, or Jean Rhys, some of whose works are set in a West Indian context.

The following extract is from Alice Walker's novel, *The Color Purple*. The novel is written in the form of a diary kept by Celie who is a young black woman living in the Deep South of the United States in the years between the First and Second World Wars.

Read the extract through carefully.

Dear God.

Harpo mope. Wipe the counter, light a cigarette, look outdoors, walk up and down. Little Squeak run long all up under him trying to git his tension. Baby this, she say, Baby that. Harpo look through her head, blow smoke.

Squeak come over to the comer where me and Mr. _____ at. She got two bright gold teef in the side of her mouth, generally grin all the time. Now she cry. Miss Celie, she say, What the matter with Harpo? Sofia in jail, I say.

In jail? She look like I say Sofia on the moon. What she in jail for? she ast. Sassing the mayor's wife. I say, Squeak pull up a chair. Look down my throat. What your real name? I ast her. She say, Mary Agnes, Make Harpo call you by your real name. I say. Then maybe he see you even when he trouble.

She look at me puzzle, I let it go. I tell her what one of Sofia sister tell me and Mr. _____.

Sofia and the prizefighter and all the children got in the prizefighter car and went to town. Clam out on the street looking like somebody. Just then the mayor and his wife come by.

All these children, say the mayor's wife, digging in her pocketbook. Cute as little buttons though, she say. She stop, put her hand on one of the children head. Say, and such strong white teef.

Sofia and the prizefighter don't say nothing. Wait for her to pass. Mayor wait too, stand back and tap his foot, watch her with a little smile. Now Millie, he say. Always going on over colored. Miss Millie finger the children some more, finally look at Sofia and the prizefighter. She look at the prizefighter car. She eye Sofia wristwatch. She say to Sofia, All your children so clean, she say, would you like to work for me, be my maid? Sofia say, Hell no. She say. What you say? Sofia say. Hell no,

Mayor look at Sofia, push his wife out the way. Stick out his chest. Girl, what you say to Miss Millie? Sofia say, I say. Hell no. He slap her. I stop telling it right there.

Squeak on the edge of her seat. She wait. Look down my throat some more.

No need to say no more, Mr. _____ say. You know what happen if somebody slap Sofia. Squeak go white as a sheet. *Naw*, she say. *Naw* nothing, I say. Sofia knock the man down. The polices come, start slinging the children off the mayor, bang they heads together. Sofia really start to fight. They drag her to the ground.

This far as I can go with it, look like. My eyes git full of water and my throat close.

Poor Squeak all scrunch down in her chair, trembling. They beat Sofia, Mr. _____ say.

Squeak fly up like she sprung, run over hind the counter to Harpo, put her arms round him. They hang together a long time, cry.

What the prizefighter do in all this? I ast Sofia sister, Odessa.

He want to jump in, she say, Sofia say No, take the children home.

Polices have they guns on him anyway. One move, he dead. Six of them, you know.

Mr, _____ go plead with the sheriff to let us see Sofia. Bub be in so much trouble, look so much like the sheriff, he and Mr. _____ almost on family terms. Just long as Mr. _____ know he colored.

Sheriff say. She a crazy woman, your boy's wife. You know that?

Mr. — say, Yassur, us do know it. Been trying to tell Harpo she crazy for twelve years – Since way before they marry. Sofia come from crazy peoples, Mr. _____ say, it not all her fault. And then again, the sheriff know how womens is, anyhow.

Sheriff think bout the women he know, say. Yep, you right there.

Mr, _____ say. We gon tell her she crazy too. if us ever do git in to see her.

Sheriff say. Well make sure you do. And tell her she lucky she alive.

When I see Sofia I don't know why she still alive. They crack her skull, they crack her ribs. They tear her nose loose on one side. They blind her in one eye. She swole from head to foot. Her tongue the size of my arm, it stick out tween her teef like a piece of rubber. She can't talk. And she just about the color of a eggplant.

Scare me so bad I near bout drop my grip. Bul I don't. I put it on the floor of the cell, take out comb and brush, nightgown, witch hazel and alcohol and I start to work on her. The colored tendant bring me water to wash her with, and I start at her two little slits for eyes –

from The Color Purple *by Alice Walker*

Progress check

1 What does this extract tell you about the kind of world Celie lives in?
2 What does the dialect form add to the narrative?

1 A world where prejudice by whites against blacks is the norm.
2 Gives a flavour of the character and makes her narrative more realistic.

Summary

1 This extract highlights the world of prejudice that Celie lives in. It is a world where the white people are dominant and the blacks are treated very much as second-class citizens.
2 The dialect form in which it is written adds an authenticity to the language – we really get a sense that this is Celie's voice speaking to us.

The sense of place or culture against which a text is set can be an important contextual influence.

KEY POINT

Progress check

If you are studying a text by a post-colonial writer or one where the sense of place or culture exerts an important contextual influence on the narrative, look carefully at the effect this has on the novel overall.

5.6 Genre, style and literary period

After studying this section you should be able to:

- *understand the importance of genre, style and literary period*
- *recognise the features in the texts you are studying*

LEARNING SUMMARY

AQA A	U4, U6
AQA B	U4, U5, U6
Edexcel	U4, U5, U6
OCR	U4, U5, U6
WJEC	U6
NICCEA	U5, U6

As well as belonging to a historical period, texts often belong to a 'literary' period too. The literary period a text belongs to will often influence the style of the writing and even the genre. Texts written in the same historical period are likely to have some similarities (although this is not always the case). For example, they may be part of a particular movement such as the 'Romantic Movement' or the 'War Poets' of the First World War or the 'Modernists' who experimented with artistic forms and styles after the First World War.

A number of 'Romantic' poets appear on the various specifications. Normally the word 'romantic' brings to mind images of romantic love or 'romance'. However, when we talk of the 'Romantic Poets' we mean something rather different. The Romantic Period refers to a specific period of time roughly between the years of 1780 and 1830. A number of writers were part of the Romantic Movement and were connected by the ideas and philosophies they shared. Not all writers of this period were 'Romantic' writers in this sense though. For example, Jane Austen wrote her novels during this period and they are not 'Romantic' in terms of the principles of the Romantic Movement at all.

'Romanticism' refers to a new set of ideas, of a philosophy which presented a new way of looking at the world, of life, of Man's place within the Universe. These ideas spread throughout Europe during the latter part of the eighteenth century and remained influential throughout much of the nineteenth. The ideas of the Romantics influenced music and painting as well as literature. Ultimately these new ways of thinking encapsulated most aspects of life including politics, religion and science. In order to fully understand Romantic writing it is important that you learn as much as possible about the historical background and events of the time because it was a time of great upheaval, revolution and war. Much of the writing of the time was influenced by these events.

In terms of English Literature the most important writers of this period were six poets divided into two 'generations'.

The 'first generation'	The 'second generation'
William Blake (1757–1827)	Lord Byron (1788–1824)
Samuel Taylor Coleridge (1772–1834)	John Keats (1795–1821)
William Wordsworth (1770–1850)	Percy Bysshe Shelley (1792–1822)

Two novelists, Sir Walter Scott and Mary Shelley, the author of *Frankenstein,* are also included as Romantic writers.

Much Romantic poetry is either:

- **lyrical** – poetry that tends to be reflective, perhaps capturing a particular moment or experience and then goes on to ponder its deeper meaning or significance, or
- **narrative** – poetry that tells a story and often encapsulates the ideas and philosophies of the Romantics. Coleridge's 'The Ancient Mariner', for example.

Another group of writers whose works you may encounter as part of your course is the First World War poets. In their case it is the war rather than a philosophical movement which influenced their writing.

Now read the following two poems.

Futility

Move him into the sun –
Gently its touch awoke him once,
At home, whispering of fields unsown.
Always it woke him, even in France,
Until this morning and this snow.
If anything might rouse him now
The kind old sun will know.

Think how it wakes the seeds –
Woke, once, the clays of a cold star.
Are limbs, so dear-achieved, are sides,
Full-nerved – still warm – too hard to stir?
Was it for this the clay grew tall?
 – O what made fatuous sunbeams toil
To break earth's sleep at all?

Wilfred Owen

The General

'Good-morning; good-morning!' the General said
When we met him last week on our way to the line.
Now the soldiers he smiled at are most of 'em dead,
And we're cursing his staff for incompetent swine.
'He's a cheery old card,' grunted Harry to Jack
As they slogged up to Arras with rifle and pack.

*

But he did for them both by his plan of attack.

Siegfried Sassoon

Progress check

These poems seem very different in many ways, but what feature do they have in common?

They both deal with the idea of the pointlessness of war.

Summary

They are both making an observation about the futility and waste in human terms of war.

> **KEY POINT**
>
> The genre, style and literary period can exert an important influence on writing and a knowledge of it can help you understand the text.

Progress check

Look at the text that you are studying. Can it be placed in a particular historical period? Does it reflect in any way what was happening at the time when it was written? Does the period have any bearing on the genre or style of the text?

5.7 Language

After studying this section you should be able to:

- understand the relationship between context and language
- see how the context can influence the language used in a text

AQA A	U4, U6
AQA B	U4, U5, U6
Edexcel	U4, U5, U6
OCR	U4, U5, U6
WJEC	U6
NICCEA	U5, U6

Language is not a static thing. It is constantly changing and evolving and the older the text the more the language is likely to have changed. For example, we can see major differences between the Middle English of Chaucer and our Modern English. The language of Shakespeare is different too, but less so than Chaucer's. Even in fairly recent texts, though, there may be elements of vocabulary and usage that are unfamiliar to us.

The following extract is taken from a very long 'epic' poem called *Paradise Lost* written by John Milton in the seventeenth century. This is from Book One and is the opening of the poem. Read it through carefully.

> Of Mans First Disobedience, and the Fruit
> Of that Forbidden Tree, whose mortal taste
> Brought Death into the World; and all our woe,
> With loss of *Eden*, till one greater Man
> Restore us, and regain the blissful Seat,
> Sing Heav'nly Muse, that on the secret top
> Of *Oreb*, or of Sinai, didst inspire
> That Shepherd, who first taught the chosen Seed,
> In the Beginning how the Heav'ns and Earth
> Rose out of *Chaos*: Or if *Sion* Hill
> Delight thee more, and *Siloa's* Brook that flowd
> Fast by the Oracle of God; I thence
> Invoke thy aid to my adventrous Song,
> That with no middle flight intends to soar
> Above th' *Aonian* Mount, while it persues
> Things unattempted yet in Prose or Rime
> And chiefly Thou O Spirit, that dost preferr
> Before all Temples th' upright heart and pure,
> Instruct me, for Thou knowst, Thou from the first
> Wast present, and with mighty wings outspred
> Dove-like satst brooding on the vast Abyss
> And mad'st it pregnant: What in me is dark
> Illumin, what is low raise and support;
> That to the highth of this great Argument
> I may assert Eternal Providence,
> And justifie the wayes of God to men.
>
> *from Paradise Lost by John Milton*

Progress check

Did you encounter any problems in understanding all of this? If so, what were they?

Summary

You might have found problems because:

- there are some archaic spellings here which might have caused some confusion
- there are some obscure metaphorical references
- some of the names are strange and do not mean anything to us
- the word order might have seemed a little odd in places.

Obviously, one of the problems in reading and understanding poetry that was written possibly hundreds of years ago is that the language we use today is not quite the same as the language that was used then. Words may have changed in meaning, hold different connotations, or may simply have been outmoded.

The second problem here is that the references or allusions used would have been understood and have held some significance to a reader in the poet's own age but often mean little to us today. Good editions usually contain notes and glossaries, though, to help you understand these more obscure references and so appreciate the text more fully. Make sure you use them to the full.

Milton uses many references and allusions to classical literature and to the Bible in his work and a knowledge of Greek and Roman mythology helps a good deal in studying his poetry. His readers in the seventeenth century would have possessed this kind of background and would understand immediately the Biblical references and classical allusions. For them the references would serve to illuminate and illustrate the work, as Milton intended. Most of us, as twenty-first-century readers, do not have this kind of background and such references can initially act as barriers to meaning rather than assisting our understanding.

Here are some things you can do to help yourself understand this kind of text more fully. These suggestions apply to any kind of text, not just poetry.

- Read the piece several times and adopt a systematic approach.
- Use the parts of the poetry that you understand as clues to help you understand more difficult sections.
- Highlight particularly difficult words, phrases, lines, images, etc.
- Look up words that you do not understand in a good dictionary.
- Refer to the notes or glossary in the text book.
- Do some background reading about the writer and their period.

> There are lots of things you can do to help become more familiar with texts written in other periods and in a language or style which is different from modern English.
>
> **KEY POINT**

Language can also change according to the place in which the text is set. For example, some writers use dialect forms to give a sense of place. D.H. Lawrence uses a dialect form to try to capture the Nottinghamshire dialect and Emily Brontë does the same for the Yorkshire dialect in *Wuthering Heights*. These language uses help to provide another kind of 'context' for the text.

Read the following extract:

> On that bleak hill-top the earth was hard with a black frost, and the air made me shiver through every limb. Being unable to remove the chain, I jumped over, and, running up the flagged causeway bordered with straggling gooseberry bushes, knocked vainly for admittance, till my knuckles tingled, and the dogs howled.
>
> 'Wretched inmates!' I ejaculated mentally, 'you deserve perpetual isolation from your species for your churlish inhospitably. At least, I would not keep my doors barred in the day-time. I don't care—I will get in!' So resolved, I grasped the latch

and shook it vehemently. Vinegar-faced Joseph projected his head from a round window of the barn.

'Whet are ye for?' he shouted, 'T' maister 's dahn i' t' fowld. Goa rahnd by th' end ut' laith, if yah went tuh spake tull him.'

'Is there nobody inside to open the door?' I hallooed, responsively.

'They's nobbut t missis: and shoo'll nut oppen 't an ye mak yer flaysome dins till neeght.'

'Why? cannot you tell her who I am, eh, Joseph?'

'Nor-ne me! Aw'll hae noa hend wi't,' muttered the head, vanishing.

The snow began to drive thickly. I seized the handle to essay another trial: when a young man without coat, and shouldering a pitchfork, appeared in the yard behind. He hailed me to follow him, and, after marching through a wash-house, and a paved area containing a coal-shed, pump, and pigeon-cote, we at length arrived in the huge, warm, cheerful apartment, where I was formerly received.

from Wuthering Heights *by Emily Brontë*

Progress check

Why do you think Emily Brontë used this dialect form for the character of Joseph? Look at the ways in which language is used in the texts that you are studying.

To add realism to the characters and give them some individuality.

Summary

This manner of speech is clearly in context with the kind of character Joseph is and it differentiates his speech from other characters such as Lockwood. Brontë gives Heathcliff his own way of speaking. Joseph's speech here is very much in context considering the kind of character Brontë was portraying and the effect that she wanted to achieve.

5.8 Readings of the text by other readers

After studying this section you should be able to:

- *appreciate the value of reading others' views of a text*
- *see how these views can help to put the text in context*
- *apply this to the texts you are studying*

AQA A	U4, U6
AQA B	U4, U5, U6
Edexcel	U4, U5, U6
OCR	U4, U5, U6
WJEC	U6
NICCEA	U5, U6

As well as knowing about the context in which a text was produced, it is also useful to know how that text has been received by different readers at different times.

It can be useful to look at the reception that the text received when it was first published. It can also be useful to look at how readers from different historical periods have viewed the text. Often the perceptions of these readers is influenced by their own context.

Finally, modern views and responses can all help to inform your responses.

The three extracts that follow are all concerned with Coleridge's *The Ancient Mariner*.

In the first one, Coleridge himself replies to a criticism made of his poem. The second one is taken from a review written when the poem was first published. The third one is from a critical essay on the poem written in 1962.

1.

Coleridge on the moral of *The Ancient Mariner*

Mrs Barbauld once told me that she admired '*The Ancient Mariner*' very much, but that there were two faults in it – it was improbable, and had no moral. As for the probability, I owned that that might admit some question; but as to the want of a moral, I told her that in my own judgement the poem had too much; and that the only, or chief fault, if I might say so, was the obtrusion of the moral sentiment so openly on the reader as a principle or cause of action in a work of such pure imagination. It ought to have had no more moral than the *Arabian Nights*' tale of the merchant's sitting down to eat dates by the side of a well, and throwing the shells aside, and lo! a genie starts up, and says he *must* kill the aforesaid merchant, *because* one of the date shells had, it seems, put out the eye of the genie's son.

Table Talk, 31 May 1830

2.

'The Poem of the Ancyent Marinere' with which the collection opens, has many excellencies, and many faults; the beginning and the end are striking and well-conducted; but the intermediate part is too long, and has, in some places, a kind of confusion of images, which loses all effect, from not being quite intelligible. The author, who is confidently said to be Mr Coleridge, is not correctly versed in the old language, which he undertakes to employ. 'Noises of a swound' and 'broad as a weft,' are both nonsensical; but the ancient style is well imitated, while the antiquated words are so very few, that the latter might with advantage be entirely removed without any detriment to the effect of the Poem.

Anonymous Review, 1799

3.

To a great extent, then, the success of the poem lies in the way it satisfies the impulse to see human fears and desires founded in and revealing universal truths. From its beginning the poem moves relentlessly toward the transformation of its action into moral statement, into an enunciation of universal law. In this connection it is interesting to recall Coleridge's famous statement of purpose in the *Biographic Literaria*: his endeavors he said were to be directed toward persons and characters supernatural, 'yet so as to transfer *from our inward nature a human interest and a semblance of truth* sufficient to procure for these shadows of imagination that willing suspension of disbelief for the moment, which constitutes poetic faith' (my italics: E.B.). The measure of Coleridge's success is indicated by the way in which from many critics he has procured not merely the willing suspension of disbelief, but the willing belief which constitutes religious faith. They are led into eagerly accepting the symbolic projection of our inward nature as the symbolic representation of objective reality.

The desire that a poem should mean, not be, is understandably strong among poets themselves, in spite of their present-day protestations to the contrary. They have an uneasy fear that to admit that a poem is an expression of attitudes which may not be rationally defensible is to concede some fatal weakness which robs it of greatness. The need for the poet to believe that he has been granted special moral insight is almost irresistible – otherwise of what ultimate worth is his eloquence? When he turns critic, therefore, the temptation is strong to justify poetry on moral grounds. This is the temptation to which Warren succumbs. He simply cannot believe that a poem so authoritative in vision, so powerful in symbolism as 'The Rime', is not morally meaningful beyond our fears and desires. As a result, he is led ironically into imposing the moral laws of what Coleridge called the reflective faculty upon a universe of pure imagination.

Edward E. Bostetter 1962

Progress check

What do you think these views add to an understanding of the poem? Don't worry if you do not know the poem. Think in terms of the context of the writers of the extracts.

Summary

In the first one it is interesting to see Coleridge's own view on a key issue concerning the poem. In the second extract it is interesting to see how one reviewer, of the time, responded to the poem. The third piece is clearly part of a longer response by a literary critic to the poem and the views expressed need to be considered from that context.

> The views of other readers from our own and other periods can help to set a text in context.
>
> **KEY POINT**

Progress check

Collect as many views on the text you are studying as you can. Try to make sure that you have some views from periods other than our own as well as modern views.

5.9 The text as part of a larger work

After studying this section you should be able to:

LEARNING SUMMARY

- *see the importance of context if your text is part of a larger whole*
- *consider the contextual influences exerted by the other parts of the text*

AQA A	U4, U6
AQA B	U4, U5, U6
Edexcel	U4, U5, U6
OCR	U4, U5, U6
WJEC	U6
NICCEA	U5, U6

Sometimes the text that you study is part of a larger body of work produced by the author. In order to understand that work fully you need to see it within the context of the larger work.

For example, it is usual to study just one of *The Canterbury Tales* by Geoffrey Chaucer. If you are studying one of the tales, though, it is important to see the tale in the context of the group of tales as a whole. It will add to your understanding of the Miller, for instance, if you know that it had been agreed that the pilgrims should each tell a tale to entertain the others and that they would go in order of rank. The Knight as the senior in rank went first and told his tale. However, although he is lower down the social pecking order, the Miller butts in and says that he will go next.

Progress check

Look at the following extract and make a note of the things that are revealed about the Miller here.

The Miller's Prologue

Heere folwen the wordes bitwene the Hoost and the Millere.

Whan that the Knight had thus his tale ytoold,
In al the route nas ther yong ne oold
That he ne seide it was a noble storie,
And worthy for to drawen to memorie;
And namely the gentils everichon.
Oure Hooste lough and swoor, 'So moot I gon,
This gooth aright; unbokeled is the male.
Lat se now who shal telle another tale;
For trewely the game is wel bigonne.
Now teileth ye, sir Monk, if that ye konne
Somwhat to quite with the Knightes tale.'
   The Millere, that for dronken was al pale,
So, that unnethe upon his hors he sat,
He nolde avalen neither hood ne hat,
Ne abide no man for his curteisie,
But in Pilates vois he gan to crie,
And swoor, 'By armes, and by blood and bones,
I kan a noble tale for the nones,
With which I wol now quite the Knightes tale'.
Oure Hooste saugh that he was dronke of ale,
And seide, 'Abyd, Robin, my leeve brother;
Som bettre man shal telle us first, another.
Abyd, and lat us werken thriftily.'
   'By Goddes soule,' quod he, 'that wol nat I;
For I wol speke, or elles go my wey.'
Oure Hoost answerde, 'Telon; a devel wey!
Thou art a fool; thy wit is overcome.'

> **KEY POINT**
>
> If the text you are studying is part of a larger work, find out as much as you can about the rest of the work.

Sample question and model answer

This question tests the candidate's ability to show:
- knowledge and understanding of the text (AO2)
- ability to communicate that understanding clearly and coherently (AO1)
- exploration of the ways the writer's choices of form, structure and language inform meaning (AO3)
- evaluate the significance of cultural, historical and other contextual influences upon literary texts and study (AO5ii).

Allow one hour for this question

With reference to the work of John Donne show how literature was changing at the end of the sixteenth century.

Student response

Opening paragraph puts the essay in context.

During the last years of the sixteenth century, literature began to emerge in a rather different light – a more critical, dramatic and complex light which provided a whole new power of expression. Much of the poetry up to the end of the sixteenth century conformed very much to a convention – the convention of courtly love. The main aim of the Elizabethan poems was not to relate individually but to conform to the convention. This convention of courtly love consisted of prescribed styles and semi-dramatic stylised behaviour, but within the convention the writer could produce his own variations. The transition from 'artificiality to realism' can be very clearly illustrated through a comparison of the poems of John Donne with some of the other, more traditional, Elizabethan poets.

Makes clear the comparison which the essay will carry out.

Comment on tradition and Donne's response to it.

However, even Donne, although he rejected the sentimentality and blatant unreality of this tradition, did not reject it entirely. He still wrote of the experiences of love in a semi-detached way, but he widened immensely its range of moods and expressions giving it a sense of reality and therefore life and meaning. His work has none of the smooth, superficial coating of poetic sweetness that his contemporaries had.

The true subject of Donne's love poetry goes much deeper than simply the experiences he had of love. The subject of love itself, and all situations concerned with love – its moods and attitudes, its experiences and experiments. His poems are concerned with complexities and incongruities and therefore expressiveness rather than beauty is the aim. The beauty of Donne's poems comes rather as a by-product, from the result of successful expression. Poems that have no convention to which they must adhere, are able to make full use of language that gives total expression and it is this language that Donne utilises to the full.

Selects an appropriate comparison.

The marked difference in the two styles, the old style and the new, can perhaps best be seen by a comparison of a Donne poem with one written in a more traditional style, for example, a poem by Thomas Campion. He was celebrated equally as a poet and composer and therefore he insisted on a union of words and music.

His poem that begins – 'There is a garden in her face' is written in the typical, traditional, Elizabethan style. The artificiality becomes immediately apparent at the opening of the poem –

Textual references back up points.

> 'There is a garden in her face
> Where roses and white lilies blow'

The metaphor that the poet uses here to liken the lady's face to a garden is very artificial and perhaps even a little absurd. What the poet has tried to

Sample question and model answer *(continued)*

do is to use the image of the garden and the roses and the lilies to convey the feeling of freshness and beauty that he sees in her face.

Although artificial and strained, the image is successful in so far as it conveys a feeling of pleasantness, the roses and lilies relating perhaps to the lady's complexion. The image of the garden is taken up in the next two lines –

> 'A heavenly paradise is that place,
> Wherein all pleasant fruits do flow'.

Ideas developed here in some detail.

This raises the image still further, speaking of the garden, and indirectly the lady's face, as a 'heavenly paradise'. However, there is a feeling that this image has been pushed too far, and it is too removed from the actual reality of the lady's face to be fully effective.

The image is carried on in the next line, taking a different turn – in the garden:

> 'There cherries grow which none may buy
> Till 'Cherry-ripe' themselves do cry.'

This refers to the lips of the lady and is broadened in the next stanza –

> 'Those cherries fairly do enclose
> Of Orient pearl a double row,
> Which when her lovely laughter shows
> They look like rosebuds filled with snow'.

Like the one in the first stanza this image is a 'pretty' one and conjures up pictures of beauty and sweetness but it lacks the depth of realism and the poem continues in this vein.

A point that should be borne in mind about a poem like this is that they were often written to be set to music and sung at court. Because of this, the poets had to work within certain bounds and their object was to produce something pleasant and pleasing to the ear rather than something that had depth and meaning.

The ideas in this poem, though, seem to be forced. It lacks depth and meaning and is, therefore, very superficial and artificial. When we compare this to a poem by John Donne the difference between artificiality and realism becomes very marked. For example, in 'The Canonisation' –

> 'For God's sake hold your tongue, and let me love,
> Or chide my palsie, or my gout,
> My five gray haires, or ruin'd fortune flout,
> With wealth your state, your minde with Arts improve,
> Take you a course, get you a place,
> Observe his honour, or his grace,
> Or the Kings reall, or his stamped face
> Contemplate, what you will, approve,
> So you will let me love.'

Direct contrast of Donne with Campion makes key point.

In this first stanza it can be seen that there is a vast difference between this, and the poem previously examined. The poem opens with a colloquial outburst which immediately creates an atmosphere that is essentially dramatic. Instead of speaking of 'gardens', 'roses', 'lilies' and 'heavenly paradise', Donne's stress lies on words such as 'palsie' and 'gout'. Donne also uses a form of short phrases but within a rather more complex structure. These short phrases add to the rather dramatic atmosphere

Development and detailed analysis on Donne's poem.

Sample question and model answer (continued)

created, add an urgency, almost a rush to express his feelings. Here the aim is not to attain sweetness, grace, or melody either for its own sake or to accommodate the musician but instead to achieve a realistic expressiveness, the like of which had never appeared before in lyric poetry.

In the second stanza Donne goes on to reinforce his argument, to be allowed to love without interference –

> 'Alas, alas, who's injured by my love?
> What merchant ship have my sighs drown'd
> Who saies my teares have overflowed his ground?
> When did my colds a forward spring remove?
> When did the heats which my veines fill
> Adde one man to the plaguie Bill?
> Soldiers finde warres, and Lawyers find out still
> Litigious men which quarrels move,
> Though she and I do love'.

Here Donne's arguments are sound, down to earth, and realistic. He uses logical reasoning to support his arguments. He does not use artificial images and he avoids the ornamental convention instead using references to wars, quarrels and the plague. From this example, then, it can be seen that Donne achieves an intensity of feeling and emotion that Campion never reaches. Donne's style achieves a truth to emotion and conveys a feeling of genuine, serious thought. The ideas and ideals embodied in the poetry of John Donne show clearly the change that was taking place in literature at the end of the sixteenth century and beginning of the seventeenth century. It typifies the changes in thought and fundamental attitudes to poetry that were the basis of the change from artificiality to realism.

Final comments clearly show the differences and refers back to question.

Overall a thorough analysis of the two poems which reflect the changes that came about in English poetry at the end of the sixteenth century. Well-chosen examples, detailed, thoughtful, perceptive work.

Exam practice and analysis

The following question tests AO5ii as the dominant objective:
* evaluate the significance of cultural, historical and other contextual influences upon literary texts and study.

Other assessment objectives that are also tested are:
* AO1 communicate clearly the knowledge, understanding and insight appropriate to literary study
* AO2ii respond with knowledge and understanding to literary texts of different types and periods
* AO3 show detailed understanding of the ways in which writers' choices of form, structure and language shape meanings
* AO4 articulate independent opinions and judgements informed by different interpretations of literary texts by other readers.

The Country Wife by William Wycherley
Remind yourself of Act II Scene i.
Explore the contemporary attitudes to marriage which Wycherley presents in this scene, paying close attention to:
* **The marriage of Mr and Mrs Pinchwife**
* **The relationship between Sparkish and Alithea**
* **The opinions expressed by Harcourt**
* **The marriage of Sir Jasper and Lady Fidget**

Assessment and Qualifications Alliance specification A

Here are some ideas to think about. They are taken from the mark scheme and relate to the Assessment Objectives for this question.
Responses in the top band would show:

* confident exploration, displaying insight and overview. Secure conceptual grasp and appropriate critical vocabulary
* a use of the text to explore illuminating connections with contemporary attitudes. Mastery of relevant textual detail.

Chapter 6

The unseen

The following topics are covered in this chapter:

- Preparing to tackle the unseen
- Writing about unseen poetry
- Writing about unseen prose extracts

Exactly where you will be tested on your ability to write about texts that you have not seen or studied before depends on the particular exam specification that you are studying. Here is a breakdown of where different boards assess your responses using unseen texts:

AQA A	Unit 6 (the synoptic module)
AQA B	Unit 6 (the synoptic module)
Edexcel	Unit 6 (the synoptic module)
OCR	Unit 6 (the synoptic module)
WJEC	a drama text linked with unseen material in Unit 6 (the synoptic module)
NICCEA	Unit 4, unseen poetry.

You will see from this that in most cases you will encounter some unseen material at least in the final unit, Unit 6 which tests all the assessment objectives for the course.

6.1 Preparing to tackle the unseen

After studying this section you should be able to:

- recognise some things you can do to prepare yourself for handling unseen material
- identify techniques that you can use when writing about unseen and unprepared materials

LEARNING SUMMARY

AQA A	U6
AQA B	U6
Edexcel	U6
OCR	U6
WJEC	U6
NICCEA	U4

The key question is – 'How best can you prepare yourself for the unseen paper?' To answer this let us look at the particular features that students who do well on this paper exhibit in their work. These include:

- having a solid level of background reading of a whole range of literature. This is not usually explicit in students' answers because the questions are not devised to show background reading. It often comes through implicitly, but clearly, when a student has read widely. Throughout the course of your studies you will have been gaining this invaluable experience of encountering literary texts of all kinds and it should stand you in good stead. Those students who achieve the higher grades are invariably those who have read well beyond the texts prescribed by the syllabus.

- having some familiarity with the techniques of literary critical appreciation. This does not mean learning by heart a whole battery of critical terms or a rigid formula which can be applied to whatever text you encounter. Rather it is an awareness that texts consist of language and that writers have used this in a particular way to achieve particular effects. The ability to describe these and the means by which they are created is essential.

- recognising that every text is individual and that there is not a 'correct' view of what a text is about but that subjective views alone are not valid. Successful students show individual and fresh responses that are firmly rooted in the text and supported by clear and detailed textual reference.

The content of the unseen paper can vary a good deal and is not necessarily restricted to a poem and a passage from a novel. Some specifications are clear to point out that a wide range of text types can be drawn upon including poetry, prose, drama and extracts from literary criticism, journalism, essays and autobiography.

Just as the material itself can vary, so can the kind of questions that you are asked. You might be asked to 'write a commentary' focusing on particular aspects of the poem or extract.

How to tackle the unseen

- Begin by carefully looking at what the question(s) asks you to do and identify and highlight the key words and phrases.
- Read the piece through carefully at least twice.
- If you do not understand certain words or phrases or parts of the piece, concentrate on the rest of the text – do not get bogged down on individual words or phrases.
- Remember that whatever the poem or passage you encounter there will be many different aspects of it to comment on.
- Look for any useful information you are given about the piece, such as when it was written, who wrote it, etc.
- Do not concentrate all your efforts on content. The examiner will be much more interested in your comments on how the piece is written and the ways in which the writer has used language to create the intended effects.

> There is a range of things that you can do to help prepare you for handling unseen and unprepared material.

KEY POINT

6.2 Writing about unseen poetry

After studying this section you should be able to:

- *plan how to approach writing about an unseen poem*
- *recognise ways of comparing unseen poems*

LEARNING SUMMARY

AQA A	U6
AQA B	U6
Edexcel	U6
OCR	U6
WJEC	U6
NICCEA	U4

Look at the following poem and write down your initial ideas about it.

What is the writer criticising and what techniques does he use?

Unknown Citizen

'JS/07/M378 This Marble Monument is Erected by the State)

He was found by the Bureau of Statistics to be
One against whom there was no official complaint,
And all the reports on his conduct agree
That, in the modern sense of an old-fashioned word, he was a saint,
For in everything he did he served the Greater Community.
Except for the War till the day he retired
He worked in a factory and never got fired,
But satisfied his employers, Fudge Motors Inc.
Yet he wasn't a scab or odd in his views.
For his Union reports that he paid his dues,

(Our report on his Union shows it was sound)
And our Social Psychology workers found
That he was popular with his mates and liked a drink.

The Press are convinced that he bought a paper every day
And that his reactions to advertisements were normal in every way.
Policies taken out in his name prove that he was fully insured,
And his Health-card shows he was once in hospital but left it, cured
Both Producers Research and High Grade Living declare
He was fully sensible to the advantages of the Instalment Plan
And had everything necessary to the Modern Man,
A phonograph, a radio, a car and a frigidaire.
Our researchers into Public Opinion are content
That he held the proper opinions for the time of year;
When there was peace, he was for peace: when there was war, he went.
He was married and added five children to the population,
Which our Eugenist says was the right number for a parent of his generation,
And our teachers report that he never interfered with their education
Was he free? Was he happy? The question is absurd:
Had anything been wrong, we should certainly have heard.

W.H. Auden

Summary

Here are some points you might have noted.

- The significance of the title 'The Unknown Citizen' is a direct reference to the Unknown Soldier – the identity of the soldier is not known – he stands for all soldiers – just as in this poem the unknown man represents millions of others.
- 'Citizen' places him in civilian society.
- The poem appears to be the state praising this man for being a model citizen.
- Auden uses irony though because his real intention is just the opposite – he is really attacking the state for the value it places on uniformity.

Now look carefully at the following two poems.

1

Since there's no help, come let us kiss and part;
Nay, I have done, you get no more of me;
And I am glad, yea glad with all my heart
That thus so cleanly I myself can free;
Shake hands forever, cancel all our vows,
And when we meet at any time again,
Be it not seen in either of our brows
That we one jot of former love retain.
Now at the last gasp of love's latest breath,
When, his pulse failing, passion speechless lies,
When faith is kneeling by his bed of death,
And innocence is closing up his eyes;
Now if thou would'st, when all have given him over,
From death to life thou might'st him yet recover.

Michael Drayton, 1563–1631

2

Mark where the pressing wind shoots javelin-like,
Its skeleton shadow on the broad-backed wave!
Here is a fitting spot to dig Love's grave;
Here where the ponderous breakers plunge and strike,
And dart their hissing tongues high up the sand:
In hearing of the ocean, and in sight
Of those ribbed wind-streaks running into white.
If I the death of Love had deeply planned,
I never could have made it half so sure,
As by the unblest kisses which upbraid
The full-waked sense; or failing that, degrade!
'Tis morning; but no morning can restore
What we have forfeited. I see no sin:
The wrong is mixed. In tragic life, God wot,
No villain need be! Passions spin the plot:
We are betrayed by what is false within.

George Meredith, 1828–1909

Progress check

Compare and contrast the two poems, highlighting their similarities and their differences.

Summary

Here are some points that you might have noted.

- The two poems by Michael Drayton and George Meredith initially appear to have the same central image. Both poets depict the failure of a relationship.
- The presentation of this image, however, is entirely different. Whilst Drayton portrays the loss of a love as something simple but not irreversible, Meredith shows the failure of a relationship as something dramatic and inevitable.
- It is the similarity between the subject of these two poems, however, that immediately strikes the reader. Both poets emphasise that the central theme in their poems is lost love. They achieve this through their use of imagery. In both pieces the concept of love is personified and described as dying. Drayton refers to, 'The last gasp of love's latest breath,' Meredith describes, 'The death of Love' and 'Love's grave'.
- This conventional theme is reflected in both pieces by their conventional structure. Drayton's poem adheres to the form of an English sonnet. The rhythm of his writing is dictated by this.
- The difference in the way that this conventional theme is presented, however, is also very striking. The reader is clearly shown that Drayton sees the loss of a love as something sad but common, whilst Meredith views the break-up of a relationship as something momentous.
- This difference in the presentation of their common theme is also reflected in the poets' use of imagery. Drayton depicts the ending of his relationship as a clean break. Much of his imagery suggests he is breaking free from some kind of restriction, 'I myself can free,' 'you get no more of me.' Drayton's use of language also illustrates that this is an amicable break. He repeats the word 'glad' giving it added impact, 'And I am glad, yea glad with all my heart'. Drayton also uses imagery of 'shaking hands' and 'kissing' which symbolises the idea of a friendly parting.

- These two poems, therefore, have very little similarity beyond their conventional theme. The poets attempt to show this subject in entirely different lights.

6.3 Writing about unseen prose extracts

After studying this section you should be able to:

- *consider ways of approaching unseen prose texts*
- *understand features you can recognise and write about*

AQA A	U6
AQA B	U6
Edexcel	U6
OCR	U6
WJEC	U6
NICCEA	U4

Look at the following two prose extracts.

Pip was still travelling up and down from Essex, the bachelor. He seemed to be happy to plan world-wide itineraries for bankers and Caribbean holidays for the classier sort of share-pusher. He learned tactfully to distinguish between what a man was prepared to spend on the firm and what was available for the wife and kids. As time went on, he grew fluently cosmopolitan: he seemed to have been everywhere. 'How did you find the Carlyle, sir?' he would ask, and, 'Was I right about the pistes at Meribel?' Who would guess that he had never left England except to play club soccer in Knokke-le-Zoute? He got a discount for Victor and Wendy when they went to Turkey, but they both contracted enteritis in Izmir, while looking for Seferis's birthplace, and their thanks were shaded. Pip took holidays with his parents in the Lake District, which his mother remembered from her childhood. Victor and Wendy could not imagine how he could endure the life he led. All he did was to read cheap thrillers and play soccer with this team of clerks and workers from a local jam factory, watch dreadful television (he would quote the commercials) and dig his parents' garden. Presumably there were girls, but it all seemed hopelessly provincial. How could he be so happy? Victor frowned when he thought about Pip, but then he frowned when he thought about most things. Wendy was always asking him what was wrong. 'Nothing,' he told her.

One day, soon after his twenty-ninth birthday, Pip rang Victor to announce that he was engaged to be married. 'Anyone I know?' asked his brother, who was waiting for a call from the Chief Secretary, to whom he had forwarded a rather sly minute. 'Most improbable,' said Pip. 'She's a girl called Maxine. I call her Max,'
'Wait a minute,' Victor said, 'I just want to make sure there isn't anybody on the line. Did you hear a sort of click just now?'

'I thought it was you, mate, disapproving.'

'Don't be silly. What is there to disapprove of? Marriage is an honourable estate.'

'She's scared stiff of you,' Pip said. 'You will be nice to her, won't you?'

'I'm nice to everybody.' Victor said. 'Where did you meet?'

'At a local hop,' Pip said. 'The Rotary have an annual do on in Chelmsford. I don't know if you remember the Dimmages, used to live along the Maldon Road?'

'It is rather a long time ago', Victor said.

'Oh I know there have been fifty budgets since then, haven't there?'

'What sort of girl is she?'

'She didn't go to university, if that's what you mean,' Pip said.

'That isn't what I meant at all. Millions of people didn't go to university.'

'Yes, but you don't know many of them, do you? She helps a vet at the moment. She's the Dimmages' niece. She's only twenty-two. I think she's rather bright. I know what you're thinking, what should I know about bright?'

'She sounds like just the girl we need', Victor said. 'Frenchie's developed a bit of a lump in one of her teats. Do you think she'd take a look at it?'

'At the usual rates, I'm sure she'd be delighted, old son;

'You'd better bring her to dinner. I'll have a word to Wendy, and see when's the best day.'

'Preferably one when you haven't got eight professors and the man who's made the big breakthrough in astrophysics, if it's all the same to you'.

'We know very few astrophysicists; Victor said. 'Would you rather it was just the four of us?'

'Max isn't a fool or anything, Vic'.

'Please don't call me Vic; I hate being confused with a cough cure.'

'Aye. there's the rub!' Pip said. 'It's simply that she's never been exposed to the full Oxbridge artillery. Any day next week, except Thursday. Thursday we're going to see her parents, in Mitcham. Tell me, how are things at the moment? I gather they're a bit sticky.'

'You have the advantage of me,' Victor said.

'I only wish I could serve an ace, then! I meant this credit squeeze and the balance of payments. If you make the travel allowance much smaller, I shall have to go out and work for a living. I wouldn't like to have your job at this stage.'

'No, well, you're not likely to get it, are you?'

'Any day except Thursday' said Pip.

Victor frowned and replaced the receiver. He lived in a state of agonized complacency. He had nothing to worry about, and it worried him. He was well thought of by his superiors and he was too firmly on the ladder ever to have to bother about the snakes. His wife was not only enviably beautiful, she was also loyal and good-natured. How could he complain if, having married a girl from whom he might have expected a life of testing anguish, he found himself with a grocer's daughter who was always there with a smile and a hot meal when he got home from Whitehall? Why was he secretly so appalled by the peace of mind to which he was treated? She had even turned down a chance to do Baudelaire in the 'Critical Studies' Series. She bought women's magazines. She said she liked the pictures of babies.

from The Glittering Prizes *by Frederic Raphael*

Now it is the autumn again; the people are all coming back. The recess of summer is over, when holidays are taken, newspapers shrink, history itself seems momentarily to falter and stop. But the papers are thickening and filling again; things seem to be happening; back from Corfu and Sete, Positano and Leningrad, the people are parking their cars and campers in their drives, and opening their diaries, and calling up other people on the telephone. The deckchairs on the beach have been put away, and a weak sun shines on the promenade; there is fresh fighting in Vietnam, while McGovern campaigns ineffectually against Nixon. In the chemists' shops in town, they have removed the sunglasses and the insect-bite lotions, for the summer visitors have left, and have stocked up on sleeping tablets and Librium, the staples of the year-round trade; there is direct rule in Ulster, and a gun-battle has taken place in the Falls Road. The new autumn colours are in the boutiques; there is now on the market a fresh intra-uterine device, reckoned to be ninety-nine per cent safe. Everywhere there are new developments, new indignities; the intelligent people survey the autumn world, and liberal and radical hackles rise, and fresh faces are about, and the sun shines fitfully, and the telephones ring. So, sensing the climate, some people called the Kirks, a well-known couple, decide to have a party.

The Kirks have, in fact, had a party at just this time of the year – the turning-point when the new academic year starts, new styles are in, new faces about, new ideas busy – for the past three autumns; and, if it had been anyone else but the Kirks, you might have said it was a custom or tradition with them. But the Kirks are very fresh and spontaneous people, who invest in all their activities with high care and scruple, and do nothing just because it has been done before; indeed they are widely understood not to have such things as customs and traditions. If the Kirks happen to have thought of a party, well, they have thought of it innocently, afresh, and from a sense of need. Evolving time signals mysteriously to those who are true citizens of it; the Kirks are true citizens of the present, and they take their messages from the prevailing air, and answer them with an honest sense of duty. They are, after all, very busy people, with many causes and issues, many meetings and conspiracies, many affairs and associations to attend to; indeed they are very lucky to catch each other in like mind, very lucky to catch each other at the same time in the same house at all. But they do know a need when they see one, and here they are, together in their own kitchen, and the idea comes, it is not clear from whom, above all, in fact, from the force of the times. Their eyes brighten, as they always do when such news comes; they say yes to each other; they set to work at once on the who, what and how of it. Howard, because he is nearest, leaves their bright pine kitchen, and goes out into the hall, to fetch, from beside their busy telephone, their busy house diary, a crucial text and record for people like themselves. They put the book between them on the kitchen table, and open it; they inspect the long, predictive tale of doings and undoings it unfolds, the elaborate, contingent plot of the days ahead of them. 'When?' says Barbara. 'Soon,' says Howard. 'Are we free on the first day of term?' asks Barbara. It is improbable, but Howard turns the pages; there is the day, Monday 2 October, and the evening is a blank. It is almost an omen; and from his inside pocket Howard takes out, at once, his pen. He holds the diary open; he writes, in his neat little hand, as if writing the start of some new story, which in a sense is what it is, the word 'Party' in the small space of white on the crowded page.

The Kirks have had parties at this time of year before, they recall, and they know a lot of people will come; they are, after all, a very well-known couple. Howard is a sociologist, a radical sociologist, a small, bright, intense, active man, of whom you are likely to have heard, for he is much heard of. He is on television a good deal, and has written two well-known and disturbing books, urging new mores, a new deal for man; he has had a busy, literary summer, and a third book is on its way. He also writes articles in the papers, and he lectures at the local new university, a still expanding dream in white concrete, glass, and architectural free form, spreading on a hillside just to the west of, and just outside, the south-western sea-coast town in which they live. The university, having aspirations to relevance, has made much of sociology; and it would be hard to find anyone in the field with a greater sense of relevance than Howard. His course on Revolutions is a famous keystone, just as are, in a different way, his interventions in community relations, his part in the life of the town. For Howard is a well-known activist, a thorn in the flesh of the council, a terror to the selfish bourgeoisie, a pressing agent in the Claimants' Union, a focus of responsibility and concern. As for Barbara, well, she is at this minute just a person, as she puts it, trapped in the role of wife and mother, in the limited role of woman in our society; but of course she, too, is a radical person, and quite as active as Howard in her way. She is, amongst her many competences and qualifications, a *cordon bleu* cook, an expert in children's literature, a tireless promoter of new causes (Women for Peace, The Children's Crusade for Abortion, No More Sex for Repression). And she, too, is a familiar figure, in the streets, as she blocks them with others to show that traffic is not inevitable, and in the supermarkets, as she leads her daily deputation to the manager with comparative, up-to-the-minute lists showing how Fine Fare, on lard, is one pence up on Sainsbury's, or vice versa. She moves through playgroups and schools, surgeries and parks, in a constant indignation; she writes, when it is her turn, for the community newspaper. When you visit the Kirks, there is always a new kind of Viennese coffee-cake to eat, and a petition to sign. And, as for the Kirks together, the well-known couple, they are a familiar pair in the high-rise council flats, going up and down in the obscenity-scrawled Otis lifts, hunting out instances of deprivation to show the welfare people, of careless motherhood to take to the family planning clinic; in the council offices, where they throw open doors behind which officials sit to thrust forward, in all their rebuking and total humanity, the fleshed-out statistic, the family that has not had its rights, not had just benefits, not been rehoused; and in the town in general, raising consciousness, raising instructive hell. The Kirks are active in the world as it is, in all its pathetic contingency; but they have higher hopes yet. They wake each morning and inspect the sky meticulously for dark hands, thunderbolts, white horsemen: evidence that the poor reality they so seriously tend has at least been wonderfully transformed, a new world, a new order, come overnight.

But in the meantime, they go on, together and separately. They have been married now for twelve years, though you wouldn't think it, to look at them, to see them, to hear them in action. They have produced, by prophylaxis, two children, bright, modern creatures, both now of school age, of whom they are reasonably fond. They live together in a tall, thin, stuccoed Georgian house, which is in a slum-clearance area right in the middle of the town. It is an ideal situation for the Kirks, close to the real social problems, the beach, the radical bookshop, the family planning clinic, the macrobiotic food store, the welfare offices, the high-rise council flats, and the rapid ninety-minute electric train service up to London, close, in short, to the stuff of ongoing life. From time to time, being passionate, liberated, consciousness-conscious people, they live apart, or with someone else, for a spell. But these always seem mature, well-thought interludes and infidelities, expressing their own separate individuality without disturbing their common Kirkness, and so somehow they always manage to be back together again within the month, and hence to seem, in the eyes of their friends, and presumably in their own eyes as well, a settled, but not an absurdly settled, couple. For the Kirks always generate excitement, curiosity. They are experimental people, intimates with change and liberation and history, and they are always busy and always going.

They look the way new people do look, this autumn. Howard, small, dark, and compact, has long hair, though not quite so long as it was last year, and a Zapata moustache; he wears neat white sweatshirts, with rousing symbols on the front, like clenched fists, and hairy loose waistcoats, and pyjama-style blue jeans. Barbara, who is big and has frizzled yellow hair, wears green eyeshadow, and clown-white makeup, and long caftan dresses, and no bra, so that her stubby nipples show through the light cotton. Howard's two books being now staple radical documents in that expanding market, their jeans and caftans are rather more expensive than those of most of the people they know. But it is invisible expense, inconspicuous unconsumption, and it creates no distances and makes them no enemies, except for the enemies who were always their enemies. The Kirks are very attractive, very buoyant, very aggressive people, and, even if you dislike or distrust them, or are disturbed by them (and they mean to be disturbing), very good company.

from The History Man *by Malcolm Bradbury*

Progress check

Compare these extracts focusing particularly on the ways in which each writer presents the characters and their attitudes.

Summary

Here are some ideas.

- In the first extract we are given some information through the narrative but we also learn a good deal about the characters through their telephone conversation.
- Frederic Raphael uses ironic contrast between the two brothers in an amusing way.
- Victor's intellectual vanity is revealed but he is also envious of Pip's happiness and contentment.
- Victor's pomposity also comes through the dialogue while Pip deliberately tries to provoke his brother's disapproval.
- Note too the role of the questioning here.
- In the second extract the characters are presented much more through the

narrative – there is very little dialogue.
- Again there is the use of irony in the description of the Kirks – their radicalism, the references to the protests, etc.
- Watch out for narrative asides like 'their jeans and caftans are rather more expensive than those of most people they know'.

> Always look carefully at the ways in which the writer has used language to achieve effects.
>
> **KEY POINT**

Here are some final reminders about the unseen.
- Read all the material including the questions very carefully several times.
- If it is suggested that you discuss areas such as theme, mood, tone, imagery, diction, rhythm, etc., make sure you do address each point.
- Do not give a line-by-line paraphrase of the poem or passage.
- Do not rush in to answering before you have absorbed the material.
- Make a range of well-thought-out points and support them with appropriate textual references.
- Avoid discussing technique without reference to the effect(s) that it creates.

Sample question and model answer

This question tests the candidate's ability to consider:
- knowledge and understanding of the text (AO2)
- ability to communicate that understanding clearly and coherently (AO1)
- exploration of the ways the writer's choices of form, structure and language inform meaning (AO3).

Read the following poem carefully and write an analysis of it showing how the poet has used language in order to achieve his effects.

The Voice

WOMAN much missed, how you call to me, call to me,
Saying that now you are not as you were
When you had changed from the one who was all to me,
But as at first, when our day was fair.

Can it be you that I hear? Let me view you, then,
Standing as when I drew near to the town
Where you would wait for me: yes, as I knew you then,
Even to the original air-blue gown!

Or is it only the breeze, in its listlessness
Travelling across the wet mead to me here,
You being ever dissolved to wan wistlessness,
Heard no more again far or near?

    Thus I; faltering forward,
    Leaves around me falling,
Wind oozing thin through the thorn from norward,
    And the woman calling.

December 1912
Thomas Hardy

Student response

Shows focus and ideas about the poem.

This poem seems to be a lament by the poet for a woman he has lost. Although the poem does not actually state that she is dead there is very much a sense through the overall tone and the bitter regret that the poet expresses that she is dead. In fact, Hardy's first wife, Emma, had died in November 1912, and in response to her death he wrote a series of poems which expressed his grief at her death.

Applies some contextual knowledge but does not let this intrude into commentary on the poem itself.

In the first stanza, the poet begins by imagining that he hears the voice of the woman he misses so much calling to him. The repetition of the lilting rhythm of 'call to me, call to me' gives a haunting quality to the opening line, as if he hears the voice, calling on the wind. In the next two lines, the imagined voice continues and the poet imagines how she was in life, when she had meant so much, everything, to him. This suggests that in some ways, before he had lost her, their relationship had changed in some way from what it was 'at first, when our day was fair'.

Good awareness of the effects of the rhythm and is sensitive to the suggestions inherent in the lines.

In the second stanza, the poet visualises his lost love and imagines her as she had been when he had arrived at the town, perhaps returning home from a trip, to be met by her waiting for him. This picture, in his mind's eye, is so vivid, that he even remembers 'the original air-blue gown' that she used to wear. In this stanza, then, the poet has moved on from hearing the voice of his loved one to imagining that he actually sees her there, as she was in the days when they were close.

Again good awareness of the effect of the poem and the way in which the poet moves on to the next stage.

Sample question and model answer (continued)

Sensitive to changing moods – the sense of illusion – good comment on vocabulary.

In the third stanza, though, the poet begins to realise that his loved one is not really there, it is merely an illusion – perhaps the sound of the wind blowing across the wet meadow. In this stanza, as he realises that the presence of the one he once loved has been evoked through his memories and imagination, there is a sense that he finds himself alone and full of sadness. This mood is reinforced through the vocabulary – 'wan', suggesting a sense of paleness, of being exhausted, tired and worn and this links with the earlier 'listlessness' suggesting that the death of his loved one has left him lacking in energy and enthusiasm in everything, including life itself. An interesting usage here is in the use of 'wistlessness'. Normally the word 'wistful' is used to mean someone who is yearningly expectant or wishful, it is also suggestive of a kind of hope. The poet turns the word around here to 'wistlessness' which accentuates the sense that he feels that there is no hope. Note also how the poet's use of alliteration here adds emphasis to this feeling as he realises that she has gone forever even though he addresses her directly –

Some interesting ideas explored here – the comments on 'wistlessness' show perception and understanding.

Comments on the use of alliteration.

'You being ever dissolved to wan wistlessness,
Heard no more again far or near?'

Well chosen textual support.

Up until this point the first three stanzas have created a regular rhythm pattern which works closely with the rhyme scheme. The repeated rhyme of 'call to me' and 'all to me' in the first stanza creates a link between the imagined caller and the poet and emphasises how much he misses her now. In the second stanza the rhyming 'Let me view you, then' and 'as I knew you then' emphasise the contrast between the poet's present pain and the happiness the couple had enjoyed in years gone by. In the third stanza the rhyme of 'in its listlessness' and 'wan wistlessness' increases the sense of pain and uncertainty leading into the final stanza.

Detailed understanding of the way in which the rhyme and the rhythm patterns work together and some perceptive comments made about the effects achieved.

The most striking thing immediately about this final stanza is the way that it breaks from the rhythmic and rhyme pattern of the first three stanzas. The caesura of 'Thus I // faltering forward' creates a halting and stumbling feel and reflects the breakdown that the poet experiences as his grief overwhelms him. The leaves 'falling' create a sense of something at an end and the sense of pain is graphically present in the image –

Good ending to the piece showing clear sensitivity to mood.

'Wind oozing thin through the thorn from the norward.'

Overall a very good response which shows a high level of sensitivity to the mood and atmosphere created by the poet and the ways in which he has used language, rhyme, rhythm and imagery to create his effects.

As the final line trails off almost unfinished we are left with the image created through the rhyme, 'falling/calling' which encapsulates the poet's feelings here and leaves us with a sense of the despair and desolation felt by him.

Exam practice and analysis

The following question tests AO5ii as the dominant objective:
- evaluate the significance of cultural, historical and other contextual influences upon literary texts and study.

Other assessment objectives that are also tested are:
- AO1 communicate clearly the knowledge, understanding and insight appropriate to literary study
- AO2ii respond with knowledge and understanding to literary texts of different types and periods
- AO3 show detailed understanding of the ways in which writers' choices of form, structure and language shape meanings
- AO4 articulate independent opinions and judgements informed by different interpretations of literary texts by other readers.

The Victorian Novel

By a close study of the passages from Jane Eyre by Charlotte Brontë and from Little Dorrit by Charles Dickens, compare and contrast some of the ways in which Victorian novelists use landscape to lend resonance to their work.

3 The Victorian Novel

(a)

Whitecross is no town, nor even a hamlet; it is but a stone pillar set up where four roads meet: whitewashed, I suppose, to be more obvious at a distance and in darkness. Four arms spring from its summit: the nearest town to which these point is, according to the inscription, distant ten miles; the farthest, above twenty. From the well-known names of these towns I learn in what county I have lighted; a north-midland shire, dusk with moorland, ridged with mountain: this I see. There are great moors behind and on each hand of me; there are waves of mountains far beyond that deep valley at my feet. The population here must be thin, and I see no passengers on these roads; they stretch out east, west, north and south – white, broad, lonely; they are all cut in the moor, and the heather grows deep and wild to their very verge. Yet a chance traveller might pass by; and I wish no eye to see me now: strangers would wonder what I am doing, lingering here at the sign-post, evidently objectless and lost. I might be questioned: I could give no answer but what would sound incredible and excite suspicion. Not a tie holds me to human society at this moment – not a charm or hope calls me where my fellow-creatures are – none that saw me would have a kind thought or a good wish for me. I have no relative but the universal mother, Nature: I will seek her breast and ask repose.

I struck straight into the heath; I held on to a hollow I saw deeply farrowing the brown moorside; I waded kneedeep in its dark growth; I turned with its turnings and finding a moss-blackenened granite crag in a hidden angle, I sat down under it. High banks of moor were about me; the crag protected my head: the sky was over that. Some time passed before I felt tranquil even here: I had a vague dread that wild cattle might be near, or that some sportsman or poacher might discover me. If a gust of wind swept the waste, I looked up, fearing it was the rush of a bull; if a plover whistled, I imagined it a man. Finding my apprehensions unfounded, however, and calmed by the deep silence that reigned as evening declined at nightfall, I took confidence. As yet I had no thought: I had only listened, watched, dreaded: now I regained the faculty of reflection.

from Jane Eyre *by Charlotte Brontë*

(b)

There was no wind to make a ripple on the foul water within the harbour, or on the beautiful sea without. The line of demarcation between the two colours, black and blue, showed the point which the pure sea would not pass; but it lay as quiet as the abominable pool, with which it never mixed. Boats without awnings were too hot

Exam practice and analysis (continued)

to touch; ships blistered at their moorings; the stones of the quays had not cooled, night or day, for months. Hindoos, Russians, Chinese, Spaniards, Portuguese, Englishmen, Frenchmen, Genoese, Neopolitans, Venetians, Greeks, Turks, descendants from all the builders of Babael, come to trade at Marseilles, sought the shade alike – taking refuge in any hiding-place from a sea too intensely blue to be looked at, and a sky of purple, set with one great flaming jewel of fire.

The universal stare made the eyes ache. Towards the distant line of Italian coast, indeed, it was a little relieved by light clouds of mist, slowly rising from the evaporation of the sea, but it softened nowhere else. Far away the staring roads, deep in dust, stared from the hill-side, stared from the hollow, stared from the interminable plain. Far away the dusty vines overhanging wayside cottages, and the monotonous wayside avenues of parched trees without shade, drooped beneath the earth and sky. So did the horses with drowsy bells, in long files of carts, creeping slowly towards the interior; so did their recumbent drivers, when they were awake, which rarely happened; so did the exhausted labourers in the fields. Everything that lived or grew, was oppressed by the glare; except the lizard, passing swiftly over rough stone walls, and the cicada, chirping his dry hot chirp, like a rattle. The very dust was scorched brown, and something quivered in the atmosphere as if the air itself was panting.

Blinds, shutters, curtains, awnings, were all closed and drawn to keep out the stare. Grant it but a chink, keyhole, and it shot in like a white-hot arrow. The churches were the freest from it. To come out of the twilight of pillars and arches – dreamily dotted with winking lamps, dreamily peopled with ugly old shadows piously dozing, spitting and begging – was to plunge into a fiery river, and swim for life to the nearest strip of shade. So, with people lounging and lying wherever shade was, with but little hum of tongues or barking of dogs, with occasional jangling of discordant bells and rattling of vicious drums, Marseilles, a fact to be strongly smelt and tasted, lay broiling in the sun one day.

from Little Dorrit *by Charles Dickens,*

Here are some ideas to think about. They are taken from the mark scheme and relate to the assessment objectives for this question.

- Candidates must show an understanding of how the passages belong within the area of the Victorian novel (AO2)
- They must demonstrate their skills of close reading by a critical appreciation of the passage (AO3)
- They must evaluate the significance of cultural, historical and social influences upon the way in which the passages may be read (AO5ii).

At the top of the mark range you should show:

- sophisticated understanding of the type of texts you are dealing with, exploring and commenting in depth on the similarities and differences and making accurate and relevant cross-reference to other texts and writers (AO2ii)
- insight into how the writers exploit description of landscape setting and use particular vocabularies and techniques (repetition, rhythm, imagery, changes of perspective and scale) to present mood, state of mind, social criticism (AO3).
- a real appreciation of the influence of historical, social, economic and cultural perspectives on their reading of these passages, noting characteristic attitudes of the context in which they were written and are set and interpreting them in the light of contemporary and later attitudes to social criticism and psychology and readings of Victorian novels (post-industrial, feminist, socialist) (AO5ii).

Chapter 7

Synoptic assessment

The following topics are covered in this chapter:

- A2 and synoptic assessment
- Different forms of synoptic assessment
- Synoptic assessment and unseen material
- Synoptic assessment and pre-release material

7.1 A2 and synoptic assessment

After studying this section you should be able to:

LEARNING SUMMARY

- *understand what is meant by synoptic assessment*
- *see how it is relevant to your studies*

AQA A	U6
AQA B	U6
Edexcel	U6
OCR	U6
WJEC	U6
NICCEA	U6

We have already mentioned synoptic assessment on a number of occasions so far in this book so it is likely that you already have an idea about what it is. Quite simply it is a form of assessment that will test all the assessment objectives that you have studied for the A2 course. It will test all these in the final module of the course.

The subject criteria for English Literature give us the following information:

> Synoptic assessment in English Literature will take account of the requirement that A Level qualifications should enable candidates to develop a broader and deeper understanding of the connections between the knowledge and understanding set out in the specification as a whole. Synoptic assessment will involve the explicit synthesis of insights gained from a close and detailed study of a range of texts important for the development of English Literature. It will require candidates to show evidence of the ways in which contextual factors and different interpretations of texts illuminate their own readings, and ensure that candidates demonstrate their skills of interpretation and expression to give articulate, well-argued responses.

Examples of synoptic assessment might include:

- a task based on **Shakespearean drama** in which candidates bring to bear their knowledge gained from previous study, to inform their interpretation of episodes from a play not previously studied as part of the course. The task might contain some additional material relating to different critical approaches or traditions of performance, e.g. the way in which Shakespeare's language and use of sources were responded to when the plays were first produced and in subsequent periods
- a task requiring the **analysis, evaluation and comparison of two texts**, drawing on candidates' study of other texts and materials from a period identified in the specification, e.g. the 1930s, the Gothic novel, medieval drama
- a task focusing on the characteristics of a **particular literary movement or period** including direct reference to and comparison between at least two writers, e.g. a study of Romantic poetry based on poems by Wordsworth and Coleridge.

> **KEY POINT**
>
> The main thing to remember is that synoptic assessment is not something to be afraid of or worried about. You will have already done all the work to cover the assessment objectives so you should be in a good position to tackle the kind of work you are likely to find on the synoptic paper.

7.2 Different forms of synoptic assessment

After studying this section you should be able to:

- *see that there are different ways in which synoptic assessment is carried out*
- *identify the kind of assessment you will have in the specification you are following*

LEARNING SUMMARY

AQA A	U6
AQA B	U6
Edexcel	U6
OCR	U6
WJEC	U6
NICCEA	U6

Different boards have all adopted different ways of presenting synoptic assessment. Here is a brief breakdown showing the differences. You should be able to see the kind of assessment pattern you will have from this.

AQA specification A: Unit 6 – Reading for Meaning. The questions here will be based on unprepared material that you are given on a specified topic. Currently the topic is War in Literature with specific emphasis on literature written about and during the First World War. It includes poetry, prose and drama.

AQA specification B: Unit 6 – Exploring Texts. This unit is based on pre-release material that students are given to study a few days before the exam. The materials are based around a topic. (An example of the pre-release approach is given at the end of this chapter.)

Edexcel: Unit 6 – Criticism and Comparison. This is divided into two sections. Section A involves the study of unseen prose or poetry. Section B involves comparative work on two texts that you have studied from the prescribed list.

OCR: Unit 6 – Comparative and contextual study. This is divided into two sections. Section A is based on passages from a reading booklet given out at the beginning of the exam. (An example of this is included later.) In Section B you answer on a topic area you have studied (the same topic area you have selected to answer on for Section A) and you answer a comparative question on two set texts you have studied.

WJEC: Unit 6 – Drama pre-1770. You answer two questions on a drama text that you have studied linked to unseen material.

NICCEA Unit 6 – Drama. You answer one question on two texts that you have studied from the pairs of text prescribed in the specification.

7.3 Synoptic assessment and unseen material

After studying this section you should be able to:

- *see how unseen material can be used as a part of synoptic assessment*
- *recognise strategies for handling this kind of material*

LEARNING SUMMARY

AQA A	U6
AQA B	U6
Edexcel	U6
OCR	U6
WJEC	U6
NICCEA	U6

As you can see from the range of synoptic assessment units offered by the exam boards, unseen material is frequently used in one form or another for assessment purposes. You will also have noted that some boards have linked this in a thematic way. The following example is taken from the OCR specimen paper, Section A, which involves selecting the studied topic area to answer on unseen material. Even if you are not studying this board's specification it can provide you with some useful practice. One of the topic areas is The Great War in English Literature.

Below are a poem and a prose extract. Read them through carefully. It may help you to look back at Chapter 6 on The unseen to remind yourself of the advice given there.

The Great War in British Literature

(a)

Bombardment

Four days the earth was rent and torn
By bursting steel,
The houses fell about us;
Three nights we dared not sleep,
Sweating, and listening for the imminent crash
Which meant our death.

The fourth night every man,
Nerve-tortured, wracked to exhaustion,
Slept, muttering and twitching,
While the shells crashed overhead.

The fifth day there came a hush;
We left our holes
And looked above the wreckage of the earth
To where the white clouds moved in silent lines
Across the untroubled blue.

Richard Aldington: Images of War *(1919)*

(b)

7.45   The barrage is now working to the right of Fricourt and beyond. I can see
       the 21st Division advancing about three-quarters of a mile away on the left
       and a few Germans coming to meet them, apparently surrendering. Our
       men in small parties (not extending in line) go steadily on to the German
       front-line. Brilliant sunshine and a haze of smoke drifting along the
       landscape. Some Yorkshires a little way below on the left, watching the
       show and cheering as if at a football match. The noise almost as bad as ever.

9.30   Came back to the dug-out and had a shave. 21st Division still going across
       the open, apparently without casualties. The sunlight flashes on bayonets as
       the tiny figures move quietly forward and disappear beyond mounds of
       trench debris. A few runners come back and ammunition parties go across.
       Trench-mortars are knocking hell out of Sunken Road Trench and the
       ground where the Manchesters will attack soon. Noise not so bad now and
       very little retaliation.

9.50   Fricourt half-hidden by clouds of drifting smoke, blue, pinkish and grey.
       Shrapnel bursting in small bluish-white puffs with tiny flashes. The birds
       seem bewildered; a lark begins to go up and then flies feebly along, thinking
       better of it. Others flutter above the trench with querulous cries, weak on
       the wing. I can see seven of our balloons, on the right. On the left our men
       still filing across in twenties and thirties. Another huge explosion in Fricourt
       and a cloud of brown-pink smoke. Some bursts are yellowish.

9.51   I can see the Manchesters down in New Trench, getting ready to go over.
       Figures filing down the trench. Two of them have gone out to look at our
       wiregaps! Have just eaten my last orange ... I am staring at a sunlit picture
       of Hell, and still the breeze shakes the yellow weeds, and the poppies glow
       under Crawley Ridge where some shells fell a few minutes ago. Manchesters
       are sending forward some scouts. A bayonet glitters. A runner comes back
       across the open to their Battalion Headquarters close here on the right. 21st
       Division still trotting along the skyline toward La Boisselle. Barrage going
       strong to the right of Contalmaison Ridge. Heavy shelling toward Mametz.

12.15 Quieter the last two hours. Manchesters still waiting, Germans putting over

> a few shrapnel shells. Silly if I got hit! Weather cloudless and hot. A lark singing confidently overhead.
>
> 1.30 Manchesters attack at 2.30, Mametz and Montauban reported taken. Mametz consolidated.
>
> *From Siegfried Sassoon:* Memoirs of an Infantry Officer

The question on page 146 is that set by the exam board on these pieces. Use it as a practice exercise.

7.4 Synoptic assessment and pre-release material

After studying this section you should be able to:

- *understand how pre-release material can be used as the basis for synoptic assessment*
- *examine some examples of pre-release material*
- *see strategies for handling pre-release material both prior to and in the exam*

AQA B > U6

The practice examination questions on pages 149–174 are taken from AQA specification B. The material is all either on, or related thematically to the play *The Crucible* by Arthur Miller.

In this paper you will be tested on your ability to:

- communicate clearly the knowledge, understanding and insight appropriate to literary study, using appropriate terminology and accurate and coherent written expression
- respond with knowledge and understanding to literary texts of different types and periods, exploring and commenting on relationships and comparisons between literary texts
- show detailed understanding of the ways in which writers' choices of form, structure and language shape meanings
- articulate independent opinions and judgements, informed by different interpretations of literary texts by other readers
- evaluate the significance of cultural, historical and other contextual influences on literary texts and study.

Sample question and model answer

By a close study of the set passages, compare and contrast their presentation of the experience of battle, and discuss how far and in what ways you see them as representative of writing from the First World War.

Student response

A sound introduction to the essay – focuses on both poem extracts.

The poem 'Bombardment' is a first-hand account of being under bombardment by the enemy for several days and the poet describes what it was like to be huddled in their holes for days on end while the shells rained down on them. The extract from Sassoon is quite different in character. It is taken from a diary or a journal and he gives an almost 'minute-by-minute' account of what is happening and what he sees. In Sassoon's account he seems to be watching events unfold from a distance. This is not the case in 'Bombardment'.

Gets to grips immediately with the poem. Shows evidence of close reading straight away.

The poem opens immediately in action as the earth is 'rent and torn' by the exploding shells. Houses are destroyed and the intensity of the bombardment is emphasised by the fact that the men dare not sleep for three nights and the tension is created through the detail of them –

'Sweating, and listening for the imminent crash
Which meant our death.'

Good reference to language use and some perceptive points made here.

By the fourth night men did sleep but it was a sleep of exhaustion, not a natural, restful sleep – their condition is emphasised through the intensity of the language –

Appropriate supporting quotation.

'Nerve-tortured, wracked to exhaustion,
Slept, muttering and twitching,
While the shells crashed overhead.'

The sense of contrast created is a sound point and shows sensitivity to poem.

The fifth stanza brings relief as the bombardment ceases and the sense of 'hush' comes as a contrast to the preceding three stanzas. The bombardment over, the men are able to emerge from the holes in which they have huddled. As they emerge the final lines form a complete contrast to the chaos of the previous lines. In contrast to the 'wreckage of the earth' the poet looks to the sky and to

'Where the white clouds moved in silent lines
Across the untroubled blue.'

Perceptive comment about the effect of nature.

It is as though nature has a calming effect on the whole atmosphere of the poem. In a sense, the sky is untouched by the brutality going on below – it is a constant and the poet seems to draw some strength and comfort from this thought.

Good comparative point made.

In Sassoon's account his language is much more 'matter-of-fact' as he reports what he sees and he includes little domestic details such as 'Came back to the dug-out and had a shave.' From his vantage point he is able to see the soldiers moving as tiny figures and this gives a sense of distance between the narrator and what he sees. The fact that there seems to be little retaliation from the Germans and that some are actually coming forward to surrender and that no casualties are being taken by the British gives a slightly more relaxed atmosphere to his writing. Even the noise of the barrage seems to Sassoon to lessen.

Sound comment on atmosphere.

Again the student shows a sensitivity to the way language is used.

However, there is still danger as he describes the shell-bursts and the flying shrapnel. It is interesting that Sassoon, too, notes some details of nature but this time the natural scene is affected by the activities of Man –

Sample question and model answer *(continued)*

'The birds seem bewildered; a lark begins to go up and then flies feebly along, thinking better of it. Others flutter above the trench with querulous cries, weak on the wing.'

Relevant support followed up by specific examples of vocabulary and its effects.

Here it is as if nature has been in some way enfeebled by the fighting and this is emphasised through Sassoon's choice of vocabulary – 'feebly', 'querulous', 'weak'.

Student shows awareness of inherent contrasts in the description of the scene.

Again we get a small detail – 'I had just eaten my last orange' but even though the British seem to have the upper hand the scene is still dangerous and he describes it as a 'sunlit Hell' and there are references to the sunlight glittering on the bayonets, creating a sense of contrast between the comforting sunlight and the uncompromising and lethal bayonets. Sassoon recognises that although viewing the scene from a distance he, too, is in some danger and he thinks, 'Silly if I got hit'. There is another reference to nature, this time immediately preceding the news that the Manchester Regiment have taken Mametz and Montauban. The reference to nature this time

Another point of contrast.

is much more positive 'Weather cloudless and hot. A lark singing confidently overhead.'

Good concluding paragraph which also addresses the final part of the question. Some interesting and relevant points made revealing ideas on First World War writers that go beyond the two pieces examined.

In many ways both these pieces are typical of writing from the First World War. The poem, like many written by other war poets, describes the horror at being caught up in war – this time from the point of view of being under bombardment. It is, perhaps, less typical of much of the poetry of people like Wilfred Owen and Sassoon himself, though, in that it does not contain an overt anti-war sentiment over and above its description. Some poems are much more openly critical of the war and its futility. Sassoon's piece is also fairly typical of this kind of writing. Other writers, such as Edward Thomas, kept a diary of their time in France. Many of them included references to nature in their writings as though this represented a kind of normality within a nightmare world.

Overall this is a strong answer that shows a good focus on the poem and extract and examines each in detail. Key issues are raised and examined and the summative comment is clear and draws the piece of writing effectively to a close.

Summary

To do well on this question you must show an understanding of how the passages belong within the genre of Great War Literature (AO2); you must demonstrate the skills of close reading by a critical appreciation of the passage and poem (AO3) and you must evaluate the significance of cultural, historical and social influences upon the way they may be read (AO5ii).

A top-range answer should show:

- sophisticated understanding of the types of text you are dealing with, exploring and commenting on the differences and similarities between the poem and the prose and making relevant and pertinent cross-reference to other writers and texts
- insight into how the writers exploit their chosen forms and use particular vocabularies to present very different views of battle
- a real appreciation of how these two extracts can be seen in relation to other texts from the Great War and the ability to make fruitful and interesting comparisons and contrasts with other texts, particularly in the way Nature is often used as a contrasting device or as a place of sanctuary.

Practice examination questions

The Crucible

Answer all three questions.
Read the unseen extract, printed after the questions.
30 minutes are allocated in the examination to the reading and consideration of this extract.

Question 1 will ask you to compare this unseen extract with the ending of *The Crucible* in your pre-release material. It would be helpful for you to read the question first, before you read the extract which follows.

Questions 2 and 3 will focus entirely on the pre-release material.

1 Compare the final scene of *The Crucible* with the penultimate chapter of *The Scarlet Letter*, examining:

- **their treatment of guilt and persecution**
- **the depictions of Salem society**
- **the ways these authors build to a climax**
- **the effects achieved by the choices of language**
- **their impact.**

(40 marks)

2 Compare and contrast *two* of the different interpretations offered in items 2, 3 and 4. Which do you find the most persuasive and why? (20 marks)

3 Using Items 5, 6 and 7, explain what sources and values most influenced Miller in his writing of the stage play of *The Crucible*. (20 marks)

This extract is taken from the penultimate chapter of Nathaniel Hawthorne's novel. *The Scarlet Letter*, first published in 1850.

Nathaniel Hawthorne was born in Salem, Massachusetts which he chooses for the setting of his novel. One of his ancestors, John Hawthorne, was one of the three judges at the Salem witch trials of 1692 which Arthur Miller uses for the subject of *The Crucible*.

This chapter marks the climax of the novel. Hester Prynne has been forced to wear a scarlet letter as a sign of her adultery. Hester had endured a forced and loveless marriage with Roger Chillingworth but Pearl, the offspring of her adulterous relationship, is seen by those in the town as 'elvish' and 'witch-like'. Chillingworth befriends Arthur Dimmesdale, the local minister, in order to gloat in his secret knowledge that Dimmesdale is the adulterer and in order to remind Dimmesdale constantly of his guilt.

At this point in the novel Hester is at the scaffold, waiting to be hanged for adultery. Dimmesdale has just preached his Election Sermon to great public acclaim and is moving from the church to the scaffold.

His subject, it appeared, had been the relation between the Deity and the communities of mankind, with a special reference to the New England which they were here planting in the wilderness. And, as he drew towards the close, a spirit as of prophecy had come upon him, constraining him to its purpose as mightily as the old prophets of Israel were constrained; only with this difference, that, whereas the Jewish seers had denounced judgements and ruin on their country, it was his mission to foretell a high and glorious destiny for the newly gathered people of the Lord. But, throughout it all, and through the whole discourse, there had been a certain deep said undertone of pathos, which could not be interpreted otherwise than as the natural regret of one soon to pass away.

Yes; their minister whom they so loved – and who so loved them all, that he could not depart heavenward without a sigh – had the foreboding of untimely death upon him, and would soon leave them in their tears! This idea of his transitory stay on earth gave the last emphasis to the effect which the preacher had produced: it was as if an angel in his passage to the skies, had shaken his bright wings over the people for an instant – at once a shadow and a splendor – and had shed down a shower of golden truths upon them.

Thus, there had come to the Reverend Mr Dimmesdale as to most men, in their various spheres, though seldom recognized until they see it far behind them – an epoch of life more brilliant and full of triumph than any previous one, or than any which could hereafter be. He stood, at this moment, on the very proudest eminence of superiority, to which the gifts of intellect, rich lore, prevailing eloquence and a reputation of whitest sanctity, could exalt a clergyman in New England's earliest days, when the professional character was of itself a lofty pedestal. Such was the position which the minister occupied, as he bowed his head forward on the cushions of the pulpit, at the close of his Election Sermon. Meanwhile Hester Prynne was standing beside the scaffold of the pillory, with the scarlet letter still burning on her breast!

As the ranks of military men and civil fathers moved onward, all eyes were turned towards the point where the minister was seen to approach among them. The shout died into a murmur, as one portion of the crowd after another obtained a glimpse of him. How feeble and pale he looked, amid all his triumph! The energy – or say, rather, the inspiration which had held him up until he should have delivered the sacred message that brought its own strength along with it from Heaven – was withdrawn, now that it had so faithfully performed its office. The glow, which they had just before beheld burning on his check, was extinguished, like a flame that sinks down hopelessly among the late-decaying embers. It seemed hardly the face of a man alive, with such a deathlike hue, it was hardly a man with life in him that tottered on his path so nervelessly, yet tottered – and did not fall!

One of his clerical brethren – it was the venerable John Wilson – observing the state in which Mr Dimmesdale was left by the retiring wave of intellect and sensibility stepped forward hastily to offer his support. The minister tremulously, but decidedly, repelled the old man's arm. He still walked onward, if that movement could be so described, which rather resembled the wavering effort of an infant with its mother's arms in view, outstretched to tempt him forward. And now, almost imperceptible as were the latter steps of his progress, he had come opposite the well remembered and weather-darkened scaffold, where, long since, with all that dreary lapse of time between, Hester Prynne had encountered the world's ignominious stare. There stood Hester holding little Pearl by the hand! And there was the scarlet letter on her breast! The minister here made a pause, although the music still played the stately and rejoicing march to which the procession moved. It summoned him onward, onward to the festival! – but here he made a pause.

He turned towards the scaffold, and stretched forth his arms.

"Hester," said he, "come hither! Come my little Pearl!" It was a ghastly look with which he regarded them; but there was something at once tender and strangely triumphant in it. The child, with the bird-like motion which was one of her characteristics, flew to him, and clasped her arms about his knees. Hester Prynne – slowly, as if impelled by inevitable fate, and against her strongest will – likewise drew near, but paused before she reached him. At this instant, old Roger Chillingworth thrust himself through the crowd – or perhaps, so dark, disturbed, and evil, was his look, he rose up out of some nether region – to snatch back his victim from what he sought to do! Be that as it might, the old man rushed forward, and caught the minister by the arm.

'Madman, hold! what is your purpose?" whispered he: "Wave back that woman! Cast off this child! All shall be well! Do not blacken your fame, and perish in dishonour! I can yet save you! Would you bring infamy on your sacred profession?"

Practice examination questions (continued)

"Ha, tempter! Methinks thou art too late!" answered the minister, encountering his eye, fearfully, but firmly. "Thy power is not what it was! With God's help, I shall escape thee now!"

He again extended his hand to the woman of the scarlet letter.

"Hester Prynne," cried he, with a piercing earnestness, "in the name of Him, so terrible and so merciful, who gives me grace, at this last moment, to do what – for my own heavy sin and miserable agony – I withheld myself from doing seven years ago, come hither now, and twine thy strength about me! Thy strength, Hester: but let it be guided by the will which God hath granted me! This wretched and wronged old man is opposing it with all his might! With all his own might, and the fiend's! Come, Hester, come! Support me up yonder scaffold!"

The crowd was in a tumult, the men of rank and dignity who stood more immediately around the clergyman, were so taken by surprise, and so perplexed as to the purport of what they saw – unable to receive the explanation which most readily presented itself, or to imagine any other, – that they remained silent and inactive spectators of the judgement which Providence seemed about to work. They beheld the minister, leaning on Hester's shoulder, and supported by her arm around him, approach the scaffold, and ascend its steps: while still the little hand of the sin-born child was clasped in his. Old Roger Chillingworth followed as one intimately connected with the drama of guilt and sorrow in which they had all been actors, and well entitled, therefore, to be present at its closing scene.

"Hadst thou sought the whole earth over," said he, looking darkly at the clergyman, "there was no one place so secret – no high place nor lowly place, where thou couldst have escaped me – save on this very scaffold!"

"Thanks be to Him who hath led me hither!" answered the minister.

Yet he trembled, and turned to Hester with an expression of doubt and anxiety in his eyes, not the less evidently betrayed, that there was a feeble smile upon his lips.

"Is not this better," murmured he, "than what we dreamed of in the forest?"

"I know not! I know not!" she hurriedly replied. "Better? Yea, so we may both die, and little Pearl die with us!"

"For thee and Pearl, be it as God shall order," said the minister; "and God is merciful! Let me now do the will which He hath made plain before my sight. For, Hester, I am a dying man. So let me make haste to take my shame upon me!"

Partly supported by Hester Prynne, and holding one hand of little Pearl's, the Reverend Mr Dimmesdale turned to the dignified and venerable rulers; to the holy ministers, who were his brethren; to the people, whose great heart was thoroughly appalled, yet overflowing with tearful sympathy, as knowing that some deep life-matter – which, if full of sin, was full of anguish and repentance likewise – was now to be laid open to them. The sun, but little past its meridian, shone down upon the clergyman, and gave a distinctness to his figure, as he stood out from all the earth, to put in his plea of guilty at the bar of Eternal Justice.

"People of New England" cried he, with a voice that rose over them, high, solemn, and majestic – yet had always a tremor through it, and sometimes a shrieked, struggling up out of a fathomless depth of remorse and woe – "ye, that have loved me! – ye, that have deemed me holy! behold me here, the one sinner of the world! At last! – at last! – I stand upon the spot where, seven years since, I should have stood; here with this woman, whose arm, more than the little strength wherewith I have crept hitherward, sustains me, at this dreadful moment, from grovelling down upon my face. Lo, the scarlet letter which Hester wears! Ye have all shuddered at it! Wherever her walk hath been – wherever, so miserably burdened, she may have hoped to find repose – it hath cast a lurid gleam of awe and horrible repugnance round about her. But there stood one in the midst of you, at whose brand of sin and infamy ye have not shuddered!"

It seemed at this point as if the minister must leave the remainder of his secret undisclosed. But he fought back the bodily weakness – and still more, the faintness of heart – that was striving for the mastery with him. He threw off all assistance, and stepped passionately forward a pace before the woman and the child.

"It was on him!" he continued, with a kind of fierceness – so determined was he to speak out the whole. "God's eye beheld it! The angels were forever pointing at it! The Devil knew it well, and fretted it continually with the touch of his burning finger! But he hid it cunningly from men, and walked among you with the mien of a spirit, mournful because so pure in a sinful world! – and sad, because he missed his heavenly kindred! Now, at the death-hour, he stands up before you! He bids you look again at Hester's scarlet letter! He tells you, that, with all its mysterious horror, it is but the shadow of what he bears on his own breast, and that even this, his own red stigma is no more than the type of what has seared his inmost heart! Stand any here that question God's judgement on a sinner? Behold a dreadful witness of it!".

With a conclusive motion, he tore away ministerial band from before his breast. It was revealed! But it were irreverent to describe that revelation. For an instant, the gaze of the horror-stricken multitude was concentrated on the ghastly miracle, while the minister stood, with a flush of triumph in his face, as one who in the crisis of acutest pain had won a victory. Then, down he sank upon the scaffold! Hester partly raised him, and supported his head against her bosom. Old Roger Chillingworth knelt down beside him, with a blank dull countenance, out of which the life seemed to have departed.

"Thou hast escaped me!" he repeated more than once. Thou hast escaped me.'

"May God forgive me!" said the minister. "Thou, too hast deeply sinned!"

He withdrew his dying eyes from the old man, and fixed them on the woman and the child.

"My little Pearl," said he, feebly – and there was a sweet gentle smile over his face, as of a spirit sinking into deep repose; nay, now that the burden was removed, it seemed almost as if he would be sportive with the child – "dear little Pearl, wilt thou kiss me now? Thou wouldst not, yonder, in the forest! But now thou will?"

Pearl kissed his lips. A spell was broken, the great scene of grief, in which the wild infant bore a part, had developed all her sympathies; and as her tears fell upon her father's cheek, they were the pledge that she would grow up amid human joy and sorrow, nor forever do battle with the world, but be a woman in it. Towards her mother, too, Pearl's errand as a messenger of anguish was all fulfilled.

"Hester," said the clergyman, ''farewell'"

"Shall we not meet again?' whispered she, bending her face down close to his. "Shall we not spend our immortal life together? Surely, surely, we have ransomed one another, with all this woe! Thou lookest far into eternity, with those bright dying eyes! then tell me what thou seest?"

"Hush, Hester, hush!" said he, with tremulous solemnity. "The law was broke! – the sin here so awfully revealed! – let these alone be in thy thoughts! I fear! I fear! It may be that, when we forgot our God – when we violated our reverence each for the other's soul – it was thenceforth vain to hope that we could meet thereafter, in an everlasting and pure reunion. God knows; and He is merciful! He hath proved his mercy, most of all in my afflictions. By giving me this burning torture to bear upon my breast! By sending yonder dark and terrible old man, to keep the torture always at red-heat! By bringing me hither, to die this death of triumphant ignominy before the people! Had either of these agonies been wanting, I had been lost forever! Praised be His name! His will he done! Farewell!"

That final word came forth with the minister's expiring breath. The multitude, silent till then broke out in a strange, deep voice of awe and wonder, which could not as yet find utterance, save in this murmur that rolled so heavily after the departed spirit.

Practice examination questions (continued)

Pre-release material

The Crucible

Contents

Item 1

Act IV of the Stage Play

(HERRICK enters with JOHN PROCTOR. His wrists are chained. He is another man, bearded, filthy, his eyes misty as though webs had overgrown them. He halts inside the doorway, his eye caught by the sight of ELIZABETH. The emotion flowing between them prevents anyone from speaking for an instant. Now HALE, visibly affected, goes to DANFORTH and speaks quietly.)

HALE Pray leave them, Excellency.

DANFORTH *(pressing HALE impatiently aside)* Mr Proctor, you have been notified, have you not?

(PROCTOR is silent, starting at ELIZABETH.)

I see light in the sky, Mister; Set you counsel with your wife, and may God help you turn your back on Hell.

(PROCTOR is silent, staring at ELIZABETH.)

HALE *(quietly)* Excellency, let –

(DANFORTH brushes past HALE and walks out, HALE follows. CHEEVER stands and follows. HATHORNE behind. HERRICK goes. PARRIS, from a safe distance, offers:)

PARRIS If you desire a cup of cider, Mr Proctor, I am sure I –

(PROCTOR turns an icy stare at him, and he breaks off. PARRIS raises his palms toward PROCTOR.)

God lead you now. *(PARRIS goes out.)*

(Alone. PROCTOR walks to her, halts. It is as though they stood in a spinning world. It is beyond sorrow, above it. He reaches out his hand as though toward an embodiment not quite real, and as he touches her, a strange soft sound, half laughter, half amazement, comes from his throat. He pats her hand. She covers his hand with hers. And then, weak, he sits. Then she sits, facing him.)

PROCTOR The child?

ELIZABETH It grows.

PROCTOR There is no word of the boys?

ELIZABETH They're well. Rebecca's Samuel keeps them.

PROCTOR You have not seen them?

ELIZABETH I have not. *(She catches a weakening in herself and downs it.)*

PROCTOR You are a – marvel. Elizabeth.

Practice examination questions (continued)

ELIZABETH You – have been tortured?

PROCTOR Aye.

(Pause. She will not let herself be drowned in the sea that threatens her.)
> They come for my life now.

ELIZABETH I know it. *(Pause)*

PROCTOR None – have yet confessed?

ELIZABETH There be many confessed.

PROCTOR Who are they?

ELIZABETH There be a hundred or more, they say, Goody Ballard is one; Isaiah Goodkind is one. There be many.

PROCTOR Rebecca?

ELIZABETH Not Rebecca. She is one foot in Heaven now; naught may hurt her more.

PROCTOR And Giles?

ELIZABETH You have not heard of it?

PROCTOR I hear nothing where I am kept.

ELIZABETH Giles is dead.

(He looks at her incredulously.)

PROCTOR When were he hanged?

ELIZABETH *(quietly, factually)* He were not hanged. He would not answer aye or nay to his indictment: for if he denied the charge they'd hang him surely, and auction out his property. So he stand mute, and died Christian under the law. And so his sons will have his farm. It is the law, for he could not be condemned a wizard without he answer the indictment, aye or nay.

PROCTOR Then how does he die?

ELIZABETH *(gently)* They press him, John.

PROCTOR Press?

ELIZABETH Great stones they lay upon his chest until he plead aye or nay. *(With a tender smile for the old man)* They say he give them but two words. 'More weight,' he says. And died.

PROCTOR *(numbed – a thread to weave into his agony)* 'More weight.'

ELIZABETH Aye. It were a fearsome man, Giles Corey.

(Pause.)

PROCTOR *(with great force of will, but not quite looking at her)* I have been thinking I would confess to them, Elizabeth. *(She shows nothing.)* What say you? If I give them that?

ELIZABETH I cannot judge you, John.

(Pause)

PROCTOR *(simply – a pure question)* What would you have me do?

ELIZABETH As you will, I would have it. *(Slight pause)* I want you living, John. That's sure.

PROCTOR *(pauses, then with a flailing of hope)* Giles' wife? Have she confessed?

ELIZABETH She will not. *(Pause)*

PROCTOR It is pretence, Elizabeth.

ELIZABETH What is?

PROCTOR I cannot mount the gibbet like a saint. It is a fraud. I am not that man. *(She is silent.)* My honesty is broke. Elizabeth; I am no good man. Nothing's spoiled by giving this lie that were not rotten long before.

ELIZABETH And yet you've not confessed till now. That speak goodness in you.

PROCTOR Spite only keeps me silent. It is hard to give a lie to dogs. *(Pause, for the first time he turns directly to her.)* I would have your forgiveness, Elizabeth.

ELIZABETH It is not for me to give, John. I am –

PROCTOR I'd have you see some honesty in it. Let them that never lied die now to keep their souls. It is pretence for me, a vanity that will not blind God nor keep my children out of the wind. *(Pause.)* What say you?

ELIZABETH *(upon a heaving sob that always threatens)* John, it come to naught that I should forgive you, if you'll not forgive yourself. *(Now he turns away a little, in great agony.)* It is not my soul, John it is yours.

(He stands, as though in physical pain. Slowly rising to his feel with a great immortal longing to find his answer. It is difficult to say, and she is on the verge of tears.)

Only to be sure of this, for I know it now: whatever you will do, it is a good man does it. *(He turns his doubting, searching gaze upon her.)*

I have read my heart this three month, John. *(Pause.)* I have sins of my own to count. It needs a cold wife to prompt lechery.

PROCTOR *(in great pain)* Enough, enough –

ELIZABETH *(now pouring out her heart)* Better you should know me!

PROCTOR I will not hear it! I know you!

ELIZABETH You take my sins upon you, John –

PROCTOR *(in agony)* No, I take my own, my own!

ELIZABETH John, I counted myself so plain, so poorly made, no honest love could come to me! Suspicion kissed you when I did; I never knew how I should say my love. It were a cold house I kept! *(In fright, she swerves, as HATHORNE enters.)*

HATHORNE What say you, Proctor? The sun is soon up. *(PROCTOR, his chest heaving, stares, turns to ELIZABETH. She comes to him as though to plead, her voice quaking.)*

ELIZABETH Do what you will. But let none be your judge. There be no higher judge under Heaven than Proctor is! Forgive me, forgive me, John – I never knew such goodness in the world! *(She covers her face, weeping.)*

(PROCTOR turns from her to HATHORNE; he is off the earth, his voice hollow.)

PROCTOR I want my life.

HATHORNE *(electrified, surprised)*: You'll confess yourself?

PROCTOR I will have my life.

HATHORNE *(with a mystical tone)* God be praised! It is a providence! *(He rushes out the door, and his voice is heard calling down the corridor:)* He will confess! Proctor will confess!

PROCTOR *(with a cry, as he strides to the door)* Why do you cry it? *(In great pain he turns back to her.)* It is evil, is it not? It is evil.

ELIZABETH *(in terror, weeping)* I cannot judge you, John, I cannot!

PROCTOR Then who will judge me? *(Suddenly clasping his hands)* God in Heaven, what is John Proctor, what is John Proctor? *(He moves as an animal, and a fury is riding in him, a tantalized search.)* I think so; I am

Practice examination questions (continued)

no saint. *(As though she had denied this he calls angrily at her)* Let Rebecca go like a saint; for me it is fraud! *(Voices are heard in the hall, speaking together in suppressed excitement.)*

ELIZABETH I am not your judge, I cannot be. *(As though giving him release)* Do as you will, do as you will!

PROCTOR Would you give them such a lie? Say it. Would you ever give them this? *(She cannot answer.)* You would not; if tongs of fire were singeing you would not! It is evil. Good, then – it is evil, and I do it!

(HATHORNE enters with DANFORTH, and, with them, CHEEVER, PARRIS, and HALE. It is a businesslike, rapid entrance, as though the ice had been broken.)

DANFORTH *(with great relief and gratitude)* Praise to God, man, praise to God; you shall be blessed in Heaven for this.

(CHEEVER has hurried to the bench with pen, ink, and paper. PROCTOR watches him.)

Now then, let us have it. Are you ready, Mr Cheever?

PROCTOR *(with a cold, cold horror at their efficiency)* Why must it be written?

DANFORTH Why, for the good instruction of the village, Mister; this we shall post upon the church door! *(To PARRIS, urgently)* Where is the marshal?

PARRIS *(runs to the door and calls down the corridor)* Marshall. Hurry!

DANFORTH Now, then, Mister, will you speak slowly, and directly to the point, for Mr Cheever's sake. *(He is on record now, and is really dictating to CHEEVER, who writes.)* Mr Proctor, have you seen the Devil in your life? *(PROCTOR'S jaws lock.)* Come, man, there is light in the sky; the town waits at the scaffold; I would give out this news. Did you see the Devil?

PROCTOR I did.

PARRIS Praise God!

DANFORTH And when did he come to you, what were his demand? *(PROCTOR is silent. DANFORTH helps.)* Did he bid you to do his work on earth?

PROCTOR He did.

DANFORTH And you bound yourself to his service?

(DANFORTH turns, as REBECCA NURSE enters, with HERRICK helping to support her. She is barely able to walk.) Come in, woman!

REBECCA *(brightening as she sees PROCTOR)* Ah, John! You are well, then, eh?

(PROCTOR turns his face to the wall.)

DANFORTH Courage, man, courage – let her witness your good example that she may come to God herself. Now hear it, Goody Nurse! Say on, Mr Proctor. Did you bind yourself to the Devil's service?

REBECCA *(astonished)* Why, John!

PROCTOR *(through his teeth, his face turned from REBECCA)* I did.

DANFORTH Now, woman, you surely see it profit nothin' to keep this conspiracy any further. Will you confess yourself with him?

REBECCA Oh, John – God send his mercy on you!

DANFORTH I say, will you confess yourself, Goody Nurse?

REBECCA Why, it is a lie, it is a lie; how may I damn myself? I cannot, I cannot.

DANFORTH Mr Proctor. When the Devil came to see you did you see Rebecca Nurse in his company? *(PROCTOR is silent.)* Come, man, take courage – did you ever see her with the Devil?

PROCTOR *(almost inaudibly)* No.

(DANFORTH, now sensing trouble, glances at JOHN and goes to the table, and picks up a sheet – the list of condemned.)

DANFORTH Did you ever see her sister, Mary Easty, with the Devil?

PROCTOR No, I did not.

DANFORTH *(his eyes narrow on PROCTOR)* Did you ever see Martha Corey with the Devil?

PROCTOR I did not.

DANFORTH *(realising, slowly putting the sheet down)* Did you ever see anyone with the Devil?

PROCTOR I did not.

DANFORTH Proctor, you mistake me. I am not empowered to trade your life for a lie. You have most certainly seen some person with the Devil. *(PROCTOR is silent.)* Mr Proctor, a score of people have already testified they saw this woman with the Devil.

PROCTOR Then it is proved. Why must I say it?

DANFORTH Why 'must you' say it! Why, you should rejoice to say it if your soul is truly purged of any love for Hell!

PROCTOR They think to go like saints. I like not to spoil their names.

DANFORTH *(inquiring, incredulous)* Mr Proctor, do you think they go like saints?

PROCTOR *(ending)* This woman never thought she done the Devil's work.

DANFORTH Look you, sir. I think you mistake your duty here. It matters nothing what she thought – she is convicted of the unnatural murder of children, and you for sending your spirit out upon Mary Warren. Your soul alone is the issue here Mister, and you will prove its whiteness or you cannot live in a Christian country. Will you tell me now what persons conspired with you in the Devil's company? *(PROCTOR is silent.)* To your knowledge was Rebecca Nurse ever –

PROCTOR I speak my own sins; I cannot judge another. *(Crying out, with hatred)* I have no tongue for it.

HALE *(quickly to DANFORTH)* Excellency, it is enough he confess himself. Let him sign it, let him sign it.

PARRIS *(feverishly)* It is a great service, sir. It is a weighty name; it will strike the village that Proctor confess, I beg you, let him sign it. The sun is up, Excellency!

DANFORTH *(considers; then with dissatisfaction)* Come, then, sign your testimony. *(To CHEEVER)* Give it to him.

(CHEEVER goes to PROCTOR, the confession and a pen in hand. PROCTOR does not look at it.)

Come, man, sign it.

PROCTOR *(after glancing at the confession)* You have all witnessed it – it is enough.

DANFORTH You will not sign it?

PROCTOR You have all witnessed it; what more is needed?

DANFORTH Do you sport with me? You will sign your name or it is no confession, Mister! *(His breast heaving with agonized breathing, PROCTOR now lays the paper down and signs his name.)*

PARRIS Praise be to the Lord!

(PROCTOR has just finished signing when DANFORTH reaches for the paper.

Practice examination questions (continued)

But PROCTOR snatches it up and now a wild terror is rising in him, and a boundless anger.)

DANFORTH *(perplexed, but politely extending his hand)* If you please, sir.

PROCTOR No.

DANFORTH *(as though PROCTOR did not understand)* Mr Proctor, I must have –

PROCTOR No, no. I have signed it. You have seen me. It is done! You have no need for this.

PARRIS Proctor, the village must have proof that –

PROCTOR Damn the village! I confess to God, and God has seen my name on this! It is enough!

DANFORTH No sir, it is –

PROCTOR You came to save my soul, did you not? Here! I have confessed myself; it is enough!

DANFORTH You have not con –

PROCTOR I have confessed myself! Is there no good penitence but it be public? God does not need my name nailed upon the church! God sees my name; God knows how black my sins are! It is enough!

DANFORTH Mr Proctor –

PROCTOR You will not use me! I am no Sarah Good or Tituba, I am John Proctor! You will not use me! It is no part of salvation that you should use me!

DANFORTH I do not wish to –

PROCTOR I have three children – how may I teach them to walk like men in the world, and I sold my friends?

DANFORTH You have not sold your friends –

PROCTOR Beguile me not! I blacken all of them when this is nailed to the church the very day they hang for silence!

DANFORTH Mr Proctor, I must have good and legal proof that you –

PROCTOR You are the high court, your word is good enough! Tell them I confessed myself; say Proctor broke his knee and wept like a woman; say what you will, but my name cannot –

DANFORTH *(with suspicion)* It is the same, is it not? If I report it or you sign to it? Why? Do you mean to deny this confession when you are free?

PROCTOR I mean to deny nothing!

DANFORTH Then explain to me, Mr Proctor, why will you not let –

PROCTOR *(with a cry of his soul)* Because it is my name! Because I cannot have another in my life! Because I lie and sign myself to lies! Because I am not worth the dust on the feet of them that hang! How may I live without my name? I have given you my soul; leave me my name!

DANFORTH *(pointing at the confession in Proctor's hand)* Is that document a lie? If it is a lie I will not accept it! What say you? I will not deal in lies, Mister! *(PROCTOR is motionless.)* You will give me your honest confession in my hand, or I cannot keep you from the rope. *(PROCTOR does not reply.)* Which way do you go, Mister?

(His breast heaving, his eyes staring, PROCTOR tears the paper and crumples it, and he is weeping in fury, but erect.)

PARRIS *(hysterically, as though the tearing paper were his life)* Proctor, Proctor!

HALE Man, you will hang! You cannot!

PROCTOR *(his eyes full tears)* I can. And there's your first marvel, that I can. You have made your magic now, for now I do think I see some shred of goodness in John Proctor. Not enough to weave a banner with, but white enough to keep it from such dogs.
(ELIZABETH, in burst of terror, rushes to him and weeps against his hand.) Give them no tear! Tears pleasure them! Show honour now, show a stony heart and sink them with it! *(He has lifted her and kisses her now with great passion.)*

REBECCA Let you fear nothing! Another judgement waits us all!

DANFORTH Hang them high over the town! Who weeps for these, weeps for corruption! *(He sweeps out past them. HERRICK starts to lead REBECCA, who almost collapses, but PROCTOR catches her and she glances up at him apologetically.)*

REBECCA I've had no breakfast.

HERRICK Come, man.

(HERRICK escorts them out, HATHORNE and CHEEVER behind them. ELIZABETH stands staring at the empty doorway.)

PARRIS *(in deadly fear, to ELIZABETH)* Go to him. Goody Proctor! There is time yet! *(From outside a drumroll strikes the air. PARRIS is startled: ELIZABETH jerks about toward the window.)*

PARRIS Go to him! *(He rushes out the door, as though to hold back his fate.)* Proctor! Proctor!

(Again, a short burst of drums.)

HALE Woman, plead with him! *(He starts to rush out the door, and then goes back to her.)* Woman! It is pride, it is vanity. *(She avoids his eyes, and moves to the window. He drops to his knees.)*

Be his helper! – What profit him to bleed? Shall the dust praise him? Shall the worms declare his truth? Go to him, take his shame away!

ELIZABETH *(supporting herself against collapse, grips the bars of the window, and with a cry)* He have his goodness now. God forbid I take it from him!

(The final drumroll crashes, then heightens violently. HALE weeps in frantic prayer, and the new sun is pouring in upon her face, and the drums rattle like bones in the morning air.)

Echoes down the corridor.

Not long after the fever died, Parris was voted from office, walked out on the highroad, and was never heard of again.

The legend has it that Abigail turned up later as a prostitute in Boston.

Twenty years after the last execution, the government awarded compensation to the victims still living, and to the families of the dead. However, it is evident that some people still were unwilling to admit their total guilt, and also that the factionalism was still alive, for some beneficiaries were actually not victims at all, but informers.

Elizabeth Proctor married again, four years after Proctor's death.

In solemn meeting, the congregation rescinded the excommunications – this in March 1712. But they did so upon orders of the government. The jury, however, wrote a statement praying forgiveness of all who had suffered.

Certain farms which had belonged to the victims were left to ruin, and for more than a century no one would buy them or live on them.

To all intents and purposes, the power of theocracy in Massachusetts was broken.

Item 2

'Mr Miller Looks at Witch-Hunting'
Richard Watts Jr.

Arthur Miller's 'The Crucible,' which opened at the Martin Beck last night, is a drama of emotional power and impact. In it, the author of 'Death of a Salesman' is contemplating the rise of mass hysteria and intolerance by the horrible Salem witch trials of 1692, and, although he clearly would not be averse to having his spectator's notice certain disquieting resemblances to present-day conditions, he doesn't press the parallels too closely. The result is a hardhitting and effective play that demands and deserves audience attention, even though it lacks some of the compelling excellence I had expected of it.

This is certainly not to say that 'The Crucible' is without the spirit and eloquence that we have come to expect of Mr Miller. Almost throughout, the play's emotional forthrightness grips the attention and holds it amid a succession of scenes of unrelenting excitement. It is written with feeling and indignation, and the importance of what it is saying by implication gives it dignity, largeness and inescapable distinction. In scene after scene, it has the sort of ringing intensity that is fairly irresistible.

Emotionally, I think it is vastly successful. Where I found it a little disappointing in its final effectiveness is in Mr Miller's inability to combine with it the kind of intellectual insight that was so notable in 'Death of a Salesman' and make it one of the most distinguished dramas of the American theater. To a certain extent, the author does not delve into the causes and motives that created the background of the terrors which marked one of the darkest spots in our history. But he is chiefly concerned with what happened, rather than why, and this neglect sometimes gives his work a hint of superficiality.

It is no doubt highly unfair to compare Miller's treatment of intolerance with Bernard Shaw's magnificent use of the theme in 'Saint Joan,' but I hope I can show what I mean by contrasting the Inquisitor in the latter drama with Deputy-Governor Danforth in 'The Crucible.' Shaw made his Inquisitor a man of great intellectual gifts and moral stature, and was all the more impressive by showing that intolerance could force even such a person into the terrible act of burning Joan at the stake. Miller's Deputy-Governor is also a well meaning man doing frightful things, but despite Walker Hampden's excellent playing, he emerges as pretty much a cardboard villain.

While there is, to my mind, an unfortunate superficiality in 'The Crucible,' the playwright deserves considerable credit for using implication, rather than too heavy an underlining to make his valuable points for today. There are, indeed, only a few moments when he doesn't let his sinister story speak for itself, and they are chiefly in the last act. But his characters tend to be dramatised points of view, or points of emotional hysteria, rather than the human beings that would have made them more striking in the theater. Nevertheless, despite such weaknesses, there is much emotional fire and indignation which can approach the overwhelming.

It seems a little fantastic to say that the veteran Mr Hampden, at his age, is improving as an actor, but I don't think I have seen him finer than he is in 'The Crucible.' Arthur Kennedy proves once more his right to be considered one of the ablest of our younger actors by the moving honesty with which he plays an outraged and unheroic man trying to fight hysteria, and there are excellent portrayals by Beatrice Straight, E.G. Marshall, Fred Stewart, Madeleine Sherwood, Joseph Sweeney, Raymond Bramley, Jenny Egan and Jean Adiar. Jed Harris has directed vigorously. Despite its frailties, 'The Crucible' is not easily to be forgotten.

Item 3

'Arthur Miller - a National Hero', by Inge Morath
(The Times Magazine)

David Thacker is an ardent admirer of Arthur Miller. He has directed more of his plays than any other director in the world, including a sort of smash hits medley of the playwright's work, at the National, on the occasion of his eightieth birthday. He has an interesting take on why Miller is so popular with English audiences, which is bound up with the tradition of our theatre. 'There are pitfalls in Miller's work. *The Crucible*, for instance, can look like a melodramatic piece if it isn't played properly. *Broken Glass* is extremely difficult. It requires an emotional empathy which is very considerable, and the text is very lyrical, almost like a dramatic extended poem. British actors are used to working with Shakespeare and plays that are both profound and very difficult. American actors don't always have that opportunity. We tend to have more of a language tradition, the language of ideas, to which theatre audiences respond very positively.'

Rhoda Koenig is one of the few critics in this country who does not rate Miller's work – early, middle or late. It is, perhaps, not entirely coincidental that she is American. 'In America,' she says, 'Miller is very much part of the American past. Any decent American is ashamed of the McCarthy period. For Miller to turn round and write *The Crucible* was a real triumph of principle overriding personal interest. It has an emotional pull which lasts. But for younger people, it's like, "OK, but what's he going to do for us now?" Why should he be expected to appeal to two and now three generations? There are plenty of novelists and playwrights who aren't any good. In his case, we're made to feel bad because he has this great social conscience.'

But it is Miller's conscience – his ability to place the most personal and human of stories in a wider social context – which is precisely what his admirers say makes his plays great. For he is the most democratic of playwrights, always striving to make his words sing to the common man – although it is doubtful he would employ such a phrase himself. If his work has had meaning for the guy in the barber shop, the harassed mother, the Willy Lomans of this world and their wives, then he feels he's done his job properly. In this sense, he was a product of his time.

'When I was starting out, and I wasn't alone in this, we thought that we were writing for the whole of the United States. My generation started to write in the Thirties and Forties, believing that was still the reality,' he recalls. 'But it was quickly wearing away. The theatres were closing down or turning into movie theatres. And this affected the way plays were written. What moved in instead was an audience that was better educated, more recondite and which also intended to be clique-ish. It resulted in a growth of highly sophisticated plays, but what was lost was the technique of doing serious work for anything like a mass audience .'

Item 4

'The Crucible' by Geoff Andrew
(*Time Out*, Feb 26–March 5 1997)

While it is true that Arthur Miller's play about the 1692 witch-hunts in Salem, Massachusetts was partly inspired by the persecution, paranoia and treachery of 50s McCarthyism, it's immediately clear from Nicholas Hytner's film version – scripted by Miller himself – that it transcends the limitations of simple analogy. As the town tears itself apart during a series of investigations testing a group of young girls' claims that their nocturnal forest gatherings were the result of Satanic possession, the story succeeds on a variety of levels: social, moral, political, psychological and philosophical. At the root of the hysteria is the sexual and emotional turmoil of Abigail Williams (Winona Ryder), bent on vengeance against Elizabeth Proctor (Joan Allen) who put a stop to the girl's affair with her husband John (Daniel Day Lewis); but that particular power struggle, with its deceit, suspicion and resentment, is as nothing to the deadly vortex that consumes Salem when Judge Danforth (Paul Scofield) arrives to take control with trials and hangings.

The ironies of the piece are savage – soon Abigail's accusations imperil John himself, while the innocent confess in order to save themselves – and well served by a top-notch cast perfectly attuned to the poetry of Miller's dialogue and the tale's fiery passions. At every level guilt, betrayal, lies and recriminations infect both the community – from infants to ancient midwives, from theological dogma to the Proctors' marriage – and the individual: Proctor is finally forced to choose his destiny according not only to truth and love but to the very purpose of existence. Hytner holds it together with solid, unflashy, well-paced direction, ensuring that this is no mere period piece but a compelling, scarily still pertinent account of human fear, frailty and cold ambition.

Item 5

'The Crucible' by Arthur Miller

The Crucible was produced by Arthur Miller in 1953, four year after his *Death of a Salesman* opened on Broadway to rave reviews, being performed 742 times, and making him into an internationally acclaimed playwright.

The sweetness of this success, however, soon turned sour as a wave of anti-Communist hysteria swept the USA in the early 50s. This affected Miller profoundly, both personally and morally. Miller himself said: 'If the reception of ... *Death of a Salesman* had made the world a friendly place for me, events of the early fifties quickly turned that warmth into an illusion.'

The House Committee on Un-American Activities had been revived in 1945 to investigate the alleged infiltration of Russian-sympathising communists into American institutions. In its search for 'enemies of the state' the Committee, under its zealous chairman Senator Joseph McCarthy, could call any witness it liked. Since they were not technically accused of anything, the witnesses were not protected by any of the usual legal procedures. They were not accused of doing anything illegal, but of being under suspicion of harbouring so-called 'un-American' beliefs and thoughts.

The Committee meetings were based on hearsay and prejudice and the widest publicity was given to 'unfriendly' witnesses. The basic issue was the interpretation of loyalty to one's country. Membership of the Communist Party was considered a treasonable act and protection of a member of the party, an unloyal act. Those investigated were imprisoned for their refusal to name others who were involved with the Communist Party.

McCarthy made a speech claiming that the State department was full of communists. This led to the ruthless smear campaign whose victims included writers and even film directors.

Miller, who was himself to become 'witch hunted', tells of the lasting effect this era had on him and how it influenced his writing of *The Crucible*:

'It was not only the rise of 'McCarthyism' that moved me, but something which seemed much more weird and mysterious. It was the fact that a political, objective, knowledgeable campaign from the Far Right was capable of creating not only a terror, but a new subjective reality, a veritable mystique which was gradually assuming even a holy resonance ... Astounded, I watched men pass by me without a nod whom I had known rather well for years; and, again, the astonishment was produced by my knowledge, which I could not give up, that the terror in these people was being knowingly planned and consciously engineered, and yet that all they knew was terror. That so interior and subjective an emotion could have been so manifestly created from without was a marvel to me. It underlies every word in *The Crucible* ...'.

The Crucible opened in New York on 22 January 1953 and ran for 197 performances. It won the Antoinette Perry and the Donaldson Prizes as the most distinguished American drama of the year, but many people saw the play as an attack on the Un-American Activities Committee and the conservative first-night audience received it coldly.

In 1955 he started working on a film which would record the work of the Youth Board of New York City in its attempt to rehabilitate members of violent street gangs. Various ex-servicemen's organisations protested about public money being sent to supplement the work of a 'known communist' and although Miller denied he was a communist he was forced to drop the project under the pressure of the smear campaign,

In 1956 when Miller applied for a passport to visit Brussels for a production of *The Crucible*, he was summoned to appear before the Committee as a witness supposedly to help them with their investigations into the illegal use of passports. When questioned, he again denied he had ever been a member of the Communist Party but admitted he had in 1947 attended meetings where some communist writers had been present. When he refused to name these writers, he was accused of contempt of Congress on 15 February

Practice examination questions *(continued)*

1957. He was fined $500 and given a one-month suspended prison sentence. He was acquitted on 7 August 1958, the day he made a public statement to the *New York Times* saying: 'The decision has made the long struggle of the past few years fully worthwhile ... I can only hope that the decision will make some small contribution toward eliminating the excesses of Congressional Committees, and particularly toward stopping the inhuman practice of making witnesses inform on long past friends and acquaintances.'

Like Proctor in the play, he wasn't concerned about the money or the sentence but his principles and his name:

'Nobody wants to be a hero ... but in every man there is something he cannot give up and still remain himself – a core, an identity, a thing that is summed up for him by the sound of his own name on his own ears. If he gives that up, he becomes a different man, not himself.' (Miller, January 1954.)

Historical Background to '*The Crucible*'

In 1620, a group of Puritans known as The Pilgrim Fathers landed in what is now Massachusetts from their ship *The Mayflower*. The word 'Puritan' was usually used as a term of abuse to mean bigoted – unloving, judgemental, intolerant, strict and harsh, although the official aim of the Puritan movement was to purify the church and world from sin. They had an unquestioning belief in their own rightness and insisted on the complete and ultimate authority of the scriptures, on the necessity of uniformity and the evil of toleration, and on the responsibility and authority of magistrates in matters of religion. Many of their leaders were opposed to democracy, attempting to prevent any independence of religious views, and had no trust in the people at large. This led to paranoia about the 'enemy within' similar to that against the communists in the 1950s.

The town of Salem was founded in 1626 and before 1692 (when the play is set) there had already been 45 cases of witchcraft and three hangings. The Rev. Cotton Mather produced a document on the effects of witchcraft, showing how the possessed victims were expected to behave. This account fell into the hands of a group of girls, and influenced by Tituba, the West Indian slave of the Rev. Parris. Abigail Williams and others started dabbling in the occult for fun. The consequences form the basis for *The Crucible*, the historical accuracy of which is outlined by Miller on the page after the character listing in the play.

Item 6
Arthur Miller's *The Crucible*: Background and Sources
Robert A. Martin

When *The Crucible* opened on January 22, 1953, the term 'witchhunt' was nearly synonymous in the public mind with the Congressional investigations then being conducted into allegedly subversive activities. Arthur Miller's plays have always been closely identified with contemporary issues, and to many observers the parallel between the witchcraft trials at Salem, Massachusetts in 1692 and the current Congressional hearings was the central issue of the play.

Miller has said that he could not have written *The Crucible* at any other time, a statement which reflects both his reaction to the McCarthy era and the creative process by which he finds his way to the thematic centre of a play. If it is true, however, that a play cannot be successful in its own time unless it speaks to its own time, it is also true that a play cannot endure unless it speaks to new audiences in new times. The latter truism may apply particularly to *The Crucible*, which is presently being approached more and more frequently as a cultural and historical study rather than a political allegory.

Although *The Crucible* was written in response to its own time, popular interest in the Salem witchcraft trials had actually begun to surface long before the emergence of McCarthyism. There were at least two other plays based on the witchcraft trials that were produced shortly before *The Crucible* opened: *Child's Play* by Florence Stevenson was produced in November, 1952 at the Oklahoma Civic Playhouse; and *The Witchfinders* by Louis O. Coxe appeared at about the same time in a studio production at the University

Practice examination questions (continued)

of Minnesota. Among numerous other works dealing with Salem witchcraft, a novel, *Peace, my Daughter* by Shirley Barker, had appeared as recently as 1949, and in the same year Marion L. Starkey had combined an interest in history and psychology to produce *The Devil in Massachusetts*, which was based on her extensive research of the original documents and records. Starkey's announced purpose was 'to review the records in the light of the findings of modern psychology,' and to supplement the work of earlier investigators by calling attention to 'a number of vital primary sources of which they seem to have been ignorant.'

The events that eventually found their way into *The Crucible* are largely contained in the massive two-volume record of the trials located in the Essex County Archives at Salem, Massachusetts, where Miller went to do his research. Although he has been careful to point out in a prefatory note that *The Crucible* is not history in the academic sense, a study of the play and its sources indicates that Miller did his research carefully and well. He found in the records of the trials at Salem that between June 10 and September 22, 1692, nineteen men and women and two dogs were hanged for witchcraft, and one man was pressed to death for standing mute. Before the affair ended, fifty-five people had confessed to being witches, and another hundred and fifty were in jail awaiting trial.

Focusing primarily upon the story of John Proctor, one of the nineteen that were hanged, Miller almost literally retells the story of a panic-stricken society that held a doctrinal belief in the existence of the Devil and the reality of the witchcraft. The people of Salem did not, of course, invent a belief in witchcraft; they were, however, the inheritors of a witchcraft tradition that had a long and bloody history in their native England and throughout most of Europe. To the Puritans of Massachusetts, witchcraft was as real a manifestation of the Devil's efforts to overthrow 'God's kingdom' as the periodic raids of his Indian disciples against the frontier settlements.

There were, surprisingly, few executions for witchcraft in Massachusetts before 1692. According to George Lyman Kittredge in his *Witchcraft for Old and New England*, 'not more than half-a-dozen executions can be shown to have occurred.' But the people of Salem village in 1692 had recent and – to them – reliable evidence that the Devil was at work: in the Massachusetts Bay Colony. In 1688 in Boston, four children of John Goodwin had been seriously afflicted by a 'witch' named Glover, who was also an Irish washwoman. In spite of her hasty execution and the prayers of four of the most devout Boston ministers, the Goodwin children were possessed by the spirits of the 'invisible world' for some months afterward. One of the leading Puritan ministers of the time was Cotton Mather, who in 1689 published his observations on the incident in 'Memorable Provinces, Relating to Witchcrafts and Possession.' Although the work was intended to warn against witchcraft, Mather's account can also be read as a handbook of instructions for feigning possession by demonic spirits. Among numerous other manifestations and torments, Mather reported that the Goodwin children were most often afflicted by 'fits':

> Sometimes they would be Deaf, sometimes Dumb, and sometimes Blind, and often all this at once. One while their Tongues would be drawn down their Throats; another while they would be pull'd out upon their Chins, to a prodigious length. They would have their Mouths opened unto such Wideness, that their Jaws went out of joint; and anon they would clap together again with a Force like that of a Spring Lock.

Four years later, in February, 1692, the daughter and niece of the Reverend Samuel Parris of Salem village began to have 'fits' very similar to those experienced by the Goodwin children as reported and described by Mather. According to Marion Starkey, Parris had a copy of Mather's book, and, in addition, 'the Parrises had probably had first-hand experience of the case, since they appear to have been living in Boston at the time. The little girls might even have been to see the hanging.'

In spite of an apparent abundance of historical material, the play did not become dramatically conceivable for Miller until he came upon a 'single fact' concerning Abigail

Williams, the niece of the Reverend Parris:

> It was that Abigail Williams, the prime mover of the Salem hysteria, so far as the hysterical children were concerned, had a short time earlier been the house servant of the Proctors and was now crying out Elizabeth as a witch; but more – it was clear from the record that with entirely uncharacteristic fastidiousness she was refusing to include John Proctor, Elizabeth's husband, in her accusations despite the urgings of the prosecutors. Why? I searched the records of the trials in the courthouse at Salem but in no other instance could I find such a careful avoidance of the implicating stutter, the murderous ambivalent answer to the sharp questions of the prosecutors. Only here, in Proctor's case, was there so clear an attempt to differentiate between a wife's culpability and a husband's.

As in history, the play begins when the Reverend Samuel Parris begins to suspect that his daughter Betty has become ill because she and his niece Abigail Williams have 'trafficked with spirits in the forest.' The real danger Parris fears, however, is less from diabolical spirits than from the ruin that may fall upon him when his enemies learn that his daughter is suffering from the effects of witchcraft.

> **PARRIS** There is a faction that is sworn to drive me from my pulpit. Do you understand that?
>
> **ABIGAIL** I think so, sir.
>
> **PARRIS** Now then, in the midst of such disruption, my own household is discovered to be the very centre of some obscene practice. Abominations are done in the forest –
>
> **ABIGAIL** It were sport, uncle!

As Miller relates at a later point in the play, Parris was a petty man who was historically in a state of continual bickering with his congregation over such matters as his salary, housing and firewood. The irony of the above conversation in the play, however, is that while Parris is attempting to discover the 'truth' to prevent it from damaging his already precarious reputation as Salem's minister, Abigail is actually telling him the historical truth when she says 'it were sport.' Whatever perverse motives may have subsequently prompted the adult citizens of Salem to cry 'witch' upon their neighbours, the initiators of the Salem misfortune were young girls like Abigail Williams who began playing with spirits simply for the 'sport' of it, as a release from an emotionally oppressive society. A proportion of the actual trial testimony given in favour of Elizabeth Proctor (John Proctor's wife) by one Daniel Elliott suggests that initially, at least, not everyone accepted the girl's spectral visions without question:

> The testimony of Daniel Elliott, aged 27 years or thereabouts, who testifieth and saith that I being at the house of lieutenant Ingersoll on the 28 March, in the year 1692, there being present one of the afflicted persons which cried out and said, there's Goody Proctor. William Raiment being there present, told the girl he believed she lied, for he saw nothing: then Goody Ingersoll told the girl she told a lie, for there was nothing, then the girl said that she did it for sport, they must have some sport. [punctuation added]

Miller's addition in *The Crucible* of an adulterous relationship between Abigail Williams and Proctor serves primarily as a dramatically imperative motive for Abigail's later charges of witchcraft against Elizabeth Proctor. Although it might appear that Miller is rewriting history for his own dramatic purposes by introducing a sexual relationship between Abigail and Proctor, his invention of the affair is psychologically and historically appropriate. As he makes clear in the prefatory note preceding the play, 'dramatic purposes have sometimes required many characters to be fused into one; the number of girls ... has been reduced; Abigail's age has been raised; ...'. Although Miller found that

Abigail's refusal to testify against Proctor was the single historical dramatic 'fact' he was looking for, there are two additional considerations that make adultery and Abigail's altered age plausible within the historical context of the events.

The first is that Mary Warren, in the play and in history, was simultaneously an accuser in court and a servant in the Proctor household. If an adulterous affair was probable, it would more likely have occurred between Mary Warren and Proctor than between Abigail Williams and Proctor; but it could have easily occurred. At the time, Mary Warren was a fairly mature young woman who would have had the features Miller has represented in Abigail: every emotional and sexual impulse, as well as the opportunity to be involved with Proctor. Historically, it was Mary Warren who attempted to stop the proceedings as early as April 19 by stating during her examination in court that the affected girls 'did but disassemble': 'Afterwards she started up, and said I will speak and cried out, Oh! I am sorry for it, I am sorry for it and wringed her hands, and fell a little while into a fit again and then came to speak, but immediately her teeth were set and then she fell into a violent fit and cried out, oh Lord help me! Oh Good Lord save me!' As in the play, the rest of the girls prevailed by immediately falling into fits and spontaneously accusing her of witchcraft. As her testimony of April 21 and later indicates, however, she soon returned to the side of her fellow accusers. On June 30, she testified:

> The deposition of Mary Warren aged 20 years here testifieth. I have
> seen the apparition of John Proctor senior among the witches and he
> hath often tortured me by pinching me and biting me and choking me
> and pressing me on my Stomach till the blood came out of my mouth
> and I also saw him torture Mis Pope and Mercy Lewis and John Indian
> upon the day of his examination and he hath also tempted me to write
> in his book, and to eat his bread which he brought to me, which I
> refusing to do, John Proctor did most grievously torture me with a
> variety of tortures, almost Ready to kill me.

Miller has reduced Mary Warren's lengthy and ambiguous trial testimony to four pages in the play by focusing on her difficulty in attempting to tell the truth after the proceedings were underway. The truth that Mary had to tell – 'It were only sport in the beginning, sir' – is the same that Abigail tried to tell Parris earlier; but the telling has become more compounded by the courtroom presence of Proctor, Parris, Hathorne and Danforth (two of the judges), the rest of the affected girls, and the spectators. In a scene taken directly from the trial records, Mary confesses that she and the other girls have only been pretending and that they have deceived the court. She has never seen the spirits or apparitions of the witches:

HATHORNE How could you think you saw them?

MARY WARREN I – I cannot tell you how, but I did I – I heard the other
    girls screaming, and you, Your honor, you seemed to believe them,
    and I – It were only sport in the beginning, sir, but then the whole
    world cried spirits, and I – I promise you, Mr Danforth, I only
    thought I saw them but I did not.

The second, additional consideration is that although Miller has raised Abigail's age from her actual eleven to seventeen, and has reduced the number of girls in the play to five only, such alterations for purposes of dramatic motivation and compression do not significantly affect the psychological or historical validity of the play. As the trial records clearly establish, individual and family hostilities played a large role in much of the damaging testimony given against those accused of witchcraft. Of the ten girls who were most directly involved in crying out against the witches, only three – Betty Parris (nine years old), Abigail Williams (eleven years), and Ann Putnam (twelve years) – were below the age of sexual maturity. The rest were considerably older: Mary Waicott and Elizabeth Booth were both sixteen; Elizabeth Hubbard was seventeen; Susanna Sheldon was eighteen; Mercy Lewis was nineteen; Sara Churchill and Mary Warren (Proctor's servant) were twenty. In a time when marriage and motherhood were not uncommon at the age of fourteen, the hypothesis of repressed sexuality emerging disguised into the emotionally charged atmosphere of witchcraft and Calvinism does not seem unlikely; it seems, on the contrary, an inevitable supposition. And it may be worth pointing out in this context that Abigail Williams was not the only one of the girls who refused to include John Proctor in her accusations against his wife, Elizabeth. In her examination of April 21, Mary Warren testified that her mistress was a witch and that 'her master had told her that he had been about sometimes to make away with himself because of his wife's quarrelling with him ...'. A few lines later the entry reads: 'but she would not own that she knew her master to be a witch or a wizzard.'

With the exception of Abigail and Proctor's adultery, the events and characters of *The Crucible* are not so much 'invented' data in a fictional sense as highly compressed representations of the underlying forces of hatred, hysteria, and fear that paralyzed Salem during the spring and summer of 1692. And even in this context Abigail Williams's characterization in the play may be more restrained in the light of the records than Miller's dramatization suggests. For example, one of the major witnesses against John Proctor was twelve year old Ann Putnam, who testified on June 30 that 'on the day of his examination I saw the bodies of Mistress Pope, Mary Walcott, Mercy Lewis, Abigail Williams ...'. In projecting several of the girls into Abigail, Miller has used the surface of the trial records to suggest that her hatred for Proctor's wife is a dramatic equivalent for the much wider spread hatred and tension that existed within the Salem community. Abigail, although morally corrupt, ironically insists upon her 'good' name, and reveals at an early point in the play that she hates Elizabeth Proctor for ruining her reputation:

> **PARRIS** *(to the point)* Abigail, is there any other cause than you have told me, for your being discharged from Goody Proctor's service? I have heard it said, and I tell you as I heard it, that she comes so early to the church this year for she will not sit so close to something soiled. What signified that remark?
>
> **ABIGAIL** She hates me uncle, she must, for I would not be her slave. It's a bitter woman, a lying, cold, snivelling woman, and I will not work for such a woman!

On a larger scale, Miller brings together the forces of personal and social malfunction through the arrival of the Reverend John Hale, who appears, appropriately, in the midst of a bitter quarrel among Proctor, Parris and Thomas Putnam over deeds and land boundaries. Hale, in life as in the play, had encountered witchcraft previously and was called to Salem to determine if the Devil was in fact responsible for the illness of the afflicted children. In the play, he conceives of himself, Miller says, 'much as a young doctor on his first call':

> *(He appears loaded down with half a dozen heavy books.)*
>
> **HALE** Pray you, someone take these!
>
> **PARRIS** *(delighted)* Mr Hale! Oh' It's good to see you again! *(Taking some books.)* My they're heavy!
>
> **HALE** *(setting down his books)* They must be; they are weighted with authority.

Hale's entrance at this particular point in the play is significant in that he interrupts an argument based on private and secular interests to bring 'authority' to the question of witchcraft. His confidence in himself and his subsequent examination of the girls and Tituba (Parris's slave who inadvertently started the entire affair) represent and foreshadow the arrival of outside religious authority in the community. As an outsider who has come to weigh the evidence, Hale also helps to elevate the issue from a local to a regional level, and from an unofficial to an official theological enquiry. His heavy books of authority also symbolically anticipate the heavy authority of the judges who, as he will realise too late, are as susceptible to misinterpreting testimony based on spectral evidence as he is:

> **HALE** *(with a tasty love of intellectual pursuit)* Here is all the invisible

world, caught, defined, and calculated. In these books the Devil stands stripped of all his brute disguises. Here are all your familiar spirits – your incubi and succubi; your witches that go by land, by air, and by sea; your wizzards of the night and of the day. Have no fear now – we shall find turn out if he has come among us, and I mean to crush him utterly if he shows his face!

The Reverend Hale is an extremely interesting figure historically, and following the trials he set down an account of his repentance entitled 'A Modest Inquiry into the Nature of Witchcraft' (Boston, 1702). Although he was at first as overly zealous in his pursuit of witches as everyone else, very much as Miller has portrayed him in *The Crucible*, Hale began to be tormented by doubts early in the proceedings. His uncertainty concerning the reliability of the witnesses and their testimony was considerably heightened when his own wife was also accused of being a witch. Hale appears to have been as tortured spiritually and as dedicated to the 'middle way' in his later life as Miller has portrayed him in *The Crucible*. Five years after Salem, he wrote in his 'Inquiry':

> The middle way is commonly the way of truth. And if anyone can show me a better middle way than I have here laid down, I shall be ready to embrace it: But the conviction must not be by vinegar or drollery, but by strength of argument ... I have a deep sense of the sad consequence of mistakes in matters Capital; and their impossibility of recovering when compleated. And what grief of heart it brings to a tender conscience, to have been unwittingly encouraging of the Sufferings of the Innocent.

Hale further commented that although he presently believed the executions to be the unfortunate result of human error, the integrity of the court officials was unquestionable: 'I observed in the prosecution of these affairs, that there was in the Justices, Judges and others concerned, a conscientious endeavour to do the thing that was right. And to that end they consulted the Presidents (Precedents) of former times and precepts laid down by Learned Writers about Witchcraft.'

In *The Crucible*, Hale's examination of Tituba is very nearly an edited transcription of her testimony at the trial of Sarah Good, who is the first person Abigail accuses of consorting with the Devil. At the time of the trials, Sarah Good had long been an outcast member of the Salem community, 'unpopular because of her slothfulness, her sullen temper, and her poverty; she had recently taken to begging, an occupation the Puritans detested.' When she was about to be hanged, her minister, the Reverend Nicholas Noyes, made a last appeal to her for a confession and said he knew she was a witch. Her prophetic reply was probably seen later as proof of her guilt when she said to Noyes: 'you are a lyer; I am not more a Witch than you are a Wizzard, and if you take away my Life, God will give you Blood to drink.' A few years after she was hanged, Reverend Noyes died as a result of a sudden and severe haemorrhage.

Largely through the Reverend Hale, Miller reflects the change that took place in Salem from an initial belief in the justice of the court to a suspicion that testimony based on spectral evidence was insufficient for execution. This transformation begins to reveal itself in Act Two, as Hale tells Francis Nurse that the court will clear his wife of the charges against her: 'Believe me, Mr Nurse, if Rebecca Nurse be tainted, then nothing's left to stop the whole green world from burning. Let you rest upon the justice of the court; the court will send her home, I know it!' By Act Three, however, Hale's confidence in the justice of the court has been badly shaken by the arrest and conviction of people like Rebecca Nurse who were highly respected members of the church and the community. Hale, like his historical model, has discovered that 'the whole green world' is burning indeed, and fears that he has helped to set the fire.

Partially as a result of Hale's preliminary investigation into the reality of Salem witchcraft, the Court of Oyer and Terminer was appointed to hear testimony and conduct the examinations. The members of the court immediately encountered a serious obstacle: namely, that although the Bible does not define witchcraft, it states unequivocally that

'Thou shalt not suffer a witch to live' (Exodus 22:18). As Proctor attempts to save his wife from hanging, Hale attempts to save his conscience by demanding visible proof of the guilt of those who have been convicted on the basis of spectral testimony:

> **HALE** Excellency, I have signed seventy-two death warrants; I am a
> minister of the Lord, and I dare not take a life without there be a
> proof so immaculate no slightest qualm of conscience may doubt.
>
> **DANFORTH** Mr. Hale, you surely do not doubt my justice.
>
> **HALE** I have this morning signed away the soul of Rebecca Nurse,
> Your Honor. I'll not conceal it, my hand shakes yet as with a wound!

At first, the witches who were brought to trial and convicted were generally old and eccentric women like Sarah Good who were of questionable character long before the trials began. But people like Rebecca Nurse and John Proctor were not. As Miller has Parris say to Judge Hathorne in Act Four: 'it were another sort that hanged till now. Rebecca Nurse is no Bridget that lived three year with Bishop before she married him. John Proctor is no Isaac Ward that drank his family to ruin.' In late June, Rebecca Nurse was found guilty and sentenced to hang after an earlier verdict of 'not guilty' was curiously reversed. Her minister, the Reverend Nicholas Noyes again, decided along with his congregation that she should be excommunicated for the good of the church. Miller seems to have been especially moved by her character and her almost unbelievable trial and conviction, as he indicated by his comments in the 'Introduction' and his interpolated remarks in Act One.

Item 7

From Arthur Miller, *Timebends*

I had known about the Salem witchcraft phenomenon since my American History class at Michigan, but it had remained in my mind as one of those inexplicable mystifications of the long-dead past when people commonly believed that the spirit could leave the body, palpably and visibly. My mother might believe it still, if only in one corner of her mind, and I suspected that there were a lot of other people who, like me, were secretly open to suggestion. As though it had been ordained, a copy of Marion Starkey's book *The Devil in Massachusetts* fell into my hands and the bizarre story came back as I had recalled it, but this time in remarkably well-organised detail.

At first I rejected the idea of a play on the subject. My own rationality was too strong, I thought, to really allow me to capture this wildly irrational outbreak. A drama cannot merely describe an emotion, it has to become that emotion. But gradually, over weeks, a living connection between myself and Salem, and between Salem and Washington, was made in my mind – for whatever else they might be, I saw that the hearings in Washington were profoundly and even avowedly ritualistic. After all, in almost every case the Committee knew in advance what they wanted the witness to give them: the names of his comrades in the Party. The FBI had long since infiltrated the Party, and informers had long ago identified the participants in various meetings. The main point of the hearings, precisely as in the seventeenth-century Salem, was that the accused make public confession, damn his confederates as well as his Devil master, and guarantee his sterling new allegiance by breaking disgusting old vows – whereupon he was let loose to rejoin the society of extremely decent people. In other words, the same spiritual nugget lay folded within both procedures – an act of contrition done not in solemn privacy but out in the public air. The Salem prosecution was actually on more solid legal ground since the defendant, if guilty of familiarity with the Unclean One, had broken a law against the practice of witchcraft, a civil as well as a religious offence; whereas the offender against HUAC could not be accused of any such violation but only of a spiritual crime, subservience to a political enemy's desires and ideology. He was summoned before the Committee to be called a bad name, but one that could destroy his career.

In effect, it came down to governmental decree of *moral* guilt that could easily be made to disappear by ritual speech: intoning names of fellow sinners and recanting former beliefs. This last was probably the saddest and truest part of the charade, for by the early 1950s there were few and even fewer in the arts, who had not left behind their illusions about the Soviets.

It was this immaterial element, the surreal spiritual transaction, that now fascinated me, for the rituals of guilt and confession followed all the forms of a religious inquisition, except, of course, that the offended parties were not God and his ministers but a congressional committee. Some of its individual members were indeed distinctly unspiritual, like J. Parnell Thomas, whose anti-Communist indignation was matched only by a larcenous cupidity for which he would soon do time in a federal prison, not far from the cell of Ring Lardner, Jr – who had been jailed for contempt of Congress – namely, for refusing to answer Thomas's questions. We were moving into the realms of anthropology and dream, where political terms could not penetrate. Politics is too conscious a business to illuminate the dark cellar of the public mind, where secret fears, unspeakable and vile, rule over cobwebbed territories of betrayal and violent anger. McCarthy's rise was only the beginning, and no one guessed that it would grow beyond the power of the president himself, until the army, whose revered chiefs he tried to destroy, finally brought him down.

My decision to attempt a play on the Salem witchcraft trials was tentative, restrained by technical questions first of all, and then by a suspicion that I would not only be writing myself into the wilderness politically but personally as well. For even in the first weeks of thinking about the Salem story, the central image, the one that persistently recurred as an exuberant source of energy, was that of a guilt-ridden man, John Proctor, who, having slept with his teenage servant girl, watches with horror as she becomes the leader of the witch-hunting pack and points her accusing finger at the wife he has himself betrayed. The story's lines of force were still tangled, but instinct warned that as always with me, they would not leave me untouched once fully revealed. And so, in deciding to make an exploratory trip up to Salem, Massachusetts, where the original court trials were still available, I was moving inward as well as north, and not without a certain anxiety in both directions.

I wanted to study the actual words of the interrogation, a gnarled way of speaking, to my ear – and some ten years later the subject of a correspondence with Laurence Olivier, who was seeking an accent for the actors in his magnificent London production of *The Crucible*. After much research he decided on Northumberland dialect, which indeed is spoken through clenched jaws. And I heard it so in the courthouse, where it seemed from the orthography to be a burred and rather Scottish speech. After a few hours of mouthing the words – often spelled phonetically in the improvised shorthand of the court clerks or the ministers who kept the records as the trials proceeded – I felt a bit encouraged that I might be able to handle it, and in more time I came to love its feel, like hard burnished wood. Without planning to, I even elaborated a few of the grammatical forms myself, the double negatives especially, which occurred in the trial record much less frequently than they would in the play.

'When I passed his house my wagon was set (stuck) in the plain road,' a complainant testified, 'and there he stood behind his window a-staring out at me, and when he turned away again the wheel was free.' A wagon bewitched by a stare. And so many other descriptions were painterly, action stopped as though by camera – a man unable to rise from his bed, caught with uplifted head by a woman who floated in through his window to lay her body on his, just like that. Reading the testimony here beside the bay was an experience different from reading about the trials in New York. Here, it could have happened. The courthouse closed at five, and there was nothing to do in the town but walk the streets. In the early darkness I came on a candy store where a crowd of teenagers was hanging out, and excited laughter went up as two girls appeared around the corner snuggled one behind the other, hopping in time with a broomstick between their legs. How, I wondered, had they known I was here? Salem in those days was in fact not eager to talk about witchcraft, not too proud of it, and only after *The Crucible* did the town begin exploiting it with a tourist attraction, the Witch trail, a set of street signs indicating where so-and-so had been arrested or interrogated or condemned to hang. At the time of my evening walk, no Massachusetts legislature had passed so much as a memoir of regret at the execution of innocent people, rejecting the very suggestion as a slur on the honor of the state even two and a half centuries later. The same misplaced pride that had for so long prevented the original Salem court from admitting the truth before its eyes was still alive here. And that was good for the play too, it was in the mood.

Like every criminal trial record, this one was filled with enticing but incomplete suggestions of relationships, so to speak, offstage. Next day in the dead silence of the little Historical Society building, two ancient lady guardians regarded me with steady gazes of submerged surprise; normally there were very few visitors. Here I found Charles W. Upham's quiet nineteenth-century masterpiece *Salem Witchcraft*, and in it, on my second afternoon, the hard evidence of what had become my play's centre: the breakdown of the Proctor marriage and Abigail Williams's determination to get Elizabeth murdered so that she could have John, whom I deduced she had slept with while she was their house servant, before Elizabeth fired her.

> '... During the examination of Elizabeth Procter, Abigail Williams and Ann Putnam both made offer to strike at said Procter; but, when Abigail's hand came near, it opened– whereas it was made up into a fist before – and came down exceedingly lightly as it drew near to said Procter, and at length, with open and extended fingers, touched Procter's hood very lightly. Immediately, Abigail cried out her fingers, her fingers, her fingers burned ...'.

The irony of this beautifully exact description is that its author was Reverend Parris, who was trying to show how real the girls' affliction was, and hence how dangerous people like Elizabeth Proctor could be. And irony, of course, is what is usually dispensed with, usually paralyzed, when fear enters the mind. Irony, indeed, is the supreme gift of peace. For it seemed obvious that Parris was describing a girl who had turned to look into her former mistress's face and experienced the joyous terror of the killer about to strike, and not only at the individual victim, the wife of a lover who was now trying to deny her, but at the whole society that was watching and applauding her valiant courage in ridding it of its pestilential sins. It was this ricocheting of the 'cleansing' idea that drew me on day after day, this projection, of one's own vileness onto others in order to wipe it out with their blood. As more than one private letter put it at the time, 'Now – no one is safe.'

To make not a story but a drama of this parade of individual tragedies – this was the intimidating task before me, and I wondered if it would indeed be possible without diminishing what I had come to see as a veritable Bible of events. The colors of my determination kept changing with the hour, for the theme of the play, the key to the compression of events, kept its distance as I groped towards a visceral connection with all this – since I knew that to simply will a play into existence was to insure a didactic failure. By now I was far beyond the teaching impulse; I knew that my own life was speaking here in many disguises, not merely my time.

I suppose I had been searching a long time for a tragic hero, and now I had him; the Salem story was not going to be abandoned. The longer I worked the more certain I felt that as improbable as it might seem, there were moments when an individual conscience was all that could keep a world from falling.

By midsummer I had found the moment when Proctor, able at last to set aside his guilty feelings of unworthiness to 'mount the gibbet like a saint,' as I had him say, defies the court by tearing up his confession and brings on his own execution. This clinched the play. One of the incidental consequences for me was a changed view of the Greek tragedies: they must have had their therapeutic effect by raising to conscious awareness the clan's capacity for brutal and unredeemed violence so that it would be sublimated and contained by new institutions, like the law Athena brings to tame the primordial, chainlike vendetta.

I have never been surprised by the New York reception of a play, and opening night in the Martin Beck, some four years after *Salesman*, was no exception. I knew we had cooled off a very hot play, which therefore was not going to move anyone very deeply. It was not a performance from within but a kind of conscious rendering. Jed indeed had intimated more than once that he detested the emotionalism of Kazan's productions and was going to do *The Crucible* with his customary style. What I had not quite bargained for, however, was the hostility in the New York audience as the theme of the play was revealed; an invisible sheet of ice formed over their heads, thick enough to skate on. In the lobby at the end, people with whom I had some fairly close professional acquaintanceships passed me by as though I were invisible.

The reviews were not as bad as I had expected, although the *Times* calling the play cold reminded me of Jed's claim to have taken Brooks Atkinson to lunch during the rehearsals of Thornton Wilder's *Our Town*, hoping to prime him for what was then the revolutionary idea of a setless play. 'I invited him into rehearsals so he could learn about the theatre, and I told him, I said, "Brooks, you don't know anything about the theatre, why don't we start giving you lessons with this play?" And he kind of chuckled and said he would love it but the *Times* critic just couldn't do anything like that.' And in fact, in his review of *The Crucible*, Atkinson could not separate the play from the cold production at all.

Business inevitably began falling off in a month or so, and Kennedy and Beatrice Straight would shortly leave for films. The rest of the cast insisted on playing even with little or no pay, especially after one performance when the audience, upon John Proctor's execution, stood up and remained silent for a couple of minutes, with heads bowed. The Rosenbergs were at that moment being electrocuted in Sing Sing. Some of the cast had no idea what was happening as they faced rows of bowed and silent people, and were informed in whispers by their fellows. The play then became an act of resistance for them, and I redirected it with Maureen Stapleton as Elizabeth Proctor and E.G. Marshall taking Kennedy's place. I had the sets removed to save stagehand costs and played it all in black, with white lights that were never moved from beginning to end. I thought it all the stronger for this simplicity. We managed to extend the run some weeks, but finally a sufficient audience was simply not there. After the last curtain I came out on the stage and sat facing the actors and thanked them, and they thanked me, and then we just sat looking at one another.

Somebody sobbed, and then somebody else, and suddenly the impacted frustration of the last months, plus the labor of a year in writing the play and revising it, all burst upwards into my head, and I had to walk into the darkness backstage and weep for a minute or two before returning to say goodbye.

In less than two years, as always in America, a lot would change. McCarthyism was on the wane, although people were still being hurt by it, and a new *Crucible*, produced by Paul Libin, opened in one of the first off-Broadway productions in New York's history, at a theatre in the Martinique Hotel. It was a young production, with many of the actors neophytes who had none of the original cast's finish, but it was performed this time as it was written, desperate and hot, and it ran for nearly two years. Some of the critics inevitably concluded that I had revised the script, but of course not a word had been changed, though the time had, and it was possible now to feel some regret for what we had done to ourselves in the early Red-hunting years. The metaphor of the immortal underlying forces that can always rise again was now an admissible thing for the press to consider.

In time, *The Crucible* became by far my most frequently produced play, both abroad and at home. Its meaning is somewhat different in different places and moments. I can almost tell what the political situation in a country is when the play is suddenly a hit there – it is either a warning of tyranny on the way or a reminder of tyranny just past. As recently as the winter of 1986 the Royal Shakespeare Company, after touring *The Crucible* through British cathedrals and upon town squares, played it in English for a week in two Polish cities. Some important government figures were in the audience, by their presence urging on its message of resistance to tyranny they were forced to serve. In Shanghai in 1980, it served as a metaphor for life under Mao and the Cultural Revolution, decades when accusation and enforced guilt ruled China and all but destroyed the last signs of intelligent life. The writer Nien Cheng, who spent six and a half years in solitary confinement and whose daughter was murdered by the Red Guards, told me that after her release she saw the Shanghai production and could not believe that a non-Chinese had written the play.

Practice examination questions *(continued)*

'Some of the interrogations,' she said, 'were precisely the same ones used on us in the Cultural Revolution.' It was chilling to realize what had never occurred to me until she mentioned it – that the tyranny of teenagers was almost identical in both instances.

Guidelines for your answers

Here are some guidelines to compare with your own work:
These are taken from the examiners' mark scheme for these questions and so should give you a good idea of the points that they would be looking for when marking this work.

Question 1
Compare the final scene of *The Crucible* with the penultimate chapter of *The Scarlet Letter*, examining:
- **their treatment of guilt and persecution**
- **the depictions of Salem society**
- **the ways these authors build to a climax**
- **the effects achieved by the choices of language**
- **their impact.**

[40 marks]

Objectives tested: AO1, AO2ii, AO3

Possible content: In order to respond to the points, candidates may draw on some of the following detail in order to form the basis of their comparisons:

Guilt and persecution:
- shifting perspective of who is/should be guilty; external and internal persecution, conflict between religious and secular criteria; guilt as private; icon as sign of guilt – publicly or personally imposed
- focus on individuals; relentless public pressure to admit guilt; role of confession; personal integrity; authorities as persecutors; role of conscience; statement in 'Echoes'

Salem society
- seen as unified mass; slow to grasp events; thinking in extremes and absolutes; unthinking; ignorant
- eagerness for convictions; individual heroism; them/us; role of judges

Building to climax
- jubilation and adulation, giving way to hints of foreshadowing; description, dialogue: the unexpected unveiling; sudden death; some heralded by language for the reader; built on dramatic ironies
- husband and wife; wider scenes; psychological complexities of individuals; frequency of exclamations

Effects through choices of language
- prolepsis; ironies; juxtapositions of Dimmesdale and Hester, pulpit and scaffold; reader engagement and address; rhetorical questions; contrasts; gothic touches; use of dramatic present; focus on main participants; archaisms for speech; parallel structures; religious epithets
- religious language; archaisms; domestic detail; Elizabeth's complexity; understatement; exclamations; heightening through stage directions; movement on stage, struggles, violent gestures; drumroll.

Question 2
Compare and contrast two of the different interpretations offered in Items 2, 3 and 4. Which do you find the most persuasive and why?

Objective tested: AO4

Assessment and Qualifications Alliance Specimen material 2000

Practice examination questions *(continued)*

Possible Content: In order to describe and conceptualise the different interpretations of the texts, candidates will draw on the following from two passages of their choice:

- **Passage 2**
  parallels drawn: spirit and eloquence; feeling and indignation; raging intensity; lack of intellectual insight; insufficient exploration of causes and motives; what rather than why; a bit superficial; inferior to *Saint Joan*; actors support textual stereotyping; depends on implication dramatised points of view rather than human beings.

- **Passage 3**
  Koenig says that Miller represents principle over-riding personal in the lack of relevance; Miller's social conscience makes people feel bad; democratic; striven to make plays speak to ordinary people; product of his time; writing for an educated audience; doubts about appeal for a mass audience.

- **Passage 4**
  film version transcends simple analogy; works on several levels: social, moral, political, psychological, philosophical; savage ironies; excellent cast; guilt, betrayal, lies, recriminations affect community and individual; no mere period piece; still pertinent account of human fear, frailty, cold ambition.

Question 3
Using Items 5, 6 and 7, explain what sources and values most influenced Miller in his writing of the stage play of *The Crucible*.

Objective tested: AO5ii

Possible content: In general terms the sources and values most influencing Miller are:
- parallel between Salem witchcraft trials and House Committees on Un-American activities
- anti-Communist/anti-witch hysteria
- Miller's personal involvement
- value of independent opinion
- value of democracy
- concern with historical accuracy
- non-conservative
- universal psychology of oppression
- reliability of justice systems
- value of drama through emotional impact
- value of metaphor transcending geographical/temporal contexts.

Candidates will support some of these by reference to specific detail, such as:
- calling witnesses not accused of anything
- meetings based on hearsay
- imprisonment for refusing to name others
- consciously engineered terror
- Puritan unquestioning belief in own rightness
- context of either works on witchcraft trials
- Mather's work on instructions for feigning possessions by demonic spirits
- issues of telling the truth
- roles of individual and family hostilities.

Focus: (i) stage play of *The Crucible*
      (ii) sources
      (iii) values
      (iv) in his writing of the stage play.

Index

The author and publishers are grateful to the following:

Translations, Brian Friel, *Faber & Faber Ltd*

A Street Car Named Desire, Tennessee Williams, *Copyright © 1947, 1953 renewed 1975, 1981 The University of the South, Published by New Directions, Reprinted by permission of the University of the South, Sewanee, Tennessee. All rights whatsoever in this play are strictly reserved and application for performance etc., must be made before rehearsal to Casarotto Ramsay & Associates Ltd, National House, 60–66 Wardour Street, London W1V 4ND. No performance may be given unless a licence has been obtained*

Naturally the Foundation Will Pay Your Expenses (from Whitsun Weddings), Philip Larkin, *Faber & Faber Ltd*

Engineers' Corner, Wendy Cope, *Faber & Faber Ltd*

Adelstrop (from Collected Poems), Edward Thomas, *OUP, by kind permission of Myfanwy Thomas*

The Four Ages of Man, W.B. Yeats, *A.P. Watt Ltd, on behalf of Michael B. Yeats*

Prayer (taken from Mean Time), Carol Ann Duffy, *Anvil Press Poetry Ltd, 1993*

The Woman in Black, Susan Hill, *Vintage, Copyright © Susan Hill, 1983*

The Remains of the Day, Kazuo Ishiguro, *Faber & Faber Ltd*

Sons and Lovers, D.H. Lawrence, *Laurence Pollinger Limited and the estate of Frieda Lawrence Ravagli*

Testament of Youth, Vera Brittain, *The Estate of Vera Brittain and Little Brown and Co*

Proverbial Ballade, Wendy Cope, *Faber & Faber Ltd*

A Room with a View, E.M. Forster, *The Provost and Scholars of King's College, Cambridge and The Society of Authors as the Literary Representatives of the Estate of E.M. Forster*

Brave New World, Aldous Huxley, *Harper Collins Publishers*

Nineteen Eighty-Four, George Orwell, *Copyright © George Orwell, 1949, Bill Hamilton, Literary Executor of the Estate of the late Sonia Brownell Orwell and Martin Secker & Warburg Ltd*

The Rainbow, D.H. Lawrence, *Laurence Pollinger Limited and the estate of Frieda Lawrence Ravagli*

Last Lesson of the Afternoon, D.H. *Lawrence, Laurence Pollinger Limited and the estate of Frieda Lawrence Ravagli*

The Color Purple, Alice Walker, *The Women's Press, David Higham Associates*

The General, Siegfried Sassoon, *George T. Sassoon*

The Nightmare World of the Ancient Mariner, Studies in Romanticism 1, Edward E. Bostetter, *Macmillan Publishers, 1962*

Unknown Citizen (from Collected Shorter Poems 1927–1957), W.H. Auden, *Faber & Faber Ltd, 1966*

The Glittering Prizes, Frederic Raphael, *Penguin Books, 1976, Copyright © Volatic Ltd, 1976*

The History Man, *Curtis Brown Group Ltd on behalf of Malcolm Bradbury, Copyright © Malcolm Bradbury, 1975*

Bombardment, Richard Aldington, *Allen and Unwin, 1929, Harper Collins Publishers*

Memoirs of an Infantry Officer, Siegfried Sassoon, *George T. Sassoon, Faber & Faber Ltd*

The Crucible, (novel), Arthur Miller, *Copyright © by Arthur Miller reproduced by the permission of the author c/o Rogers, Coleridge and White Ltd*

The Crucible, (play), Arthur Miller, *Copyright © 1952, 1953, 1954 by Arthur Miller, copyright renewed 1981 reproduced by the permission of the author c/o Rogers, Coleridge and White Ltd*

Timebends, Arthur Miller, *Copyright © 1987 by Arthur Miller reproduced by the permission of the author c/o Rogers, Coleridge and White Ltd*

'Arthur Miller – a National Hero' Inge Morath

They are also grateful to the attributed Exam Boards whose questions are reproduced with the kind permission of the Assessment and Qualifications Alliance (AQA), Edexcel, The Welsh Joint Education Committee (WJEC), Northern Ireland Council for the Curriculum, Examinations and Assessment (NICCEA), and Oxford, Cambridge and RSA Examinations (OCR). The author accepts responsibility for the answers, commentary and ways of working given: these have not been provided by the Exam Boards.

Every effort has been made to trace the copyright holders and to obtain their permission for the use of copyright material. The author and publisher will gladly receive information enabling them to rectify any error or omission in subsequent editions.